# Masters
# Without
# Slaves

# MASTERS WITHOUT SLAVES

*Southern Planters in the Civil War
and Reconstruction*

*JAMES L. ROARK*

*W · W · NORTON & COMPANY*

*New York · London*

*To my mother and my father*

Published simultaneously in Canada by
Penguin Books Canada Ltd,
2801 John Street, Markham, Ontario L3R 1B4.

W. W. Norton & Company, Inc., 500 Fifth Avenue, New York, N.Y. 10110
W. W. Norton & Company Ltd., 37 Great Russell Street, London WC1B 3NU

LIBRARY OF CONGRESS CATALOGING IN PUBLICATION DATA

Roark, James L.
  Masters Without Slaves.

  Bibliography: p.
  Includes index.
  1. Reconstruction.     2. Plantation life—Southern
States.     3. Slavery in the United States—Southern
States.     4. Southern States—Social conditions.
I. Title.
E668.R64     1977          976'.04          76–47689

ISBN-0-393-05562-0

ISBN-0-393-00901-7 pbk.

7 8 9 0

# Contents

# Preface

For more than a century, Americans have been fascinated by the antebellum world of plantation slavery. Novelists, whether they have come to praise or to revile, have transformed the cotton kings, rice barons, and sugar lords into legendary figures. In recent years, this nation's foremost historians have been drawn to the Southern plantation, often with immensely important results. But historians have tended to follow Southern folk tradition and divide the South's history into halves—"before the war" and "after the war." With only a few notable exceptions, studies of plantation slavery break off abruptly with the firing of the first shot at Fort Sumter. It is unfortunate that historians have paid so little attention to the behavior of planters after 1860. The Civil War was the critical moment in the planters' history, and their responses to events provide valuable insight into the mind and character of the South's antebellum aristocracy. To some degree, of course, wars and revolutions distort and refract traditional values and behavior, but more significantly, they magnify essentials. The intensity of extreme situations triggers primary values. Ideology, which in normal times often remains obscured, is thrust to the surface. As the whirlwind of the Civil War made a shambles of the world of the plantation elite, it forced planters to establish their priorities and thereby reveal the fundamental social values of their class.

Even more importantly, the years of the Civil War and Reconstruction form precisely the moment of transition from the Old to the New South. Historians have for decades debated the issue of whether continuity or rupture characterized nineteenth-century Southern history. Was the Civil War in effect a chasm dividing one South from another, or was it a temporary disruption followed by the restoration of old ways? What exactly changed and what remained the same? A full discussion of whether or not the Civil War was revolutionary is far beyond the scope of this investigation. But because planters participated successively in both the Old and the New South, because they were masters both with and without slaves, they can tell us much about the slaveholding and free-labor ways of life and the relationship between them. The impact of secession, war, defeat, emancipation, and Reconstruction upon the fundamental beliefs and everyday behavior of the Southern planter class is the subject of this study. It seeks to discover the perspective of the master, to achieve an unfiltered view from the "big house."

I have relied heavily upon primary sources—planters' letters, diaries, and notebooks. I have tried to listen carefully to what planters said about their circumstances, and have discovered that they left lucid, even dramatic, testimony to what was significant in their lives. It has been frequently noted that Southerners have not been particularly devoted to introspection and self-analysis. The overwhelming majority of planters, certainly, were working farmers, not professional writers or ideologues. Only a few consciously adopted the role of defender of their region or class, and most thought primarily in terms of the defense of their own domains. They often had only slight formal education, and most did not and many could not articulate a complete or rigorous world view. And yet, while they never expressed a unified philosophy, over juleps or otherwise, a philosophy was implicit in their thoughts and actions. War magnified their essential values, although it also insured that their thought would be roughhewn and incomplete. Chaos was not conducive to reflection, even for those who were in the habit, and disruption rarely allowed for careful exposition. If the vaunted leisure of the planter class had ever existed for more than a few, it evaporated during the war. But while their writings do not add up to a complete social ideology, their words and actions do illuminate their interior worlds.

Personal, contemporaneous sources not only have the sharp impact of immediacy, but in this case provide the only reliable guide to the transformations that occurred in planters' inner lives. The old Chinese proverb—"The palest ink is clearer than the best memory"—was never more true than when applied to the emotional issues of slavery, secession, and Southern independence. Postwar reminiscences and memoirs were heavily influenced by new circumstances and needs, and are, therefore, often highly untrustworthy guides to the Southern past.

On the eve of the war, the planter class numbered about forty-three thousand Southerners, more than 90 per cent of whom were male and almost all of whom were white. Fortunately, Southern manuscript collections contain magnificent accumulations of their papers—more in fact than the most diligent scholar could possibly read. The embarrassment of riches inevitably presented problems of selection, and I chose sources with two criteria in mind. First, I wanted them to reflect the distribution of planters in the eleven Confederate states. I read more in materials from Louisiana and South Carolina, therefore, than in those from Texas and Florida. And second, I attempted to deal with a cross section of the planter class. That is, I sought out the small planter as well as the large, the politically inert as well as the politically active. In all, I mined about 160 family collections. In defining the planter, I have adopted the common antebellum standard—ownership of twenty or more slaves and employment of them in the production of agricultural goods. Though somewhat arbitrary, this criterion assures that the individual had a considerable involvement with slavery and makes it likely that he or she organized production around the plantation system.

The plantation South was not the entire South, of course. The story of the South during these years is not just that of masters, or even masters and slaves, but also that of yeoman farmers, merchants, poor whites, free blacks, urban artisans, herdsmen, and others, who together made up the majority of the South's people. Each group presumably had a related but distinctive view of events in these decades, and each perspective would be valuable. But planters merit special attention, not only because of their relative neglect in this period but also because of their primacy in Southern affairs.

Moreover, the plantation South itself encompassed variations —between the tidewater and the piedmont, between rice and cotton country, between Virginia and Mississippi. But as David Potter once remarked wryly, historians can be divided into two categories—"lumpers" and "splitters"—those who choose to search for similarities and aggregates and those who seek differences and distinctions. In this study I have chosen to lump, not because there were no differences and distinctions among planters—and I hope I have not obscured those which did exist—but because what they shared was so fundamental. It was these shared qualities that largely determined their responses during the years in question, and it is these shared qualities that I wish to examine. Planters were situated at a particular place in the Southern social order, and their position provided the point of departure for their essential values, assumptions, and beliefs. Their world view was more than a matter of individual preference. As a Cooper River, South Carolina, planter declared on the eve of the war, he was a "Plantation Man."*

With the maturation of the slave system in the South, planters increasingly coalesced into a powerful and distinctive social class. Inhabitants of a region in which fully two-thirds of the white population had no direct connection with slavery, and citizens of a nation which was publicly committed to freedom and equality, planters achieved a new self-consciousness as slaveholders. They were more and more bound to each other and to slavery by their class position, racial fears, and conservative social philosophy. The large profits returned by cotton, rice, and sugar in the 1850s were reflected in the growing cultural and political power of the slaveholders. The voice of the South was never entirely the voice of its elite, but influence was heavily concentrated in planters' hands. Their hegemony was not complete and did not eliminate the gulf between slaveholding and nonslaveholding whites, but as Eugene Genovese has argued convincingly, it did mean that class antagonism, which became increasingly sharp, was confined to struggles which did not jeopardize the basis of Southern society. The South's white population accepted slavery, the planters for their own reasons and the nonslaveholding white majority because it insured white supremacy and white democracy, and offered the promise of white equality.

Planters also revealed a growing cohesiveness and unanimity on fundamental principles, a coming together ideologically. Central was the conviction that no people had ever had more at stake in the maintenance, in all its integrity, of the relationship of master and

*Alfred Huger to R. Bunch, Oct. 20, 1857, Alfred Huger Papers, Duke.

slave. With respect to the central issues of slavery and blacks, Southern agriculture and Southern civilization, they displayed a remarkable consensus. Well-known ideologues like John C. Calhoun and later George Fitzhugh led the way in fashioning the argument that slavery was beneficial to both whites and blacks, and while not all planters explicity accepted their premises, few denied them. The convergence of planters around the positive-good defense of slavery still left considerable room for differences on specific policies. In the 1850s, questions regarding the reopening of the slave trade, the place of free blacks in Southern society, and the expansion of slavery into the territories divided planters. But the war demonstrated that they shared a basic unity, that they agreed on first principles.

The proslavery ideology was itself internally contradictory—planters, for example, often indiscriminately adopted clashing race and class arguments in slavery's defense. And it also often contradicted the reality of their everyday lives—where, for instance, paternalistic sympathies warred with crass exploitation of labor. Like most ideologies, therefore, it was inconsistent, contradictory, and self-serving. And yet, for planters it sufficed. It provided justification for the master-slave relationship with which they had grown to maturity, and it told them there was virtue in their lives and social system.

When one individual enters the world of others by way of personal documents, when he is at their bedsides for both birthing and dying, he cannot help but ache for their suffering and destruction. I have been moved by the planters' experience and have felt a deep involvement in their lives, but I also feel that as an author I have an obligation to be as clear as I possibly can be about my own moral position. In letting planters speak largely for themselves, I do not intend that the reader succumb to the planters' own poignant and self-defending rhetoric. This is not an apology or a requiem for the planter class. Their civilization was flawed, their morality blighted, and they were themselves largely responsible for pulling down the pillars of their own temple. The South and indeed the entire nation paid a heavy price for their devotion to plantation slavery. Rather, this is an effort to write the history of that moment when they became masters without slaves. It is my attempt at a Mathew Brady photograph of the planter, a portrait which, I hope, informs us of the character of the antebellum master class and explains important features of the postwar South. While it is history through planters' eyes, therefore, it is not necessarily history on planters' terms.

The debts that I have incurred in the course of this study are such that I am tempted to paraphrase a certain Englishman and to say, never has so little owed so much to so many. Some of the individuals who provided assistance were friends, whom I could easily exploit, but others were at the time strangers, who simply responded generously to my request for criticism. This study began in 1970 as a doctoral dissertation at Stanford University, where it benefited in its early stages from the wise counsel of David M. Potter and was directed by Carl N. Degler. For Professor Degler's careful criticism, warm encouragement, and sustaining friendship, I am deeply indebted. More recently, I have received advice from a number of other scholars. I wish to thank the following individuals for reading the entire manuscript and for offering valuable suggestions: Michael P. Johnson, Jack P. Maddex, Jr., Michael Perman, Louis S. Gerteis, George P. Rawick, and Paul Seaver. I would also like to thank several others for their helpful comments on portions of the manuscript: Joel Williamson, Robert Gilmour, James M. McPherson, John S. Rosenberg, Jerry Cooper, Charles P. Korr, and Arthur H. Shaffer. I have also profited from the excellent editorial advice of James L. Mairs and Esther Jacobson at W. W. Norton & Company.

I have been the recipient of unfailing courtesy and expert guidance from the staffs of the following libraries and archives: the Alabama State Department of Archives and History, Duke University, Emory University, the Georgia Historical Society, the Louisiana State Department of Archives and History, the North Carolina State Department of Archives and History, the South Carolina Historical Society, the South Caroliniana Library at the University of South Carolina, the Southern Historical Collection at the University of North Carolina, Tulane University, the University of Georgia, and the University of Virginia. I wish to thank Mrs. Dorothy Hogue for her skillful and conscientious typing. I would also like to thank the Danforth Foundation and Stanford University, which provided financial support at the dissertation stage, and the American Philosophical Society and the University of Missouri for grants which allowed me to complete the study and to prepare it for publication.

Finally, I would like to express my gratitude to Martha, whose contribution has been greater than she imagines.

*PART I*

# PRELUDE

# CHAPTER 1

# The Planters' Revolution

"The prospect before us in regard to our Slave Property, if we continue to remain in the Union, is nothing less than utter ruin."

JOHN BERKLEY GRIMBALL
*December 19, 1860*[1]

The Southern struggle to preserve slavery was as old as the nation itself. The task had from the beginning involved Southerners in stiff political conflict, and with the election of Abraham Lincoln to the presidency, they entered a dangerous political crisis. The Republican victory compelled planters to reassay the value of the Union. Demands for Southern independence, moreover, forced them to consider the health of their own region, to take measure of its internal stresses and fissures. Confident in their own minds of the necessity and legitimacy of slavery, planters worried that other Southerners would not perceive the institution as clearly. The secession debate embroiled planters in the issues of sectionalism and nationalism, race and class, and slavery and freedom. In the winter of 1860–61, they debated the fundamental identity of their region. When they emerged from the secession crisis in the spring, planters had launched a revolution, as, in the words of Robert Toombs, "the best guarantee for liberty, security, tranquility, and glory." [2]

I

Southern planters were divided on the issue of secession, but only because their fundamental agreement to defend slavery could be expressed in different ways. United in their belief in the indispensability of slavery and in the legitimacy of secession, they differed on the advisability and necessity of Southern independence. For more than a decade, the vast majority of planters had resisted the arguments of that tiny group of Southern nationalists who beat the drums for secession. They rejected the logic that Southern nationhood offered the only protection from an aggressive, abolition-minded Northern majority. When the storm clouds gathered in 1860 and the cries of the secessionists reached a new intensity, Southern Unionists mounted the stump once more to put down the demands for independence.

In their battle with the secessionists, Unionist planters drew upon an arsenal of arguments, the sharpest of which had been honed over the years. Like modern revisionists who deny the inevitability of conflict and the insolubility of differences, many Unionists argued that the national crisis was merely another fabrication, the work of "demagogues" who "generally have nothing to lose." [3] A Louisianan declared that the "Abolitionists and the Nullifiers were uniting to destroy the Union." The "leaders (not the groundlings) of these great calamities," he explained, were "the basest men that God permits to live." [4] James M. Willcox of Virginia regarded "the whole of this evil to be attributed to corrupt politicians and having in a very great degree been produced by a portion of the Democracy and not alone by Abolitionists." [5] The commotion was due entirely to politicians struggling for "the loaves and fishes," John Hartwell Cocke of Virginia declared. [6] A Tennessee gentleman agreed, arguing, "We are pushed into this predicament by bad politicians north & south." [7] And from Virginia came a simple solution: "If the people would discard the politicians, all would be well, they made the fuss, but they can't stop it, the first step towards peace is to cast the whole of that soulless set overboard." [8]

Unionists lamented the declining political leadership of the nation. Longing for the days of reasonable compromise, when slavery was guaranteed and Union preserved, anti-secessionist planters praised the old pacifiers. "Webster and Clay are gone," Daniel Perrin Bestor mourned, "and God has given us over to fools and mad men." [9] "Our Washingtons, Jeffersons, Madisons, Monroes, Jacksons, Clays, Websters, all dead and none like them in this our day of trouble," added John Houston Bills of Tennessee. Now they were victims of the "Yanceyits" * and other "traitors of the Union." [10] A young Louisiana planter complained that there was "no national figure to calm and moderate us as in the past." "Passion and prejudice," he said sadly, "are to be our only guides." [11] Alfred Huger of South Carolina declared, "Undue violence practised by very 'small men' on both sides has brought us to this state of things—the 'People', who are the acknowledged sovereigns, and who, in my firm belief, love their Country, have had but little to do or to say in this matter! The politicians, for there are no longer any Statesmen, love themselves. . . . Great God, that Pigmies should sit in judgment over the works of Giants!!" [12] With proper guidance, Unionists believed, emotions could be soothed and solutions found.

As for the fire-eaters' central argument that disunion offered the only defense of slavery, Unionists responded that this was just so much moonshine. Secession was "perfect madness," William J. Minor of Natchez asserted, for unquestionably secession "would lead to war" and "war" to "emancipation." [13] James Lusk Alcorn, a prominent Mississippi planter-politician, pleaded with the extremists to reflect for a moment on the realities of regional power. He sketched a dreary picture of a beaten South, "when the northern soldier would tread her cotton fields, when the slave should be made *free* and the proud Southerner stricken to the dust in his presence." [14] An Alabama slaveholder called for restraint and caution in a situation in which, despite the fire-eaters' claims, no one could discern the future. "The God of all only knows when and where it is all to end," he said. "The result may be to deprive us of all our negroes. If so, we must summon a stout heart to feed and clothe ourselves." [15] In July, 1860, the tough-minded Georgian Alexander Stephens summed up the common feeling when he declared simply, "I consider slavery much more secure in the Union than out of it if our people were but wise." [16]

---

*Bills's spelling. All unpublished material has been transcribed exactly as written. Gross errors are normally not followed by "*sic*"; the more subtle and less obvious errors are.

Secession not only threatened slavery, but endangered all property, and the prosperity of the 1850s as well. In the first few weeks after Lincoln's election, Unionists denounced loose talk about Southern independence and pointed to its depressing effect on Southern business. A Tennessee planter complained that the agitation had "greatly injured Commerce, destroyed the price of Cotton and now scared the banks into suspension." [17] The owner of a sugar plantation in Louisiana was furious because the "rash and hasty actions" of secessionists in New Orleans had driven away "a large sugar buyer . . . though his pockets were well lined with money." [18] A Yazoo, Mississippi, planter denounced the jingoist hubbub, arguing, "If Revolution and secession is the result[,] property I think will go down especially in the south." [19]

Southern Unionists did not need to defend the North or Abraham Lincoln; they simply had to convince Southerners that the fire-eaters' cure was worse than the Republican disease. Secession, a Tennessee planter argued in December, 1860, would "destroy the Very best government on Earth for some good reason it is true, but not Enough yet to justify so great a sacrifice of good. . . . Henceforth all is to be Confusion, distress and trouble till we are worn out and then a government no better I fear." [20] Striking a responsive cord in many planters, one anxious Virginian counseled that Southerners had "better bear the evils that we have, than fly to others that we know not of." [21]

What some today consider one of the supreme ironies of the slaveholders' revolution—that the first gun fired on Fort Sumter should have ended Southern slavery and the prosperity derived from it—was clearly recognized and foreseen at the time. But beyond predictions of emancipation and poverty, Unionist planters argued that the fire-eaters' agitation could easily set the spark to anarchy and revolution, the sort of bloody insurrection that "was seen in France in 1792." One plantation mistress wondered how Southerners could consider secession when "we have an enemey [sic] in our bosoms who will shot [sic] us in our beds." [22] With the planters perched atop a slave population numbering more than 3.5 million, it seemed to some highly unlikely that any revolution could be worth its costs.

Probably no one was more interested in educating Southerners about the dangers of revolutions than the historically minded Alexander Stephens. All societies, but particularly those built on slavery, abhorred revolution, he argued. "We have nothing to fear from anything so much as unnecessary changes and revolutions in government. The institution [of slavery] is *based* on *conservatism*," Stephens declared. "Everything that weakens this has a tendency to weaken the institution." In a special warning to the South's elite, he said, "Revolutions are much easier started than controlled, and the men who begin them, even for the best purposes and objects, seldom end them." "Human passions are like the winds," he explained, "when aroused they sweep everything before them in their fury." Stephens knew that wars fought on home grounds were transforming; the usual result was either "general anarchy" or "despotism." He drew analogies with the English revolution of 1640 and the French revolution of 1789, pointing out that they had begun with proclamations of liberty and had ended with the reigns of Cromwell and Napoleon. "To tear down and build up again," the Georgian concluded, "are very different things." [23]

Revolution risked anarchy, while continued membership in the American nation provided quite practical benefits. Unionists compared the dismal future of a puny independent South, a "second or third rate nation," with that of a powerful and united "American Empire." [24] Secession also risked Balkanization and falling prey to foreign nations. [25] And there was the continual refrain that all of the South's "prosperity is connected with, and dependent on, an eternal copartnership." [26] But it was one thing for Unionists to point out the advantages of copartnership and another entirely to explain how Southerners could continue to harmonize and balance their loyalties to slavery, state, and nation.

No one was more willing or better suited by experience to instruct Southerners on the pleasures and perils of simultaneous loyalties than Alfred Huger of Charleston. The owner of Cooper River estates and a personal friend of James L. Petigru and Hugh S. Legaré, this old Federalist had supported Andrew Jackson during the nullification crisis and thus cut himself off from South Carolina political life. Just as he had resisted nullificationists in the 1830s, he battled secessionists in the 1850s. "I never consented to regard my Country as bounded by the Savanna River on one side and Pee-dee on the other," he said in 1856. "South Carolina is my home; she is my mother; she is dearer than my country. I owe *her* everything, but my Country is either that which Washington left or I have none! What a Revolution may do towards procuring me another or a better I know not." [27]

In an eloquent letter to a confused and questioning young friend in 1858, Huger explained, "You are an American citizen but you are an inhabitant of the South—discriminate between the Social feeling which binds you and your affections to this side of the Potomac, and the Political feeling which must eminate [sic] from your own consciousness of 'Right' vested in you by the Constitution. They are entirely different but they are not antagonistic! and it is by their combination that the importance & validity of each is developed." "Our government," he continued, "differs from all that the World has ever seen before and our allegiance is a divided one & our attachments must be regulated accordingly." The loyalties of Southerners are divided—"as are our affection for our father & mother! so are our faculties of body & mind"—but "these are parts that would be valueless alone, mere particles of existence, but *together* they make the grand mosaic! & a perfect 'whole.' "

Huger admitted that the North and the South were different, but like James Madison in his famous *Federalist* No. 10, he transformed difference into strength. "Why suppose we all dealt in slave labour, suppose we all furnished the same productions, suppose our particular interests were all alike, suppose Congress agreed always on these cardinal points! why then, we should be all government & no People." This "unnatural similarity" would lead to "barbarism! inexpressibly bad in our extended Empire, but immeasurably worse in a 'Southern Confederacy.' " John C. Calhoun had understood "the twin-like affinity between the two Constitutions, state and Federal," Huger argued, "but his followers have mistaken his digressions for his conclusions." [28]

Unionism was widespread in the South, but it was usually conditional. As Carl Degler has said, it was a "peculiar Unionism." [29] Whether the attachment of even so staunch a supporter of the nation as Alfred Huger would continue rested upon the degree of danger to Southern society that he perceived flowing from the North. In 1856 Huger had exclaimed, "The abolition of slavery! that only foundation for reclaiming the Barbarian!! Oh! that fools should rush in where angels fear to tread! Should the Black Republicans succeed, & they do half that they threaten, we shall be in a State of Revolution forthwith." He added, "If the people of the North drive me to the necessity of going with my 'section' against my Country, *they* are responsible &

not *me.*" [30] Slavery, South Carolina, and the United States together formed the "perfect whole." But the loyalties were in delicate equilibrium, and whether they could remain balanced, as they had during the 1850s, depended largely upon the behavior of Northerners.

Finally, when separation and subjugation appeared the only alternatives, most planters, but not all, submerged the Northern part of their loyalties and rallied to the Southern standard. They made their choice at different times, some with Lincoln's election and many more with the firing on Sumter and the secession of their states. Unionists did so reluctantly and with great pain. In a letter to James L. Petigru after the war began, Alfred Huger declared, "We have differ'd about the 'necessity' of this unhappy Revolution, and it is impossible for me to retrace those steps which 'developments' of each succeeding day seem to justify! *I* would gladly have died to save the 'Union'—but God has decreed that we were not worthy of a Great Empire—and I *must* say, I hold the North to be responsible, as the instrument of its dissolution! beyond this I am with you—and will stand with you, or fall with you!" [31]

Tearing up deep-rooted allegiances was odious. After reluctantly casting his vote for secession in the Louisiana convention, Andrew McCollam declared that disunion "was the bitterest pill that I ever took." Thinking back to his vote, he admitted, "There are moments when the thought brings over me almost a sickening sensation." [32] John Houston Bills jotted in his diary, "No Compromise, no recognition of our rights by the North. I go with my section Come what will—but give up the government as I would an old friend; in sorrow." [33] From "Rural Rest" in Tennessee, William Henry King explained after he heard the news from Sumter, "I am opposed to secession and disunion. But war has been declared; our homes, our interests, our all is here in the South. We have to take sides, and we cannot go against our State and Country." [34]

With a mixture of anger and resignation, the great majority of Unionists admitted after Sumter, and many much earlier, that the time for debate had passed, that the die had been cast. The action of South Carolina was detestable, a Virginian asserted, "but now we have to meet the consequences; causes claim no part of our duty at present. 'Twould be folly not to put out a fire instead of wasting time to find the incendiary!" [35] Another Virginian, who believed it was a "politicans' war," conceded that "this is no time now to discus [*sic*] the causes, but it is the duty of all who regard Southern institutions of value to side with the South, make common cause with the Confederated States and sink or swim with them." [36] A Tennessee planter declared that "however wrong the leaders may have acted, no one will see the South Coerced into submission to such a Motley Abolition Crew as is headed by Lincoln." The "best government on earth" has been sacrificed to the "unholy prejudices of the North." And he added without much conviction, "I hope we may be able to build up as good upon the ruins. We shall see." [37]

Who were those planters who argued against secession in the crisis of 1860–61? Why had they found the logic of Unionism persuasive, at least temporarily, while so many others had not? These are simple questions, but unfortunately, they are without simple, or even adequate, answers. Some things can be said, however. For one, the presidential contest in November revealed that Unionism, most clearly represented in this election by John Bell and the Constitutional Union party, was strongest in the upper South. But Bell also showed strength in several plantation areas in the deep South—along the Mississippi River in Arkansas, Mississippi, and Louisiana, in central Georgia, and in the black belt of Alabama. Constitutional Unionists were likely to have been Whigs, as were most Unionists before the demise of the Whig party in the mid-1850s. The correlation between Whiggery and Constitutional Unionism was highest in the upper South, but it was positive in the deep South as well. [38]

In addition, planters may have tended to divide on the issue of secession along the lines of age and wealth. One scholar has argued recently that in the 1850s the upper echelons of the planter class became increasingly closed. The rising prices of slaves and the concentration of wealth at the top meant younger and lesser planters found their aspirations thwarted. Because Southern independence offered the hope of renewing the expansion of slavery and restoring upward social mobility, younger, less wealthy planters favored secession. [39] However helpful this political and social profile proves to be in answering questions about who supported Unionism and why, complete answers inevitably lie deep in the personality and experience of individuals, ultimately beyond the historian's reach for the majority of the planter class.

Planter Unionists fought against secession, but few were willing to fight against the Confederacy. They had not questioned the right of secession; they had merely doubted its necessity. But after the bombardment in Charleston harbor, secession became an accomplished fact in eleven Southern states. The fragile balance of loyalties had been upset, and the individual had nothing left to do but act upon his priorities. Despite the fire-eaters' taunts, most of the planters were not true "submissionists." To be sure, they had championed a variety of means of establishing Southern rights. "Co-operationists," a majority of the planter Unionists, had urged united Southern action or no action at all. "Reintegrationists," a much smaller group, had viewed secession as temporary, a tool by which Southerners could force the reconstruction of the Union on a more satisfactory basis. A relatively few planters sorted out their priorities differently and remained loyal to the Union throughout the war, often actively resisting Southern efforts at independence.[40] But the vast majority, friend or foe of secession, after April, 1861, saw no alternative; they were all Confederates. Whatever their feelings about the timing and wisdom of the Southern revolution, they were all revolutionaries.

## II

Opposing the Unionists in the debate that raged across the South in the winter of 1860 and spring of 1861 was a formidable collection of planters who favored secession. The issue was potent enough to convulse neighborhoods, destroy friendships, and eventually divide families. "Here is gall and wormwood infused into a hitherto peaceful community," one plantation mistress observed. "Bitterness and strife are the fruits of political difference."[41] Some plantation folk perceived the alternatives with a Manichaean sharpness, but many others saw only shades of gray. "Some say, this is the darkness that precedes the dawn of the *malenium* [sic]," a Georgian remarked in March, 1861, "others say *the judgment day is coming; I* say, it is damn difficult to tell what is to be inaugurated."[42] But it was the secessionists' task to convince confused Southerners that the preservation of the Union would eventually demand the sacrifice of Southern civilization. Northerners, they argued, were taking aim at the institution of slavery. Secessionists, therefore, set about explaining why the South should secede and how it could secede legitimately.

As advocates of change, secessionists assumed the burden of proof. Locked in debate with the Southern Unionists, they met their arguments point by point. Continued Union, not separation, threatened

Southern slavery, they maintained. Rather than impoverishing the
South, independence would cut it loose from the bloodsucking Yankees, allowing it to flourish. Foot-dragging Southern politicians with
national ambitions, not men of rash and hasty temperaments, were
the ones who jeopardized the South's security. Whereas the election
of a "sectional President" promised social chaos, nationhood would
preserve liberty and order. "Submission is revolution," the Richmond
*Examiner* declared, "secession will be conservatism." [43] Compromise, not forthright action, was dangerous and suspect. "I need not
say that that miserable humbug of pretended compromise is regarded
with scorn and contempt by every man true to the South & to his
rights," Edmund Ruffin proclaimed. [44] And Southerners would not
face crushing defeat, as anticipated by Unionists, but rather would
win their national independence. Northerners would probably not
even fight, secessionists asserted, and if they did, Southern men would
make short work of the Yankees.

The secessionists' most forceful argument was that the Southern
minority had finally come face to face with a permanent antislavery
Northern majority, dooming the dream of the coexistence of slavery
and Union. Fiery John Perkins, a Louisiana planter and later a
Confederate senator, had concluded as early as 1856 that because of
the "Republican hatred and detestation toward the people and institutions of the South," the election of a Republican president would be
equivalent to a declaration of abolition. [45] And in February, 1861,
Catherine Edmondston of North Carolina declared that the Republican victory in November had transformed the United States into an
"idealistic" and "Utopian Union." To her the scenario was obvious:
"Union now means Conquest—and Conquest, Confiscation. So we
go!" [46] "We were born under the institution and cannot now change
or abolish it," William Kirkland of Mississippi declared. He had
rather "be exterminated" than be forced to live in the same society
"with the slaves if freed." [47]

In addition to proving that the South should secede, Southern
nationalists needed to show Southerners how they could justify their
secession. The independence movement could have been constructed on either of two theoretical bases—the Constitution of 1787
or the Declaration of Independence of 1776, constitutional law or
natural law. Most planters rather casually adopted both. They agreed
with Alfred Huger's description of secession "as a withdrawal from a

compact in which all parties are equal, and in which the *'parts' only* are sovereign, & the *'whole'* merely 'representative'!" [48] And at the same time, many approved of the idea that "the right of self-government" was "a revolutionary right." [49] The arguments left some planters spinning. "Men call secession a constitutional remedy or act," David Gavin of South Carolina noted in the fall of 1860, "and yet say we are in the midst of a revolution[;] how a legal or constitutional act can be revolutionary I cannot imagine. . . ." [50]

That planters should have invoked the natural right of revolution at all is curious. When the legal tradition of 1787 was readily available, why was it necessary for the conservative plantation elite to raise a "revolution"? After all, for more than three decades conservative Southerners had busied themselves burying Thomas Jefferson and his concepts of natural law, replacing them with the more congenial ideas of John C. Calhoun. Words like "revolution" and "natural rights," therefore, seem jarring and out of place in the planter vocabulary.

There are probably several explanations for the planters' adoption of the natural right of revolution as their rationale. A few individuals may have had private misgivings about the Southern reading of the Constitution and the doctrine of state sovereignty. Probably many more recognized that the Southern interpretation of the relationship between the "parts" and the "whole" was contradicted by most Northerners. But if Northerners could deny the legitimacy of secession under the Constitution, they could hardly deny the right of a people to revolt against oppression. The legitimacy of the entire American experience rested upon the validity of the ideas in the Declaration of Independence. And, certainly, many Southerners in 1860 believed that they constituted a separate and distinct people, different from Northerners in institutions, habits, attitudes, values, and character. As a separate people, Southerners were entitled to self-determination. "This is all we have asked," Andrew McCollam declared in May, 1861. "We hold that all peoples have a right to govern themselves." [51] A Georgia woman asserted that Southerners claimed "nothing from the North but—*to be let alone*—and *they*, a people like ourselves whose republican independence was won by a rebellion, whose liberty was achieved by a secession—to think that they should attempt to coerce us—the idea is preposterous." [52]

In addition, it was important that planters link their revolution to the conservative revolutionary model of 1776, rather than letting the anti-secessionists carry the day by conjuring up the frightening specta-cle of France in 1792. Opponents of secession had hammered away on the fact that revolutions were dangerous and unpredictable, that they had a way of throwing their riders, replacing them with new, and that they often ended by destroying the very institutions they were designed to protect. The American Revolution, however, offered planters a safe, sane, usable revolutionary tradition. The First Ameri-can Revolution, in fact, became the metaphor for what the planters were about, the analogy that supplied unquestionable legitimacy, the historical precedent that provided practical instruction, and the glori-ous example of victory that lifted Southern hopes for their own "great experiment."

In the opinion of Southerners, the political issues were the same as in the Revolution—a liberty-loving minority was going to war to protect its freedom against the encroachments of a conspiratorial and tyrannical central government. During the war, Alfred Huger, that reluctant Confederate from Charleston, proclaimed that "we have fallen back on the identical principles that were put in motion by Patrick Henry in 1765—the present contest is one of the same charac-ter." And because "the issue is the same, intrinsically, the conse-quences will probably be the same also." [53]

The two situations also seemed nearly identical in military terms. Like the colonists, Southerners could win by not losing; a solid defense would assure victory. Planters realized they were fighting the census returns, but hadn't the Founding Fathers? "Britain could not conquer three millions." Daniel Perrin Bestor of Louisiana reminded his doubting son, and the "world cannot conquer the South." [54] Like colonial patriots, Southerners would fight fiercely "for our homes, our lives—the honor & safety of ourselves, our families & our property. . . ." [55] To those who argued that the South had miscon-strued the intentions of the Republicans, Bestor replied, "The British said they were not going to make war upon Massachusetts[;] they were only going to punish the Rebels. So they marched up Bunker Hill, and these Rebels shot back again. Now what do you call it?" [56]

Especially appealing to the planter elite was the conservatism of the American Revolution. Indeed, according to their reading, it had been so conservative that it hardly deserved the title of revolution at all. The goal had been simple political independence, and the issue of home rule had not expanded to include the dangerous question of who should rule at home. The men who made the revolution had maintained control in victory. Even Alexander Stephens, who had warned his fellow Southerners that those who begin revolutions seldom end them, added, "The American Revolution of 1776 was one of the few exceptions to this remark that the history of the world furnishes." [57] Rather than threatening internal order, property, status, or power, the war had actually worked to promote unification of the fragmented colonial society and to weld distinct political units into a single nation. To an elite which worried about rifts in its society, the example of the previous century was heartening. [58]

The American Revolution of 1776 provided Southerners with a tradition that was appropriate but also ill-defined. Its very malleability allowed its use by both conservative slaveholders and radical abolitionists. While planters were attracted by the example of a conservative and successful war for independence, abolitionists adopted the egalitarian and universalistic social theory expressed in the Declaration of Independence. Both Northerners and Southerners rested their case in 1861 on a common heritage—the Constitution of 1787 and the Revolution of 1776. But that did not mean that the peoples of the two sections saw eye to eye, of course, for Southern planters argued that, when these precedents were properly interpreted, secession was shown to be constitutional and revolution traditional.

Secessionist planters argued during the crisis of 1860–61 that the creation of a separate Southern nation was both necessary and proper. Nationhood was necessary because "black Republicanism," abolitionism in political form, had swept into power, threatening Southern slavery and Southern society, and it was proper according to America's most sacred documents. The Founding Fathers had provided a perfect model of a conservative revolution. Understood properly, it would allow the most timid and conservative Southern planter to step up and proudly endorse the South's "revolution."

III

By the late spring of 1861, the matter of Union or secession had been settled in favor of the Confederacy. But the character of the new Southern nation had not been so sharply resolved. The secession debate had forced planters to produce blueprints for revolution. They were rarely penned in ink, with every interior line fully drawn; more

often, they were merely pencil sketches, outlines rather than com-
pleted plans. But those outlines reveal what planters were fighting for
and what they were fighting against. A good many, probably a substantial majority, viewed the formation of the Confederacy as simply an
attempt to preserve the Southern way of life as it existed on the eve of
the war. They sought to protect their slave society against the encroachments of the nineteenth century. Since they perceived all
disturbing forces as coming from outside the South, they believed a
quick, surgical political separation would adequately protect the
South from the threats of the North, the embodiment of the modern
world.

But a considerable number of planters were eager to do more than
simply redraw political boundaries. For this group, consisting largely
but not entirely of aristocrats concentrated along the eastern seaboard,
independence alone was inadequate as a war aim. In their opinion,
existing social reality in the South did not define the social ideal.
These planters believed that rather than standing astride a perfectly
ordered, conservative slave society, they were shakily perched upon an
unstable social pyramid, with deep fissures only thinly papered over.
Instead of trying to protect the society as it existed in 1861, they hoped
to remold it according to the pattern of an earlier age. We are great not
for "what we *have*," Alfred Huger said in 1858, "but for being what we
have *been*. . . ." [59] They were not conservatives trying to perpetuate a
successful society, but reactionaries attempting to turn back to an
earlier social perfection.

"The usurpers will certainly fail," Alfred Huger said in 1862,
referring to the Lincolnites, "but the Confederacy may not
succeed." [60] What the Charleston gentleman meant was that
achievement of political independence was only a prerequisite to
success, not success itself. Curiously, these reactionary gentlemen
hoped to raise a revolution that looked beyond the simple Lockian
affair envisioned by their merely conservative friends. For these
champions of order and stability, nothing less than a drastic reordering
of Southern society could provide the security which was at the heart
of their search in 1861. The South was risking all for independence,
and it must not come away with the thorn still in its side.

Unease and apprehension were not sectional phenomena in mid-
nineteenth-century America. For conservatives in every part of the

country, it was an age of anxiety. Men of property and standing were disturbed by the disorder and instability of American society. The legacy of the Jacksonian era seemed to be constant change, an erosion of traditional restraints and a rejection of traditional authority, and a decline of respect for reason and order. Conservatives sought to harness the spirit of "boundlessness," that spirit of endless aspiration and possibility, to re-establish limits and reimpose control.[61] Each section, as David Brion Davis has recently shown, came to blame the other for its disintegration. Perceiving patterns of conspiracy, Southerners battled the Abolitionists, and Northerners confronted the Slave Power.[62]

While anxiety was a national, not a sectional, malady, the anxiety of conservatives in the North was faint compared to that of the traditionalist conservatives in the South. No one else was quite in their position. No other group had to defend a society constructed upon the institution of slavery. Planters were occasionally blind to reality, but they were not oblivious to the peculiarity of their slave society. Just after the firing on the *Star of the West*, South Carolina planter J. Motte Alston asked Unionist James L. Petigru how it all would end. "Alston," he replied, "don't you know that the whole world is against slavery? So, if the South is to fight for that, rest assured it is lost, never mind which side wins." [63] Few accepted Petigru's conclusion, but slavery's anachronistic peculiarity and the repugnance with which it was viewed could not be ignored.

Other factors added to planter anxiety. Opponents of secession had foreseen a gruesome fate for the South if it seceded, and their predictions could not be conveniently forgotten once secession was accomplished. Unionists had asserted that war would loosen the hinges of Southern society, possibly opening the door to class conflict and social upheaval of a magnitude to threaten even the South's "peculiar institution"—slavery. And there was the North, massive and powerful. Most planters agreed that if war came it would be a war about slavery, an abolitionist war, despite the official statements of Lincoln's government. Southerners could not help reflecting that "we are so few in numbers, compared to the non-slave states." [64] Even if Northern armies did not free the slaves, there was always the threat of action by the slaves themselves. Rumors of insurrection raced across the South, and white men scrutinized the conduct of blacks more closely than ever. "A little offence of a negro may cost him his life," one planter observed.[65] Mixing reality with fantasy, planters feared that John Bull, Billy Yank, Johnny Poor White, and Nat Turner were all lurking in the shadows. That vision knotted the stomachs of more than just the cowardly.

Dangers of a more subtle and less direct character also bedeviled the minds of traditionalist planters. The most salient feature of the Jacksonian era was ebullient democracy, and the perils of free, white manhood suffrage were obvious. In some ways, Jacksonianism had made fewer inroads in the South than elsewhere. South Carolina's state government, for instance, was still an aristocratic structure, as was much of the South's local government, the county-court system having remained largely unmodified. But in another way, the South was more vehemently Jacksonian than the North. Planters themselves loudly proclaimed the equality of all white Southerners—everyone was made equal, they said, by virtue of their race in a society built on racial slavery. But despite their public pronouncements, and despite the shallowness of their own aristocratic roots, most members of the planting class supported strongly antidemocratic values. While the disillusionment with democracy among many Southern Rights Democrats sprang entirely from the threat of a free-state majority, many old Whigs were especially prone to skepticism about democracy in any form.[66] Frederick Law Olmstead in his travels along the eastern seaboard found that "the Democratic theory of social organization is everywhere ridiculed and rejected." [67] If planters in the Old South seemed to display the most virulent antidemocratic feelings, slaveholders everywhere were critical of democracy.

Southerners had learned to fear "King Numbers" early in the nineteenth century, studying at the knee of John C. Calhoun. The South Carolinian spent much of his life in a tortured search for a scheme to protect slavery from Northern majorities and to preserve the Union. Even the pro-Union and anti-Nullification South Carolinian Alfred Huger honored Calhoun for his efforts "to discover how he could prevent a *Confederated Republic* from running wild—declining to a *National Democracy*." [68] Twisting on the horns of the South's dilemma, Calhoun devised an intricate contractual arrangement which he hoped would insure sectional harmony, but without its acceptance, most planters in 1861 felt that they faced a hostile Northern majority. The American nation, according to one Mississippi planter, was governed by "an unprincipled, bankrupt majority, made up of the odds and ends of the very most offscourings of creation, especially the Old World." [69] Tobias Gibson of Louisiana said defiantly, "Better That we should be exterminated than to have to submit to a Government of the Mob—with a Baboon at its head." [70] Outnumbered, the South fell back to the traditional check on the national majority—the principle of local self-government, a defensive posture which ironically traced its roots back to Thomas Jefferson.

As the star of Calhoun and conservatism rose in the South, Southern admiration for Thomas Jefferson and liberalism declined. Actually, the Jeffersonian legacy was ambiguous. There was the Jefferson of 1798, with his support of the rights and autonomies of communities, and occasionally a planter spoke fondly of that Jefferson. But much more often the Virginia sage was remembered and condemned for his advocacy of the principles of equality, democracy, and personal liberty. Jefferson was attacked not because he was interpreted as favoring black equality, but because he favored equality at all! "Thanks to Mr. Jefferson," Huger said, "we have made a mistake . . . and pushed the love of democracy too far. . . . The doctrines of Mr. Jefferson have left this country under a fatal delusion. . . . a vulgar democracy & a licentious 'freedom' is rapidly supplanting all the principles of constitutional 'liberty'! When shall the American people perceive that all our difficulties arise from the absurdity of deciding that the 'pauper' & the 'landholder' are alike competent to manage the affairs of a Country, or alike entitled to vote for those who shall?" [71] Conservative planters could not react against their liberal heritage without reacting against liberalism's ideological father.

Jefferson was made to bear a heavy burden for his words "All men are created equal." Crotchety old David Gavin, a Colleton District, South Carolina, planter who named his horse "Democrat," even held Jefferson responsible for the stock missing from his plantation. "I have no doubt some democrat, not perhaps haveing [sic] any, put his political doctrine into practical operation with me, for as 'all men are by it equal,' and he or they had no beeves and I had, he took mine to be on an equality with me. I thought it bad enough for them to take my hogs but it is certainly worse to take my cattle and hogs both, but as this is a democratic country and government, and all men free and equal, an age of progress and improvement, I must submit to it for I cannot help myself. . . ." [72] Thus, the man of Monticello was finally brought to the level of the neighborhood cattle rustler.

But usually planters did not treat Jefferson's notion of equality in a jocular way, for they viewed the doctrine as a two-edged sword, with each edge sharp enough to cut down Southern slavery. Jeffersonian principles denied the very legitimacy of the South's peculiar sort of property—property in men. One plantation mistress was struck by the "inconsistency" of a Southern slaveholder's writing "Whereas all men are born free and equal." [73] Howell Cobb was more charitable to Jefferson but not to his interpreters. Cobb explained that the expression "All men are born equal" had been "perverted from its plain and truthful meaning, and made the basis of a political dogma which strikes at the very foundations of the institution of slavery. Mr. Lincoln and his party assert that this doctrine of equality applies to the negro, and necessarily there can exist no such thing as property in our equals." [74]

Moreover, Jefferson's ideas threatened property by opening the gates of unlimited suffrage. Giving "men without property the privilege of deciding how far property can bear to be taxed" endangered all property, Alfred Huger thought. But he was particularly concerned about the fate of slave property under that "pernicious leveling system" of democracy. "Slavery is essentially conservative," Huger once said, "but even slavery with all its advantages cannot endure extreme democracy which [presents] the 'rich' with the necessity of buying up the 'poor' when the polls are open." [75] David Gavin agreed that "popular self-government and Universal suffrage" were the "most pernicious humbug of this humbug age." On the relationship of democracy to abolitionism, Gavin said flatly, "Democracy is the principle of abolition." It is "democrats alias mob-o-crats alias Abolitionists." The "demon democracy" was "sapping the foundations of the rights of property in everything." [76] It was not surprising, therefore, that when Lincoln explicitly portrayed the war as being for democracy, some planters automatically read "for abolition."

Had democracy been confined to the North, the planters' problem would have been relatively simple, but they saw shoots of democracy all around them. One South Carolinian, while admitting that the "ideas of *conservatism* . . . still prevail to a greater extent [in the South] than in other sections of the country," asserted that the "tendency of our whole country at present is to extreme democracy." [77] Alfred Huger pointed out that along with democracy would come its two detestable companions, "passion" and "higher-lawism," and he logically concluded that "if you propose to carry these 'causes' into the Southern Confederacy, why you will only transplant the noxious weed into a richer soil & only bring the pestilence nearer home!" [78] The South needed permanent immunization against the epidemic of "mobocracy."

That the "noxious weed" was already well rooted in the South was obvious. White manhood suffrage was universal, and David Gavin had counseled against secession for that very reason. Formation of the Confederacy, he said, was no more than "a leap from the frying pan into the fire" because it contained within it "the seeds of dissolution and civil War by leaving universal suffrage." Until the South recognized that "the only proper representation in governments should be property," an independent Confederacy would offer no more protection than the old Union. [79] Alexander Stephens also viewed secession as a step from bad to worse, and for partly the same reasons. "There is a general degeneracy confined not to one section or the other," he said. "The people by nature are prone to error. Their inclinations in politiks [*sic*] are that way as in morals they are to sin." Secession would only lead to "a race between demagogues to see who could pander most to the passions, prejudices and ignorance of the people . . . just such a sort of thing as was seen in France in 1792." [80]

Secession, nevertheless, came and was followed closely by war. While planters like Huger and Gavin opposed Southern independence, once it arrived they hoped Southerners would take the opportunity to make those fundamental readjustments which were imperative if the Second American Revolution was not to go the way of the First. Occasionally, Southern planters turned back to the Revolutionary era, not simply for justification and a practical model, but for the true principles of social organization. Gavin hoped to restore the nation "as the signers left it," for he was convinced that the Fathers had never intended that "the industrious prudent and honest should support the lazy, idle, vicious and dishonest." [81] Huger envisioned a society in which honesty would replace venality, reason uproot passion, and constitutionalism supplant "higher-lawism." Only by getting back to first principles could the Confederacy avoid "the shoals, and quicksands." [82] Gathering their images of the future from the past, searching in that mythical past for an ideology of social perfection, they hoped to recast Southern society along pre-Jacksonian lines.

Like Northern abolitionists, planters sometimes displayed an almost messianic vision of the war and its potentiality. It was first of all a war for self-determination, but it provided a wonderful occasion for communal regeneration and self-transformation. A Georgia woman believed that because the luxury of plantation life had softened and tarnished Southern character, the younger generation especially would gain from the war's testing and toning.[83] To his sister, who had expressed concern about the disruption of her education, Randall Lee Gibson of Louisiana replied that while it was true that the young women of the Confederacy would not have the advantages of traditional education while the war lasted, "how like the women of the First Revolution they will become!" Adversity would reveal their hidden strengths and neglected virtues. "I am more of an Athenian that a Spartan in my views of life," Gibson said, "but I do not believe we shall be without some good results from even this Revolution besides gaining independence." [84] Young planters themselves felt they were entering into the most character-building experience of their lives. More than one young aristocrat who had drawn fort duty complained, "I scarcely know how a battle is conducted, or how a soldier lives in camp; I lose all the valuable experience that revolutions give young men." [85] Southerners recognized that war could galvanize and rejuvenate a people, and they hoped theirs would be that kind of struggle.

Practically speaking, of course, the members of the planter class could not institute internal changes at will, and would have been unable to do so even if they had been united in the need. But the action taken by some secession conventions made it clear that more than just a handful of individuals were interested in restoring nature's conservative equilibrium. Conservative Virginians, for instance, thinking the time was ripe to reverse the democratic trend, approved several antidemocratic amendments to the state constitution, which the voters later rejected.[86] There were few changes in the Confederate constitution, but Southerners constantly reiterated that they wanted to restore and not overturn the law. As Alexander Stephens pointed out, the changes that were made were all of a conservative nature. Howell Cobb added that they were all prompted by careful attention to past evils and predicated on future protection.[87] Even the reactionary David Gavin had some praise for the new constitution, although he was disappointed that it did not protect suffrage with poll taxes and the requirement that voters possess both land and Negroes.[88] Southern planters could rarely match the purity and intensity of George Fitzhugh's dream of a full-blown "Reactionary Enlightenment," but more than a few joined him in seeking "a great conservative reaction." [89] In their opinion, looking backward offered the only hope of real progress in a slave society.

In the decade before the war, major proslavery thinkers proclaimed the existence of perfect harmony between Southern classes. They adamantly denied that there were sharp cleavages between white slaveholding and nonslaveholding Southerners. [90] But in reality planters occasionally encountered disgruntled small farmers. During the secession crisis in Virginia, for instance, a planter reported confronting several of his poor neighbors who were angrily claiming that "cotton planters & negro traders as a general thing keep up the excitement & they put down the prices of negroes which they wish to buy." [91] Encounters like these worried planters and stimulated their fears that the ties which bound the two classes together would not hold in the face of jarring interests. They realized full well that for slavery to survive it must have a community consensus, that the loyalty of nonslaveholders was crucial to the success of any strike for independence.

Even when they had not experienced personal confrontations, many planters lacked faith that the proslavery dogma was firmly entrenched in the small farmer class. "Last April I would have said, almost any body would have said, that such a change as has taken place over the south was impossible," Henry Watson, Jr., of Alabama remarked in March, 1861. He told of hearing a leading secessionist say during the crisis, "I tell you it is *impossible*, gentlemen. I tell you that the Union is stronger than slavery." The majority of Southerners were after all nonslaveholders, this fire-eater had lamented, and he was sure that they would be willing to abolish slavery rather than destroy the Union. "Yet to the astonishment of all of us," Watson said, still shaking his head, "the Union is dissolved . . . by the *voice of the people.*" [92]

The degree to which nonslaveholders were truly loyal to slavery is not entirely clear. As Eric Foner has recently observed, the social history of the Old South is still largely in its infancy, and doubtless, nonslaveholding whites have been studied least of all. All we can say now is that in assessing their loyalty to slavery, the proslavery ideologues were probably more correct than the doubtful planters.

That there was some hostility, even hatred, toward planters for their power and pretensions is apparent, but that the two classes were bound by kinship, sometimes by friendship, and by the social and economic aspirations of the small farmer class is equally obvious. Most powerful of all in securing the allegiance of the Southern masses to slavery, moreover, was the binding force of race. However deep their resentments of the planter class, nonslaveholding whites, certainly those living in plantation areas with large concentrations of blacks, were likely to fear the social and economic consequences of emancipation even more. [93]

Whenever planters expressed confidence in the loyalty of non-slaveholding whites, they rested their argument on the power of race. "In fact, it is not a question of slavery at all," William Cabell Rives said in 1861. "It is a question of race." [94] From North Carolina, Catherine Edmondston reported a conversation in which she was asked by a neighbor if she could possibly expect "the West, and the white population who have none, to fight for our negroes?" She answered smartly, "I certainly do. . . . I call it patriotism, for I should like to know what is to become of the country when our slaves are free. How will the west like such a neighbor? Or the white folks, who have none, to be governed by them?" Three months later she was still arguing her case. "It is not 'a few negroes,' " she told her doubting neighbor. "It is the country, for I should like to know who could live here were they freed?" [95] Planters hoped that there was no disentangling the issues of race control and of slavery in the South, for their own self-interest depended upon the inseparability of the two.

In the end, planters, the majority of them at least, did lead the South out of the Union. The strike for independence was predicated in part on the belief that the South would not fly apart along its class or caste seams. The centripetal force they relied most heavily upon was white supremacy, the patriotism of race which Catherine Edmondston spoke of and which U. B. Phillips later identified as the central theme of Southern history. That there was debate about the adhesive power of caste and the disruptive power of class, however, indicates that planters entertained doubts about the cohesion of Southern society, especially under the pressure of war.

Although most planters recognized the "distinctiveness" of the South and argued the existence of a "people," very few relied to any degree on Southern nationalism to provide strength and solidarity in the new Confederacy. Apparently, nationality was recognized for what it was—incipient, only weakly developed, and only partially functional. Planters, in fact, hoped war would become the instrument of national unification, as it had during the First American Revolution. Catherine Edmondston said that the Southern states were similar "in blood, in soil, in climate and in institution." [96] But until the furnace of war had forged a true nationality, most planters would rely on the "institution," and more particularly the institution's promise of continued race control, to unify the Southern people.

Recognizing that race was a dominant theme in discussions of slavery on the eve of the war, some historians have concluded that planters valued slavery primarily as a means of race control. Because Southern slavery was racial, there is no easy way to disentangle its racial aspects from its economic, political, and cultural aspects in the thoughts of planters. But very likely a substantial part of their rhetoric about slavery as an institution for white supremacy grew out of their realistic perception that it was the racial aspect of slavery that most firmly bound nonslaveholders to the institution. Their own commitment to slavery was far more profound than a simple fear of black equality.

Even as they pursued the racial argument to its fullest, planters were apprehensive that nonslaveholding whites were unreliable, that this line of reasoning might fail to convince, that the lower class might opt for its own economic self-interest. There was also some fear that economic self-interest might split the master class itself. Realizing that slavery was less secure economically in the Border States, some planters in the deep South worried about a sellout by Border State planters. If slavery was ever perceived as expendable, deep-South planters reasoned, masters in the Border States might take advantage of their unique position of being able to get rid of slavery and get rid of blacks at the same time. [97] At bottom, planters like Alfred Huger were disciples of Madisonian federalism; they believed that society was made up of factions and that factions represented differing economic interests. Under stress, individuals were likely to revert to first principles and protect those things in which they had direct and substantial interest. As the stresses and strains of war increased, therefore, the specter of class warfare kept pace.

The secession debate turned largely on the question of how to make slavery safe in the South. Some planters, however, wanted to broaden the discussion to include the question of how to make the South safe

for slavery. To these men, the South looked too much like the North.
It stood in need of a social revolution as well as a separatist
revolution—of a revolution within a revolution. While the majority
of the planter class did not fully share this perspective, a significant
number of the gentry hoped that the Confederacy would roll back a
large portion of modern history. The South would become a consistent slave society, without any admixture of Jeffersonian liberalism. It
would become a society of *"conservatism,"* as one South Carolinian
proclaimed in 1860, a society which was "better classified" and in
which "distinctions between classes are better marked." Power would
lie entirely "in the hands of the men of property & of education, who
from the very fact of ownership of the soil and its production and from
their education are alone qualified to be the ruling class." [98] In the
end, of course, the Confederacy did witness a social revolution, but
one that failed completely to satisfy these planters' dreams.

## IV

Twenty-five years before Fort Sumter, a South Carolina planter
left his plantation to travel south on a business trip. From Georgia,
Iveson L. Brookes wrote home to his wife about a strange and frightening dream that repeatedly disturbed his nights. "The substance," he
explained, "is that in some twenty or thirty years a division of the
Northern and Southern States will be produced by the abolitionists
and then a war will ensue between the Yankees and slave-holders
—that the army of the Yankees will be at once joined by the
n-----s who will show more savage cruelty than the blood thirsty
Indians—and that the southerners with gratitude for having escaped
alive will gladly leave their splendid houses & farms to be occupied by
. . . those who once served in them." Because it was such a "plausi-
ble dream," Brookes concluded that "judicious foresight" required
that every planter "should within two years sell every half of a negro &
land & vest the money in western lands—so as to have a home &
valuable possessions to flee to in time of danger." Then, fully conscious of the contradiction, he announced that earlier that same day
he had bargained for a new farm—in the Georgia plantation
country. [99]

When Brookes's prophecy of civil war finally came to pass, he was
the owner of three plantations, one in South Carolina and two in
Georgia. His slaves numbered more than a hundred and his estimated

wealth exceeded $170,000.[100] He had been able, apparently, to bury his youthful nightmare, for he had neither cut his involvement in slavery by half nor provided a Western escape hatch. By 1861, Brookes, like the Southern planting class as a whole, was more deeply committed to plantation slavery—financially, socially, and intellectually—than ever before. Just as the planters' overriding allegiance to slavery had determined their response to the secession crisis, their continuing allegiance to slavery would shape their behavior during the war.

Despite a full generation of sectional hostility, the plantation gentry was shocked by the outbreak of fighting. Lincoln's proclamation calling for 75,000 troops to put down "combinations . . . too powerful to be suppressed by the ordinary course of judicial proceedings" stunned most planters. Fire-eaters, however, such as Susan L'Engle of "Palarmo" in Florida, were "ecstatic" and "jubilant" over the prospects of settling the issue of Southern nationhood once and for all.[101] Southern Unionists, on the other hand, were devastated. They had worked and prayed for years for compromise, and had failed. Now they were face to face with the hateful alternatives they had hoped to avoid. One North Carolinian knew exactly what Lincoln's call would mean. North Carolina, he lamented, would "slide out of the Union like a shot out of a shovel," and he knew, too, that he would go with it.[102]

The people of the Confederacy understood perfectly the significance of Fort Sumter. By mid-April they knew they were at war. On April 14, 1861, Edward Fontaine, an Episcopal rector and Mississippi plantation owner, wrote with keen perception that "Civil War commenced . . . at Fort Sumter in Charleston Harbor."[103] Hope did linger in a few hearts, of course. Catherine Edmondston still thought that the Union "may fall apart from its own want of cohesion & we may be spared a protracted civil struggle."[104] But most planters recognized that the war had finally come.

Planters and their sons raced one another to enlist, to buy Confederate bonds, to outfit the smartest company. They thrilled at the thought of finally doing battle with the Yankees. Everyone knew that one Southerner could lick at least five Yankees. One plantation woman grew lyrical over the prospects of a triumphant South. "I feel as tho' I could live poetry," she cried.[105] And yet others evidently expected a tougher contest. It was with knit brows and clenched teeth that they slipped on their Confederate gray. "The die is cast the deed is done and I'm a volunteer in the state of Mississippi regularly mustered into the service of the state. . . . I am going now from a sense of duty more than a love of adventure," William Kirkland announced soberly.[106] Samuel David Sanders of Georgia showed no more enthusiasm. It was his "duty to go," he explained. "I would be disgraced if I staid at home, and unworthy of my revolutionary ancestors." [107]

From the beginning, therefore, some planters had a premonition that the war would be neither brief nor easy. The euphoria expressed by Annie I. Jones over the Charleston victory lasted only a day. "I felt so happy last night thinking that would be an end of war," she said, "but it seems to be only the beginning." [108] A week later, Everard Green Baker of Mississippi was in an equally somber mood. "I fear there are terrible times ahead of us," he declared, "the bloodiest civil war that has ever darkened the page of history." In a matter of months, "we will be fighting for our homes our lives. . . ." [109] Later in April, John S. Dobbins of Georgia agreed that the war would be "a desperate one, unless the Lincolnites back down," an occurrence he thought unlikely. The Georgian promised, however, that the South could "never be whiped [sic] into Lincoln rule or subjution [sic]." That could happen only "by killing us all." [110] Never a man to waste words, Charles Smallwood could only scratch, "Expect awful times ahead." [111]

With the firing on Fort Sumter, planters not only realized that they were at war, and that the contest was likely to be a stiff one; they were also clear about the nature of that war. Well before Lincoln's Emancipation Proclamation, most were convinced that a Union victory meant the destruction of plantation slavery. Because a "black Republican" sat in the White House, Southern planters were sure it would be a "black Republican" war. Even especially careful and restrained observers quickly accepted this premature but prescient interpretation of Northern war aims. Henry Watson, Jr., Massachusetts-born but for more than thirty years an Alabama planter, argued on July 15, 1861, that the object of the Federal Government was the maintenance of the Union. He added, however, that "public opinion is gradually changing & if the war is continued a year it will become a raid against slavery—a war for the abolition of slavery." Only two weeks later he discarded his first timetable. "I have become satisfied of one thing," he announced, "that this war is to be a crusade against slavery—that the emancipation of our negroes will soon be avowed as an *object* of the war and that it will be waged with all the fanaticism, zeal & rancor of a Religious War." He ordered his manager to subscribe one-half of his cotton crop to the Confederate cause. For "if emancipation takes place," he said, voicing the sentiments of almost the entire planter class, the plantations "will be worth nothing." [112]

Despite the somber predictions of a tough fight and the realization that the fight was for the highest stakes, many planters greeted the war with a sigh of relief. Fort Sumter broke the suspense. It ended the agony of waiting. The dread which preceded the event had become insufferable for some, particularly for those who waited in pressure cookers such as Charleston. In February, Henry Selby Clark had admitted, "In truth, if it must come, I wish it would come soon for the State of suspense which has prevailed for the last 4 or 5 weeks is worse than a very disasterous [sic] reality." [113] Acquaintance with the reality would change his mind, but like many Southerners he almost welcomed the first shots for the relief they brought.

War promised to do far more than soothe jangled nerves. It apparently offered the means to heal the dangerous divisions that had opened among Southerners during the secession crisis. As members of a society based on racial slavery, Southerners believed white solidarity obligatory, and abhorred public dissension. And yet, the winter had seen white Southerners openly battling one another on the most crucial questions. But while the secession debate has fostered division, war promised to produce Southern unity. At last, they could end the debate about the future extent of the Republican challenge. Aggression was no longer potential; it was real, and it was at their doors. Now Southerners would stand shoulder to shoulder to defend their liberties. Lincoln's action sickened many, but they could at least look forward to a united white South.

The degree to which the divisions within the South had troubled planters was revealed in their response to the outbreak of fighting. "*Now* we can have no political differences; *now* we can have no Union men; *now* we must have a united and harmonious South," declared the Memphis *Avalanche*. [114] Edward Fontaine of Mississippi reported that the people there were "preparing for war." The "whole South is now United," he declared joyfully. "All the South is now a unit." [115]

William Wallace White of North Carolina was exuberant. Those were "stirring times—South rising as one man for resistance." [116] In October, a contented Louisiana politician reported that elections were no longer a contest of "principle." Now they were a "mere choice of men." There were "no differences of opinion in the South." Southerners were all "of one mind." [117]

One expects, of course, to find secessionists rubbing their hands in anticipation of muffling their anti-secessionist opponents, but even former Unionists expressed relief that the debate was over. While certainly not welcoming war or ready to declare it a blessing, they often joined their secessionist brothers in the belief that war would reunify the South. An outspoken Tennessee opponent of secession, John Houston Bills, received the news of Lincoln's "proclamation of war against the South" sadly, but concluded that however "wrongly the leaders may have acted, no one will see the south Coerced into submission to such a Motley Abolition Crew. . . . *Now* the South will be a unit." [118] Another anti-secessionist, Henry Watson, Jr., thought that the most elementary desire—"the defense of his home"—would weld every Southerner to his fellows. [119]

Once war had clarified the alternatives, the overwhelming majority of Southern planters lined up behind their new flag. Four Border States, those with the least stake in slavery, remained in the Union, but the important states of the upper South, including indispensable Virginia, joined the Confederacy. Planters' enthusiasm may have been tempered—by reverence for the old Union, by fear of the future—but even the staunchest opponents of Southern nationhood could come around. Within a matter of months, in fact, Henry Watson, Jr., would declare that Southerners were "engaged in a holy war." [120] Another opponent of secession, Tobias Gibson of Louisiana, came to believe that the entire world was following the American Civil War because the Confederacy represented "the last remains of free government." [121] That eloquent Unionist Alfred Huger of Charleston was slow to warm to the cause, but once he did, he burned with white heat. Late in 1861 he declared, "Our Duty is in one word 'fight' fight to the last! and if the word is to be changed let it be 'die' and 'die' without asking for quarter or for mercy." For to "perish is definite" he reminded his fellow Southerners, but "to suffer under subjection to Ruffians, is a condition without an end." [122] The blistering fire that Huger had once leveled at secessionists would for the remainder of the war be directed at the "Lincolnites."

Their cause was holy and it was just, and victory was a certainty. Despite widespread forebodings, Southern planters were generally confident. A triumphant Confederacy was assured by the South's superior civilization, its lofty cause, and its unsurpassed character. They believed that the soil of the South had produced a better man. Slavery, the plantation, and the experience of command were factors in his making. Planters believed that there could be no question about the outcome of a contest between lean, hard Southern fighting men, defending family, property, and liberty, and soft, flabby Yankee mechanics, waging an unconstitutional and utopian war of aggression and tyranny.

As important as their cultural arguments were, planters' faith in a Southern victory rested, at bottom, on their estimation of the economic power of their staple crops, particularly cotton. When William Howard Russell, a correspondent of the London *Times*, arrived in Charleston just after the bombardment of Fort Sumter, he found that the concept of King Cotton was "the fixed idea everywhere." It was the "all-powerful faith without distracting heresies or schisms." [123]

The dominance of cotton, planters proclaimed, was undeniable at home and abroad. For years, Southerners had argued that Northern prosperity depended on the South's agricultural production. If the valve were shut off, the entire Northern economy would grind to a halt. Without Southern cotton, Northern textile mills would stand idle. Without Southern markets, New England manufacturers would drown in their own surpluses. Without the foreign exchange earned by the overseas sales of Southern cotton, the financial structure of the North would collapse. In time, one planter argued, "those accursed northern villains" would learn that "their entire wealth" was "imparted to them through Southern labor." [124] Edmund Ruffin spoke for most of his class when he declared that in the South's ability to "withhold the benefits of our trade, we hold a power over the North more powerful than a powerful army in the field." [125]

King Cotton could not only decree the destruction of the North's economy, but also order European intervention on behalf of the Confederate nation. England's economy, after all, depended nearly as much on cotton as did the North's. When the Federal Government moved during the summer to close off Southern ports to foreign traffic, a Louisiana planter predicted that the English and French governments would "pay no regard to the pretended bloccade [*sic*]" because their own "interest," almost "absolute necessity," demanded that they "buy our cotton." [126] A year and a half later a Georgian, Henry L. Graves, remained confident that "sheer necessity" would bring help from overseas. But he felt compelled to explain the delay. "*Cotton certainly is King,*" he said. "He however requires time to assert his supremacy, but that he will assert it in time is *inevitably certain.*" [127] Through the final days of the war, cotton remained at the heart of planters' hopes for victory.

Most planters, then, paid proper homage to the power of the South's staples, and accepted, in theory at least, the logic and necessity of cotton diplomacy. From the first, however, there were a few heretics. Testy David Gavin of South Carolina belittled the influence of cotton. He thought the Confederate government's decision to embargo cotton, made during the first summer of the war, was "very silly." How, he asked, could a "cotton famine" persuade "England to acknowledge our Independence, when by that and arms they have not succeeded in compelling the North to acknowledge our Independence?" [128] The Reverend C. C. Jones of Georgia was critical of the policy that "relied most blindly" on the "single articles of cotton and tobacco" to gain the intervention of Europe. A "kind of Providence," he explained, "has so adjusted the provisions for man's necessity that any one product, no matter how largely soever cultivated and used, may be struck out, and after a little temporary inconvenience the world eats, sleeps, and clothes itself and goes about its business as aforetime." [129] For most of the war, however, these doubters remained a minority.

A corollary to the general belief that both the North and Europe were economically dependent upon the South was the notion that the South was dependent upon no one. Anti-secessionists had argued that the South's prosperity rested upon its connection with the rest of the American nation. But most planters believed that independence would mean that the South was free to enjoy "a direct trade with our *best* customer, England," without the "fools and swindlers" of "Wall Street as our mediators." Again, the crucial factors were cotton and tobacco, the products of the plantations. Because the South raised "what the whole world required, and what England is always willing to pay for," it was economically independent. [130] Planters expected that secession would cause temporary economic dislocation, but few doubted that the Confederacy rested upon a solid economic foundation.

To protect the life they knew in the South, planters took their states out of the Union and created a new nation. Many were, at first, reluctant revolutionaries, questioning the necessity of Southern nationhood; but after the commencement of the war, most no longer doubted that their crucial interests lay in the successful defense of that new nation. In unprecedented unity, they lined up behind the Confederacy, expecting that their solidarity, their armies, and their cotton would bring them victory. And yet, while the spirits of Southern politicians and publicists soared, planters were conspicuously sober. Rather than tossing their hats in the air, they squared their shoulders in anticipation of the fight of their lives. The stakes were the highest; all agreed that the outcome would be "rule or ruin."

From the moment Edmund Ruffin pulled the lanyard that sent one of the first shells toward Fort Sumter, historians have debated the essence of the American Civil War. "War for Southern Independence," "War between the States," "War of the Rebellion," "Second American Revolution," "Last Capitalist Revolution"—each name represents a theory about its central thrust. Historians have sometimes reached their conclusions about causes by referring to the war's consequences. Some calculations have hardly taken account of the participants' original aspirations. But if it is important to know what Southerners were about when they launched their insurrection, it is important to take seriously what they said they were about.

The crisis of 1860–61 revealed significant variety even within a regime as unified as that of the plantation gentry of the Old South. To some, secession was merely a Lockian withdrawal of consent, forced upon the South by Republicans and intended to preserve a good society. Others hoped secession would be accompanied by a truly transforming revolution, one that would create a fresh society as well as a new nation. And to the small band of steadfast Unionists, secession was unnecessary and imprudent, and risked duplication of the chilling events that had issued from the French Revolution.

There is a name for the Civil War, however, which encompasses the variety of opinion in the Southern planter class. For the vast majority of planters, it was the War for Southern Security.[131] To make secure the way of life associated with plantation slavery was their primary motivation. They disagreed about what was required for this end, whether revolution was necessary and how deeply it should cut. The revolution was not raised for racial reasons, although race was important, or for profit's sake, although that too was part of their calculations. Slavery was an indivisible entity in their lives; unlike a matter such as the tariff which could be bargained up a little or down a little, slavery was inviolable, uncompromisable. Randall Lee Gibson of Louisiana declared that the purpose of the Southern Revolution was to "guarantee order, security, tranquility, as well as liberty."[132] Events would soon transform the planters' revolution beyond recognition, however. As some anti-secessionists had prophesied, it would end in the destruction of the very institution it was intended to make secure.

*PART II*

# WAR-STORM

# CHAPTER 2

# Plantations under Siege

". . . heretofore farming was a pleasure; now it is different."

JAMES M. WILLCOX
*June 10, 1863* [1]

Planters brought to the Civil War an implacable commitment to the preservation and perfection of the Southern world of plantation slavery. That the plantations crumbled and slavery disintegrated was not the result of a slackening of fealty on the part of the masters. Those results were determined elsewhere. The plantation was the heart of the master's world. It was the source of wealth, status, power, and often identity itself. The plantation was for the master the concrete expression of what was for many others an elusive abstraction—the "Southern way of life." Many years after the war, Philip Alexander Bruce said, "Each large estate presented in itself all the features common to the whole system, and was in itself a reflection in miniature of the entire civilization of the Southern States." [2] Bruce clearly exaggerated, but it was more than mere egotism that caused planters to interpret a threat to their particular interest as a threat to the whole order. The plantation was both the reality and the symbol of what the planters' revolution was all about, and its preservation became the touchstone of the planters' wartime experience.

The secession crisis had found planters in essential agreement on fundamental principles but divided on the specific issue of the Southern Revolution. To some the revolution was a threat; to others, a promise. To some it conjured up visions of the bloodiest slaughter and destruction; to others it meant a courageous defense of home and liberty; and to still others it was a grand clash of ideologies, a forging of a flawless Southern society. Whatever their blueprints and dreams, war became for all an agonizing ordeal. The whirlwind of revolution descended upon the South. It disrupted and transformed lives, relationships, and values; it crushed old institutions and created new ones; it produced economic catastrophe and political impotence; and it introduced into every home the miseries of destruction and death. But what the challenge of war revealed, or rather what it underscored in the blackest of ink, was the allegiance of the planters to plantation slavery.

In a curious and somewhat paradoxical fashion, the Civil War drove Southern planters at once away from and back to their plantations. On the one hand, it expanded horizons and drew individuals away from their everyday duties. Plantation folk were transported far from their homes, either physically by the military or mentally by the epic struggle which swept across the South. A North Carolina man reported in 1861 that he continued "to note farming operations" but that he had "almost lost interest in everything except war news." [3] A Georgia woman explained that events of such importance were transpiring elsewhere "that the little every day occurences that make up a day fade into utter insignificance." [4] In mid-1862, another plantation mistress thought back to the beginning of the war, when her diary was "but a record of domestic incidents, trifling in themselves, but interesting to us, because they made up our lives." But now, she thought, "how different! My garden, that great source of interest, passes unnoticed & my housekeeping, which absorbed so large a portion is not deemed worthy of a single entry; but battles and sieges, bloodshed, and the suffering of a mighty country occupy every thought." [5]

On the other hand, planters were drawn back to their plantations. Indifference to "farming operations" and "domestic incidents" proved a luxury that barely survived the first year of the war. There quickly "came into our lives an intenser interest in what was before us so constantly," one plantation woman remembered. [6] The rigors of war penetrated the farms, forcing men and women to give increased attention to the most mundane, but crucial, matters. In late 1862, a Marietta, Georgia, woman reported that the "leading topics" in her neighborhood were "political and domestic economy, state of the country, and molding candles, spinning, and weaving." [7] By 1864 the attention of Alexander McBee, a North Carolinian with extensive properties, was riveted on survival. "As you well know," he wrote his brother, "the all important matter now in this Confederacy is to raise something to live on." He was "straining every nerve" trying "to get out of the weeds." [8]

As the war gradually turned planters "inward," a change occurred in the context of their discussion of important issues. The secession crisis had been a hothouse for debate and rhetoric, and had encouraged the growth of abstract analysis and interpretation. The war, on the other hand, plunged planters back to earth. It channeled their thinking to the personal, the tangible, the immediate. The sobering environment of a Southern plantation under siege replaced the rarefied and heady atmosphere of the independence debate. Southern thought was not paralyzed by war, as some have charged; it was simply redirected. Ideology did not disappear; it revealed itself in the handling of practical problems revolving around family, lands, crops, and labor.

The fate of any particular plantation rested upon a thousand variables, from the accidents of geography to the vagaries of nature. But whatever happened to individual planters, their experience during the war had a common denominator in their effort to defend the plantation. As they struggled to isolate their farms from the chaos bubbling up around them and to insulate their homes from the disaster unfolding before them, they faced essentially similar problems. Each had to contend with the disruptions of war: the attack on cotton; the loss of white, male management; the shortages of supplies and markets, of tools and livestock; the intrusion of government; the animosity of the white nonslaveholding class; the encroachment of poverty. And, ultimately, most faced the staggering problems brought by the clash of armies, the erosion of confidence, the growth of anxiety and depression, and above all, the disintegration of the institution of slavery. It was on the plantation—in the fields, the slave quarters, and the "big house"—that the lineaments of revolution revealed themselves most graphically to the planter class.

I

The Civil War began quietly enough for most plantation dwellers. As always, the summer sun baked the countryside, slowly ripening the crops and turning the fields white with fleecy cotton. Planters worried about worms and grass, weather and prices, while their black slaves moved up and down the long rows, cultivating and picking, baling and bagging. But this year there was a difference. Plantations were under siege, and the smooth routine of Southern agriculture was disrupted. Among the early casualties was royalty itself. King Cotton, the key to the planters' prosperity and to Confederate strategy, was struck a hard blow and nearly fell.

As early as the fall of 1860, the secession scare had squeezed cotton by disrupting the normal marketing and financial arrangements upon which the planters relied. The dislocation was severe enough to leave the South still in the midst of marketing the 1860 crop when the war came in the spring. The war further choked off the regular channels of commerce, causing many planters to move into the new season with large amounts of unsold cotton on their hands. But by then huge acreage had again been sown with cotton, for despite the tight money, most planters had managed to put in their usual crop. William A. Hardy of Louisiana reported in June that the planters in his neighborhood were generally in good shape, but those who "aren't are in trouble because money and credit are scarce." [9] James Sparkman of South Carolina learned just how scarce when he applied to his Charleston factor for credit and learned that not a "dime" was left to be lent. [10]

That first summer, planters faced not only credit and marketing difficulties but a Federal blockade and a Confederate embargo. From the outset the Federal navy undertook to seal off the entire coast of the Confederacy, shutting off imports and denying the South any revenue from exports. But even before the Northern blockade became effective, the Confederate government adopted a strategy of "cotton famine." It reasoned that by withholding all cotton from Southern ports (thereby making the Federal blockade truly effective), it could compel certain European nations to break the blockade and free Southern trade. Crushed between the policy of the enemy and that of their own government, planters shipped little cotton through Confederate ports after 1861.

In addition to the tremendous obstacles they faced in trading cotton, planters were confronted in the early months of the war with a popular demand that they cease growing it. For decades, reformers had called on the South to break the spell of cotton, to diversify its agriculture and rely more on its own resources. The cry for agricultural independence was far older than the demand for political independence. But war meant that the old arguments for diversity took on a new urgency. The *Southern Cultivator*, long an advocate of "mixed husbandry," declared the blockade a blessing in disguise. The South had no choice but to reform its agriculture. The greatest deficiency of the Confederacy, the *Cultivator* declared, was not "the want of arms. IT IS THE WANT OF BREAD." [11] One Southern newspaper put the alternatives bluntly: "Plant Corn and Be Free, or plant cotton and be whipped." [12] Food would win the war. A self-sufficient South could hold out forever. Once assured of the South's staying power, England would intervene to get its cotton. The logic was irrefutable, "corn" and "bread" men argued. To continue to plant cotton under such circumstances was to flirt with treason.

Some planters accepted the "bread" policy from the first. A Mississippi planter reported that his neighbors had marked their state's secession by cutting their cotton acreage in half. [13] Louisiana sugar growers had begun to switch to corn as early as January, 1861. [14] And in Alabama, a plantation manager noted in his report to the owner, "the disposition is to plant more grain[,] raise meat & stock," and "in the large majority of cases to spin & weave their own clothes [and] make their own shoes" as well. [15]

Crucial in some planters' decisions to switch to food crops was the argument of patriotism. In June, 1861, a Louisiana man declared that the South could never be whipped if the planters would only devote their resources "to the exclusive raising of provisions." [16] Mrs. C. C. Clay, Sr., of Alabama, ex-first lady of the state and an able manager of her family's plantation, believed that a Confederate victory was impossible without the transformation of the plantations. She cut back her own cotton crop and recommended to her son in Richmond that the Confederate Congress force others to do the same. [17] Planters in Warren County, Georgia joined together to resolve that in order to "achieve a national existence and independence," they would devote their "best energies to the raising of grain." In their opinion, "no true and enlightened patriot will plant a full crop of cotton." [18]

Simple, self-interested economic calculations, however, appar-

ently convinced more planters to switch from cotton to provisions. A
Georgia woman explained that since "there is no market for cotton,"
she had no choice but to plant corn. She heartily "disliked doing it
however." [19] An Alabama planter predicted that all "cotton planters
will diminish their cotton crops largely unless there is a prospect for
sales between this & planting season in April." [20] Others explained
their decision by pointing to the likelihood that war would disrupt the
vital Mississippi River trade in provisions, making them expensive, if
available at all. [21]

More intricate, but no less solidly based on hard economic calculations, was the logic that led a Liberty County, Georgia, planter to
decide to limit his cotton planting to only an acre per hand. "We have
the present crop on hand," he explained to his son in March, 1862,
"which will be sufficient if sold this or the coming year to pay expenses
for two years. If not, why add to it? And if not, our only dependence is
upon a provision crop. . . ." He went on to observe, projecting
ahead, that if the coming of peace "finds us with a provision crop, we
can sell it for something. And then peace will bring some little credit if
we need it." [22]

Whatever the reason—patriotism or economic necessity—planters
began slashing the acreage devoted to staples. Cotton production
plummeted from 4.5 million bales in 1861 to 1.5 million bales in
1862. Individual states showed even sharper declines. Georgia, for
instance, harvested a cotton crop in 1862 that was less than one-tenth
as large as its previous year's crop. Sugar production also declined
drastically, from 459 million pounds in 1861 to only 87 million
pounds a year later. At the same time, production of food crops rose
rapidly. [23] Planters proved amazingly nimble and adaptable, if reluctant, in making what was a revolutionary transformation of the plantations.

And yet, enough planters continued to show attachment to staples
to convince some Southerners that the decision to plant food crops
could not safely be left to the individual. Coercion, mild and respectful at first but then increasingly severe, was employed. Planters themselves often attempted to convince others to cut back staples. The
president of the Southern Planters' Convention in 1861 promised that
the task would be nearly painless. By "decreasing the quantity of
cotton, tobacco and sugar but little," perhaps by only one-quarter, he
argued, "we can raise abundant supplies of food." [24] When voluntary

compliance lagged, local planters sometimes established vigilante committees. David C. Barrow of Georgia did not want "to incur any odium in the matter" and switched to provision crops. "I do not want them coming to survey my fields," he said. "I do not want meetings held on my conduct." [25] Members of an Alabama women's group pledged themselves to "pull up, cut up, and destroy" every acre of cotton that was cultivated in violation of the guidelines. [26] When some planters stood on their rights to plant what they pleased, legal coercion was adopted. The Confederate Congress refused to enter this mare's-nest and asked for state action. Every state but Texas and Louisiana passed statutes regulating the amount of cotton that planters could legally cultivate, and Virginia followed with restrictions on its staple, tobacco.

Although the crop was reduced to a mere 500,000 bales by 1863, cotton remained a strong pretender to the throne throughout the Civil War. Planters served the new ruler, corn, but many found it profitable to bend a knee to the old sovereign as well. One planter responded to war by simply reversing the proportions of the traditional six hundred acres of cotton and two hundred acres of corn. [27] But more often, planters felt their way through the confusion, guessing about future developments. Rumors of peace might be greeted with a flurry of cotton planting. Planters often continued to grow as much cotton as they thought they could sell. The decline in cotton production during the war probably reflected the severe constraints of government coercion, inadequate capital, the need felt by individuals to supply their own provisions, and the disruption and destruction of war more than it reflected voluntary crop restrictions by the planter class.

The cotton that was produced during the war found its way to a variety of destinations. Within the South, the Confederate government acquired vast stores of cotton, private Southern manufacturers greatly increased their consumption, and private speculators roamed the countryside buying up crops in anticipation of future profits. Cotton also continued to move outside the South. While only a trickle went out through the regular Southern ports, some made its way across Texas and Mexico to Europe, and even more crossed the battle lines to Northern buyers. A good deal of the cotton grown during the war never found a buyer at all. Planters sent it off to the wharves and warehouses of the market centers, or kept it on the plantation, where it was packed into sheds or buried in a distant corner of the estate.

Those who continued to plant and sell cotton sometimes explained their actions. When the committee of "Public Safety" in Randolph County, Georgia, attempted to curtail the cotton acreage on Robert Toombs's plantations, Toombs directed his manager to plant a full crop. The disposition of his property, he said hotly, was his own business. "My property, as long as I live, shall never be subject to the orders of those cowardly miscreants. . . ." [28] The Reverend C. C. Jones of Georgia felt compelled to justify his selling cotton to a local speculator. "This cotton is *not sold to go out of the country*," he explained. "This I would not do. But if men buy and store on speculation and wait the opening of the ports, and we can afford to sell at their offer, I think we may do so." [29] Others sought to turn to their own advantage the strategy advocated by the "bread" men. To lure England into intervening, they argued neatly, the South needed not to cut back its production of cotton but to stockpile it in vast amounts. So tempting a prize would prove irresistible, whereas concentration on food crops would make it certain that England would never intervene. [30]

Other planters eschewed justification entirely. They simply planted cotton and sold it. One of the most successful practitioners of calculated realism was James Lusk Alcorn of Mississippi. His plantation, "Mound Place," was situated on rich delta land in Coahoma County and had prospered during the decade before the war. By 1860 Alcorn owned nearly a hundred slaves and held property valued at a quarter of a million dollars. That winter he argued vigorously against secession on the very practical ground that war would destroy plantation slavery. When his state seceded, he only grudgingly joined the defense of the South, hoping always for a reconciliation that would include protection of the peculiar institution. [31]

Old antebellum political quarrels surfaced immediately in the Confederacy, and Alcorn, a Whig, quickly found himself rejected by his fellow Mississippian and long-time Democratic enemy Jefferson Davis. Sensitive and inordinately ambitious, Alcorn grew bitter. Unrewarded by the new government, whose very existence he had opposed, and threatened by the government he had never wanted to leave, Alcorn was alienated from both the Confederacy and the Union. This dual alienation was painful, but it freed him from inhibiting political attachments. Unfettered, he was at liberty to define his identity as a Southerner however he wished. He chose to think of it in terms of the protection of his family and his farm. His defense took the form of cultivating and trading as much cotton as he could.

Federal troops reached "Mound Place" in a matter of months, but rival armies swept back and forth across Coahoma County until 1865. Alcorn sent his family to central Alabama to wait out the war, while he stayed on the plantation to do what he could to save his property. For the next three and a half years Alcorn was busy "hiding and selling" his cotton and dodging both Federal and Confederate soldiers. The "smuggling business" was risky but profitable. He told his wife in late 1862 that he had just sold 111 bales at forty cents a pound and had another 90 bales ready to ship. When she begged him to quit and to come to Alabama, he said he would, but first "I wish . . . to fill my pockets." The longer he managed to steer the narrow course between Federal and Confederate destruction, the more confident he became. "If . . . the sky should clear up," he said in 1862, "I can in five years make a larger fortune than ever; I know how to do it, and will do it."

When he first began, smuggling cotton was a lonely affair. But by the end of 1862, Alcorn noticed that some local people were "beginning openly to trade." Operating beneath the moon had become almost "popular," he said. He had seen nights "when near four hundred bales of cotton were openly sold and full fifty men were on the bank participating." He could not help reminding his wife of how his neighbors had once talked about him. "It would astonish you to witness the reaction," he said smugly. Now, he thought, there was "scarcely an exception in the country." Up and down the Mississippi River, in fact, in Natchez, Memphis, Vicksburg, wherever Federal troops opened up the cotton markets, local planters, after some hesitation perhaps, flocked to the market place.

Alcorn once said cynically, "It is a bad wind that blows no good," and much of his wartime activity appears equally devoid of principle. He was ingratiating and shrewd, making "many agreeable acquaintances" among the occupying Federal troops. He bribed Confederate raiding parties, men whose features were "sharpened with hunger." "The adjustment is made, the deal struck. Tomorrow night, another trip." He learned to play on the network of dislocation and suffering. So successful was he that not only did "Mound Place" survive, but Alcorn wrung a fortune from a war that hamstrung most of the South's planter class.

Through it all, Alcorn never once showed the slightest indication that he was ashamed of his behavior or thought he was acting contrary to his own principles. And he did have principles; he did display a commitment to something higher than his own self-aggrandizement. While he bowed to Federal power in Mississippi, he did not take the oath of loyalty, though it was in his interest to sign. He was proud that he was known as the "Old Secesh Chief." In 1864 he reported laughingly to his wife that the slaves were complaining that "others fare better," and that they constantly nagged him, saying, "Other people take the oath, why can't you?" How Alcorn could trade with the Yankees and yet refuse to sign their paper was beyond his slaves. How he could trade with the enemy and still consider himself a true Southerner was beyond many others.

No doubt, some of the planters who traded across the lines were simply greedy. John McVea of Louisiana claimed they all were. "The necessity urged in its behalf," he said, "is that of food and clothing." In his opinion, however, the excuse was "fictitious and false," for short-ages never existed.[32] But another observer, a Confederate cotton agent who should have been less than sympathetic to the smuggling, offered an explanation that raised the planters' behavior above mere avarice. "Many of these people were in great straits," he told another Confederate official, "and they reasoned that what they wanted for their cotton was as necessary to their existence as was that which the government wanted for cotton necessary to its existence."[33] Rather than just lining their pockets, then, they were fighting for survival. Although sometimes specious and merely self-serving, the argument was also a genuine reflection of the planter elite's belief that its needs were paramount, that what served its interests served the general interest of the society of which it was a part. From the beginning, after all, planters had made it clear that the preservation of their plantations was the *raison d'être* of the Confederacy.

What was at stake was the survival of the plantations. Whether a planter saw this survival as obtainable through compliance with or in defiance of government edicts depended on his capacity for abstraction and his confidence that immediate sacrifices would assure eventual security. From the perspective of many, obedience to the government's injunctions appeared to mean collaboration in their own destruction. Cotton had built their plantations, and few had any

faith that corn could sustain what cotton had fashioned. They understood that corn was a domestic crop, while cotton was an international
staple. Under Confederate policy, the production of cotton became
unpleasant, unpatriotic, and even unprofitable. However, when the
needs of the plantation clashed with the demands of the Confederacy,
planters usually chose the homestead over the homeland. One planter
attempted to explain the situation to General Leonidas Polk. "The
party that controls the river," he said matter-of-factly, "will secure the
trade of the people on the banks, and nothing can be done to change
the order of things but whip the Federals away or whip the natives out
of these counties." [34] The needs of the plantation and the demands of
the Confederacy would clash repeatedly during the war. The cotton
question was one of the earliest, but whenever planters were forced to
choose between the two loyalties, they tended to make the same
decision.

## II

Planting was a demanding life in the best of times, and in wartime
the demands reached impossible proportions. The struggle for survival began earlier in some areas than in others, but by 1862 the war was
being brought home in earnest to most plantations. The dilemma of
whether to plant cotton or corn assumed its place in a long list of
troubles: skyrocketing taxes and prices; shrinking markets and incomes; the impressment of crops, tools, livestock, and labor; conscription; rampaging and ransacking armies; restive slaves; and the inevitable visitors—disease and death. The larger Southern aspirations and
goals which had been on so many lips before the war faded as the
planters battled to save their beleaguered plantations. And from the
planters' perspective, they were being abandoned in their efforts, even
by the Confederate government itself.

In 1864 a young Northerner came south to take up the Federal
Government's offer to manage an abandoned plantation in occupied
Mississippi. Brought to his knees in a matter of months, this "Yankee
planter" concluded that planting was not for him. For a man "to be
able to cope with all he encounters in this business," he grumbled, he
"should have the faith of Abraham; the patience of Job; the wisdom of
Soloman [sic]; the perseverance of Washington; and the indomitable
pluck and courage of old Jackson." Not even the prospect of selling

cotton at a dollar a pound could tempt him to stay. As he headed northward, he noted ruefully that his plantation adventure had turned out "quite as foolish and more disastrous than my Pikes Peak trip." [35]

The typical planter was probably no more heroic than the young Northern adventurer, but as a Southerner he was already at home, and to him running the plantation was infinitely more than a lark for Pikes Peak gold. Planting was a means of earning money, certainly, but it was often an affair of the heart and mind as well. The plantation was his way of life. It was no wonder, then, that the Southern planter stayed to fight, as a soldier in the battlefields and as a farmer in his own fields.

The war penetrated the South's plantations in innumerable ways, and one of its most visible effects was the rapid exodus of adult white males. Fathers, sons, and overseers rushed to the colors to do battle with the Yankees. Mary Govan of Mississippi saw her husband and all five sons serving in the Confederate armies at the same time. Those who were less enthusiastic about volunteering were, in time, encouraged to join the forces in other ways. One lonely plantation mistress noted that "conscription has hobbled almost every household," including her own.[36] Women sometimes found that their courage "all oozed out" [37] when a son was called to the front, but nevertheless, by the end of the first year of war, much of the rural South approached a matriarchy.

A good many planters, however, displayed real ingenuity in discovering ways to remain on their plantations. Charles Smallwood of North Carolina took advantage of the Confederate substitution law which allowed a conscripted man to hire someone else to fight for him. Drafted in January, 1862, he searched until April before finding a substitute. And substitutes were notoriously slippery. A few months later he was again looking, and when he found another, he took several days off to deliver him personally to the army in the field.[38] Another North Carolina planter, Alexander McBee, advised his son to remain his county's representative at the General Assembly because "if you hold on to *that office* you may not be liable to do some other harder duty." [39] In 1864, Richard Ivanhoe Cocke of Virginia sought exemption as an "agriculturalist." His case was coming up soon, he told a friend, and fortunately, it was going to be heard by a "board of Powhattan gentlemen." [40]

Probably most heavily relied upon, however, was the "twenty-negro" law. Adopted by the Confederate Congress in October, 1862, it exempted from service one white man for every twenty slaves on a plantation. Originally passed to increase the Confederacy's food supply and to provide police protection in the slave counties, the law allowed planters and their sons to avoid conscription. In Alabama, for instance, of nineteen categories of exemption, only medical disability was invoked more frequently than slaveholding. In all, nearly fifteen hundred exemptions were issued to slaveholders in that state.[41] The law also enabled planters to protect their overseers from military service. While most planters could not get along with their overseers, many also believed they could not get along without them. A year before the war, a Virginia planter explained why he was "compelled to have one." Without "such a person, little as I think of them in the main, the negroes will make nothing, not corn to feed themselves & no tob. to buy meat and clothes." He tried it once, he said, and he knew "they can do nothing without a white manager."[42] Because of its obvious class bias, the "twenty-negro" law was one of the Confederacy's most unpopular measures, and planters constantly feared it was in danger of repeal. They were kept on edge wondering "whether I should have to go to the army or not" and worrying about "how much longer we are to be exempted."[43]

Planters no doubt attempted to evade military duty for every reason from cowardice to conviction, but they usually explained their actions in terms of higher patriotism. They adopted the argument used by one plantation mistress who tried to coax her husband back home after he had volunteered. "You have no right to throw away your life," she asserted, "you can do more for your country at home in other ways."[44] Both "prudence and patriotism" required that planters remain at home, a Georgian declared.[45] There they could accomplish what the "twenty-negro" law exempted them for—the increase of food production and the control of slaves.

An old gentleman from Georgia maintained in July, 1863, that a planter "at home is two fold yes five fold as valuable as in the field." Everyone knew, he said, that the "question of food . . . is today the most important question before us." But because so many planters were leaving "their plantations without a male person," he argued, "we are today in greater danger of whipping our selves than being whipped by our enemy." Without white men supervising the farming, the "crops will all or nearly all be wasted." It would be far better to "shut up every shop in town than stop the planting interest. The women can keep shop." Nineteen out of every twenty women knew nothing about planting anyway. "Everything is moved by the planters," he concluded, "ruin them or even cripple them & we are done." [46]

In June, 1862, Brigadier General Richard Winter of the Mississippi militia expressed the other half of the planters' argument. After the defeat at Shiloh, Mississippi "minute men" had been called up to stem the Federal tide. The order had netted many reluctant planters, and Winter reported that in "the richer portion" of his brigade "the question is constantly asked 'what is to become of my wife & children when left in a land swarming with negroes without a single white man on many plantations to restrain their licenciousness by a little wholesome fear or visit with condign punishment any act of wrong or insubordination?' " [47] Both halves of the planters' case were succinctly stated in 1862 by a Georgia planter who pleaded for exemption because there was "danger of Negro riots and starvation unless a few energetic men are allowed to remain upon the plantations." [48]

Hundreds of planters successfully evaded military service, but even larger numbers eventually left to fight the Yankees. As white men grew scarce on the plantations, white women increasingly assumed managerial responsibilities. Women planters were, of course, not new to the South, having been on the scene since the earliest Southern settlement. On the eve of the war, thousands of women legally owned plantations, and scores actually managed them. But for most women, total responsibility for a plantation was "a new and a strange business." After the death of her husband in 1863, Mary Jones of Georgia found that "this cruel war imposes strange duties upon us all," but she added, "I am willing to stand in my lot." Her lot was three plantations and more than a hundred slaves, and each day she followed her late husband's footsteps in the "grand rounds." [49]

To ease their wives' burdens, planters would often gather their slaves around them for a final word before they bid good-by. A. H. Boykin told his bondsmen in May, 1861, that he expected "them to do their duty & if ever there was a time to make an effort now is it." [50] Catherine Edmondston heard her husband tell their bondsmen "to remember their duty to me and give me no trouble." She thought "they were much affected" by the speech. [51] Husbands also kept up heavy correspondences with their wives on plantation affairs—the wives sending streams of questions and reports and the husbands feeding back instructions on everything from weddings to whippings. Routine and tradition, as well as the assistance of knowledgeable and responsive slaves, provided additional support for the new management.

Plantation husbands obviously believed their wives could handle the plantations in their absence. Not one would have voluntarily left had he not thought his wife could take care of both the crops and the slaves. And the women's performance largely substantiated the men's faith. The results certainly disproved the old gentleman's claim that nineteen out of twenty knew nothing of farming, for not only did Southern women keep the plantations going during wartime, but it was largely under their management that the formidable adjustment was made from cotton to food production.[52]

However, the deeply rooted images which surrounded plantation women were not easily overturned. Despite the women's performance and the men's trust, Southern men continued to cling to the old portrait of the Southern lady, even when it clashed with the reality of their own plantations. George Hairston, master of a Lowndes County, Mississippi, estate, still saw Southern women as all crinoline and curls. He admitted that they were involved in the war effort, but regarded their contribution as largely vocal. They talked of "nothing else," he said. "Their friends and sweethearts being in the army," he explained understandingly, "their hearts are with them and their tongues are proportionately influenced." And he offered the reassuring observation that they still "look as charming[,] their eyes sparkle as brightly & they smell as sweetly & graciously as if they're devoid of care."[53]

But women could hardly remain carefree, or sweet-smelling for that matter, when charged with the wartime management of a slave plantation. Regardless of their skill, the rigors of war eventually penetrated the most ably run farms. At first, perhaps, adjustment may have been a matter of learning to do without favorite luxuries—silk dresses and fashionable sunbonnets, oolong tea and French wine. But the plantation folk learned quickly that war meant that "we can neather export our produce or import our needfuls."[54] Complaints grew more strident when such "needfuls" as salt, medicine, and cotton cards grew scarce. And in time, the most urgent cries came from formerly prosperous plantations. The inhabitants of "Magnolia" in Louisiana had "no shoes, no clothing[,] nothing to eat," the owner reported in December, 1862. "Famine stares us in the face I fear." [55] Another plantation dweller described her life as "anxiety about something to eat, something to wear, and anxiety about everything." [56] Those who owned slaves usually suffered less than the average white Southerner, especially in the early years of the war, but still, a North Carolinian was not alone when he wailed, "Who can stand it?—How long—oh! how long shall this thing last?" [57]

As the war disrupted staple production, incomes shriveled. James Heyward of South Carolina owned four plantations, with more than four thousand acres of cleared land. By 1864 he was planting barely a tenth of this property—331 acres in rice and 90 in provisions. [58] Another South Carolinian, James Gregorie, produced eighty-two bales of sea-island cotton on his place in 1862; by 1865 he had trouble putting together two small bales. [59] A Mississippi woman announced that her cousin did not have "a single dime" because "not a bale of cotton can be sold," and explained that she had "bought nothing for the best of reasons—nobody buys—because nobody has any money." [60] Sally Sparkman of Mississippi explained early in 1862 that "we cannot sell our cotton," and "consequently we have no money for that is all we have." [61]

And yet the planters' problem was not always money. "I have hundreds of dollars in my pocket book," one woman reported, "& yet cannot buy a yard of calico. . . . a great many other things are among the things money cannot buy in the Confederacy!" [62] Even when a planter had money and found the goods he wanted, he could still run into trouble. In January, 1865, William Cooper discovered that Mississippi merchants were refusing to take "any amount of Confederate notes nor Bank notes except Greenbacks." Cooper was fortunate, for a friend lent him five dollars in greenbacks to buy two bushels of corn for his family. [63]

Shortages of food and clothing, of credit and money, became common on most plantations. They made life difficult and harsh, but they were understandable concomitants of war, and as such, were usually accepted as part of every Southerner's burden. Another intruder into plantation affairs was not so stoically received. The Confederate government became increasingly entangled in plantation management. At first, planters regarded irritating government policies as temporary and minor, part of the confusion of the times, but when the irritation became constant, many planters believed that they discerned a policy of conscious disregard for the plantation interest.

For many planters, the primary contact with the war came through a Confederate official. These encounters were rarely pleasant. It was a government official who told the planter what he could plant, how much, and what and with whom he could trade. It was an official who burned the cotton or sugar crop when he deemed it necessary. It was an official who dragged the plantation supervisors off to war, and impressed the planters' food, their livestock, their tools, and even their slaves. Confederate officials in Richmond created discriminatory currency and tax systems, encroached upon valued civil liberties, and provided inadequate relief from hardship. Confederate troops ransacked and pillaged rural estates. Although the long war vastly increased Southern hatred for the Yankees, it did not automatically swell affection for the Confederacy.

Few Confederate policies escaped criticism, but planters leveled especially heavy fire at those that touched cotton. Robert Toombs, for instance, warned the government to keep its hands off the crop. "Let the production and distribution of wealth alone," this lover of Ricardo and Smith demanded. "Producers have nothing to do with morality. That is a question for consumers, and not then for the legislative power." [64] Another planter warned the influential South Carolinian William Porcher Miles that the Confederate cotton policy could lead to open revolt. Because of the embargo, he explained, the planters were not able to sell their cotton, and "having nothing else to sell which will bear transportation," they could not pay their exorbitant Confederate war taxes. If the government tried to sell their plantations "under the hammer," they would rise in resistance. [65]

The Confederate government also had an annoying habit of burning the planters' cotton and sugar whenever Federal troops approached. When Northern soldiers closed in on Memphis in May, 1862, for instance, General P. G. T. Beauregard burned three hundred thousand bales of cotton and poured thousands of barrels of molasses into the streets—not only making it difficult to get around the city, but wiping out many planters who had stockpiled their goods at the wharves and warehouses. One planter wrote a restrained appeal to a Confederate senator, expressing hope that the Confederate government could see its way clear to buy cotton rather than to burn it. He would gladly have sold his seven hundred bales at only seven cents a pound, he said, rather than watch Beauregard send it up in flames. If the government would adopt his plan, "then we would have some means to live on, and aid the cause in a measure more commensurate with our wishes." Without government assistance, he said mildly, "I fear there will be much inconvenience, if not distress, and suffering." [66] The habit of burning cotton hardly endeared the government to the gentry.

Planters acquiesced, at first, in inconvenient and cramping government regulations partly because they believed the government would compensate them for their suffering. In October, 1861, a Mississippi woman told a friend that she was not selling any cotton because the "Government forbids it," but she was confident that they would "make arrangements as early as possible to relieve the planters all they can." [67] One gentleman was sure that the Confederacy would increase its relief when it understood that without cotton "we will not be able to feed & clothe our families with the actual necessities of life." [68] But even when the government responded, as it did when it established the "produce loan," which allowed planters to obtain Confederate loans by mortgaging their crops, planters claimed they were victimized by ruinously low prices for their produce.[69] And sometimes the government was slow to pay at all. When that happened, the typical response was likely to be that of Louisianan Lemuel P. Conner: *"Our plantations must not furnish the government any more corn."* [70] Whether planters disregarded or obeyed the laws pertaining to the cultivation and trade of cotton, they felt increasing bitterness toward the government that interfered so blatantly in their primary activity and offered them so little in return.

The Confederate government not only adopted a heavy-handed approach to the plantations but jeopardized Southern liberties in general. That acerbic critic Robert Toombs accused Jefferson Davis of a degree of authoritarianism that would make the recovery of "public liberty hereafter impossible without another bloody revolution." [71] Ella Clanton Thomas, a peppery supporter of the Southern cause, claimed that the Confederacy had become a "Despotism" where "no man dare express an opinion of his own." [72] A Georgia planter noted the bitter irony of this "terrible sacrifice of freedom in our War for freedom." [73]

Catherine Edmondston of North Carolina was one of those plantation dwellers who began by heaping praise on the Confederate government and ended by damning it to hell. This fiery woman hated all things Northern and welcomed immediate secession. The Yankees were "vile money worshippers," "pragmatical, insufferable, detestable," "quarrelsome, defiant, selfish," a "puritanical, deceitful race." In short, "We detest you!" In December, 1861, she explained why the Southern people chose to risk secession and war. "Men & women looked the alternative stern in the face and preferred death, extermination, anything to being conquered, subjugated, our God given blessing of self government infringed or even tampered with, and determined to resist to the last, to be free!" The issue could not be simpler or more frightening. The South fought "for home, for freedom, for independence," while the North battled "for conquest & tyranny [*sic*]." [74]

She entered the struggle eagerly, proud of her new country and new government. She was enraptured with President Jefferson Davis, whose style and charm she constantly contrasted with the crudity and gracelessness of the "railsplitter" to the North. "What a blessing that our exponent, our head, is a gentleman, a man not only of good sense but of good breeding." She congratulated the South for electing an entire government of "Gentlemen." And as late as 1863 she still believed that "our *Government* unlike the Yankee despotism does not lie. Its official Dispatches are all true, for they come from Gentlemen. . . ."

In 1862 her North Carolina plantation began to feel the impact of the war. When her husband left for the front, the dreary struggle for food and clothing and money fell to her. The usual hardships, including surly and disobedient slaves, came her way. She tried to convince herself that her privations could not be "what our fore fathers endured in the Revolution!" But by the end of the year she began to find fault with the Richmond government. At first she allowed herself to criticize only Confederate military strategy. She chided that the "rears of our two armies may yet meet if they fall back far enough!"

But by 1864 her government of gentlemen had become that "weak and imbecile Congress." She noted that in their last session they had passed "the suspension of the Act of Habeas Corpus . . . [and] the Military, the Currency, and the Tax Bills." Reviewing their labors, she concluded, "The first puts our liberties in the grasp of a simple man; the second resolves us with a Military despotism by putting all men between seventeen and fifty five into the service[;] . . . the third repudiates one third of the currency now in circulation[;] . . . & the fourth taxes us so heavily that after the Government has taken what it wants it leaves us little else to live on. . . ." Then, touching on what was at the heart of her anxiety and criticism, she described the "owners of slaves," those "whose money is invested in farming," as "so heavily mulcted that it almost amounts to an abolition of Slavery entirely so far as the profits are concerned."

In the last year of the war, she fired as many salvos at her own government as she did at the Yankee invaders. In March, 1865, she finally decided that "our ills spring not from the Yankees but from bad Government which has crippled our resources & thus allowed them to gain ascendency over us." And with the Northern soldiers at her door, she cried, "When we gain our Independence it will be in spite of our rulers!" The path of disillusionment and estrangement that Catherine Edmondston followed was crowded with members of the planter class.

The crux of the difficulty between the Confederate government and the planters lay in the difference between their ultimate goals. As the war lengthened, the government grew increasingly single-minded in its commitment to political independence and was more and more willing to subordinate all other interests to that end. A Virginia planter, Charles Ellis, in March, 1865, noted the rising criticism of the Richmond government but claimed that the people would fight on and suffer anything "for separation from the Yankees." [75] This Virginian was not representative of the planter class as a whole, however, for its members were primarily committed to the preservation of the plantation slavery system. They had called the Confederacy into being to preserve their interests, and by 1865 it appeared to many that their own creation was threatening what it had been established to defend. To found an independent nation and lose the plantations would be no victory. It would be utter defeat.

By 1865, therefore, a large portion of the planting community was alienated from its own government, having reached a position similar to the one James Lusk Alcorn achieved six months after the war began. And Southern planters were increasingly tempted to follow his example and wish a pox on both Washington and Richmond. They were certainly willing to join Robert Toombs in declaring that the "revolution" had been made "odious" by the Confederate government. [76] But in the end, they could not withdraw their commitment to Southern independence or their allegiance to the Confederacy, for they understood very well that their individual fates were welded to the fate of the Southern nation. They could only pull back into their rapidly crumbling sanctuary of family and farm and shake their fists at the destiny fortune had dealt them.

### III

Of the many changes in the social landscape of the South, few were more distressing to planters than the fragmentation of white solidarity. Planters feared that the entire social order was about to become unhinged. War had promised to heal the rifts between white Southerners, but instead it apparently produced even deeper divisions. Planters believed the South was divided along two axes—that of political loyalty and that of class affiliation. Unionism, withered by Lincoln's policy of coercion, stubbornly refused to die. It actually gained strength with each year of the war. Class animosity, denied by antebellum Southern spokesmen, was also a rising specter. Planters thought they perceived a growing class consciousness among non-slaveholders and feared the result would be class warfare. In time, planters came to believe that the two cracks in Southern unity —disloyalty to the Confederacy and disloyalty to the Southern social order—were caused by the same element: nonslaveholding, white Southerners.

In the winter of 1860–61, several different categories of political opinion coexisted in the South. Unionists opposed secession and Southern nationhood; secessionists supported immediate withdrawal and national independence; and "co-operationists" counseled united Southern action and secession only if injured. Secession dumped the co-operationists into the Confederate camp, and war pushed many Unionists into a defense of Southern liberty. While winter saw the South divided over its proper course of action, summer found white Southerners generally unified in their commitment to beat back Northern aggression.

Rock-ribbed Unionists persisted, nevertheless, and were found in every segment and class of the Southern population, including the plantation gentry. It is difficult to determine the actual number of planters who remained loyal to the Union. Frank Klingberg has discovered that in the 1870s, hundreds turned in claims to the Southern Claims Commission, established after the war to repay Southern Unionists for damages caused by Northern troops. More than 700 filed claims in excess of ten thousand dollars, of which 191 were eventually upheld, and almost 800 others filed claims in amounts of five thousand to ten thousand dollars, of which 224 were sustained.[77] Taking into account the Commission's stringent requirements for proof of loyalty and loss of property, as well as the attrition over time, Klingberg estimates that approximately four times this number—that is, about 1,660 planters—were actually eligible for recompense. According to the United States census of 1860, approximately 43,000 Southerners in what became the Confederate states owned more than twenty slaves. Using these two figures, we find that some 3.8 per cent of those in the planter class were active Unionists during the war.

Why some planters permanently cast their lot with the Union rather than with their class is not always readily apparent. Often, they were tied to the North by sentiment, education, business, or blood. For whatever reason, these Southerners could not bring themselves to participate in the Union's destruction, and actively opposed those who did. There was no ambiguity in the Unionism of the woman in Issaquena County, Mississippi, who was driven off her plantation for stubbornly flying a United States flag, or of the planter in Lexington County, South Carolina, who urged his son to escape to the North to join the Union army and defeat the rebellion.[78] But few Unionists could match the fury of James Madison Wells of Louisiana, owner of four plantations and nearly a hundred slaves. He denounced the conflict as a rich man's war and a poor man's fight, gathered more than a hundred men around him in the woods of Rapides Parish, and made forays to trap and destroy Confederate wagon trains. Finally, in November, 1863, he fled to the safety of the Union lines, from which he continued to wage war on the Confederacy.[79]

Nor was there any doubt about the loyalty of J. F. H. Claiborne, historian, politician, and master of "Laurel Wood," on the Gulf coast of Mississippi. He had hoped to remain neutral, but when forced by war to choose sides, he chose the Union, serving as a spy for the Federal forces that invaded his neighborhood in 1862. In a letter to the general of the Union forces, Claiborne explained the plight of the Southern Unionist, incidentally indicating why the historian has difficulty establishing the Unionist credentials of any particular individual without conclusive contemporary evidence. "Surrounded here by armed men, mostly of desperate character & fortunes, my person in danger, and my property liable to be plundered, I have been compelled to be circumspect," Claiborne explained. "But," he added, "I have neglected no means to further the cause." By being circumspect, he meant that he had kept his Unionism under his hat and had lent some support to the Confederate government—purchasing Confederate war bonds, for example.[80]

Though planters were certainly numbered among the Unionists of the rock-ribbed variety, it is possible that even the small percentage found by Klingberg is exaggerated. The evidence accepted by the Southern Claims Commission after the war as proof of Unionism was sometimes ambiguous and inconclusive, despite the Commission's efforts to weed out the states'-rights Southerner who had merely been disaffected with the Confederacy and the war-weary Southerner who had merely wanted an end to the conflict. As the Claiborne example demonstrates, the purchase of Confederate bonds was not necessarily evidence of warm-hearted support of the Southern cause. It may have been, as it was in his case, a cheap way to obtain protection for a highly visible, highly immobile, and therefore highly vulnerable planter. Likewise, refusing to sell provisions to the Confederacy, selling goods to the Yankees, and evading service in the Confederate military, all of which were accepted by the Commission as partial proof of active Unionism, may not have been evidence of Unionism at all. The motivation of these acts did not invariably have political components. While some individuals may have been inspired by resolute national affection, others may have been self-interested planters just seeking their own survival.

That is not to say that the planter class was unanimous in its support of Southern independence. However, it is significant that the planters, who were very sensitive about such things, expressed no concern about rampant Unionism within their own class, at least after the outbreak of war sharpened the issues. Unionism was certainly rarer among members of the planter class than in any other segment of the Southern population. Many planters, of course, maintained a deep affection for the Union and writhed at its tragic destruction. They railed at the agitators, Northern and Southern, who had brought on "this sad, useless, politicians' war." But when faced with the apparent alternatives of independence or subjugation to "black Republicanism," they overwhelmingly chose independence. True Unionism, the Unionism that had a real effect on the fortunes of the Confederacy, was concentrated in those areas where nonslaveholders predominated—northern Alabama, the mountain counties of Georgia, eastern Tennessee, and western North Carolina. When the planters identified Unionism with the white laboring class, they were largely correct.[81]

Persistent Unionism shattered the dream of white solidarity in the South and posed problems for the planters' comfortable view of the Southern cause. Planters wanted to see themselves as defending a whole regional way of life, not simply their class right to exploit black and white labor. Unionist sentiment among white nonslaveholders threatened to make the entire myth unbelievable, even to Southerners, by exposing the reality. More concretely, planters feared that persistent Unionism would give rise to an active fifth column for the Northern cause. At the very least, planters thought, divisions at the top among whites might spark "servile insurrections" among the blacks below. In a society based on racial slavery, white unity was imperative. But just as menacing in the eyes of some planters was the division they perceived taking place along another seam. Planters believed that they saw a growing class consciousness and belligerence among nonslaveholders, whether they were Unionists or not. In the cry that it was a rich man's war but a poor man's fight, planters perceived a deterioration of their hegemony. They feared that whites of the lower class might actually attempt to wage class warfare against the plantations.

Thinking in terms of classes came naturally to planters. They had been raised in an environment in which class distinctions were in the air, taken for granted as reflections of the established social order. The tendency was more pronounced among the older, eastern lowland aristocracy perhaps, but planters everywhere exhibited a self-conscious elitism. They were the legitimate guardians of the lesser classes, black and white, the arbiters of the economy, culture, and government of the South.

At the same time, however, the South was a self-professed democratic society. George Fredrickson has called the South a "*Herrenvolk* democracy," democratic for the master race but tyrannical for the subordinate race.[82] But the democratic and egalitarian ethos did not sit easily with the planters' aristocratic philosophy or the actual distribution of power and wealth in Southern society. Their continued hegemony demanded that they publicly proclaim their democratic convictions, but planters were self-conscious about their position in Southern society and worried that it was fundamentally insecure. They argued vigorously that the existing social order served *all* Southerners' interests. Racial slavery provided every white man membership in the ruling class and also the means by which non-slaveholders could advance into the gentry. In 1854, Alfred Huger succinctly explained how slavery operated in this dual fashion to unify whites. Speaking of land and slaves, he said, "Those who have neither & are disposed to work are in every respect on a footing with their wealthy neighbors." [83]

Because every white man had a stake in slavery, therefore, Southern spokesmen during the secession crisis promised that every white Southerner would fight to the death to defend his way of life. But whatever the public dialogue, planters also expressed doubts about the security of slavery and the stability of class relationships in the South. Perhaps their anxiety was prompted by the ambivalence of their position as aristocrats in a democracy. Certainly, during the secession crisis planters had revealed their fears that Southern society was badly out of joint. The disjuncture, they thought, was largely the result of certain notions, Northern in origin and democratic in spirit, which infected the white laboring classes. Some planters had opposed secession for the very reason that the upheaval of war would surely fan the flames of class dissension. And others had looked upon the war as an opportunity to exorcise those ideas which were poisoning Southern society.

Whatever the final impact of the war on class relations in the South, its immediate effect was to bring white Southerners closer together —much closer, in fact, than many planters desired. For the war not only helped unite the South against the "Lincolnites" but also brought white Southerners elbow to elbow in the Confederate military service. The plantation had apparently shielded many young planters from contact with poorer whites, for when army life brought them together, they often found the indiscriminant mixing of classes repugnant.

While some young aristocrats—notably the sons of Robert E. Lee, P. G. T. Beauregard, and James M. Chestnut—volunteered as privates in the Confederate armies, scion after young scion complained of the mingling of the classes in the camps. One young planter declared that the "dignity of Office is becoming lowered in our Army.

Our transportation is so limited that Co. Officers are about on a par with privates in point of dress and sociability." [84] Another glumly reported to his family that "there are very few of the officers who are our equals in society." [85] Young Cadwallader Jones was angry about his reassignment because "there is such a difference between the men composing that company, and these, this company; there they were mostly educated men—nearly all gentlemen, here they are a set of men that can scarcely read." But, to give them their due, he admitted that they were "clever in their way." [86]

More fortunate in his military service, apparently, was Charles C. Jones, Jr. Son of a prominent upcountry planter and himself mayor of Savannah, this young officer extolled his Chatham artillery as "a company of companions and of gentlemen," each of whom had "large private interests at stake." To gain admittance to this august assembly, one had to possess "character, blood, and social position." The candidate also had to be vouched for by two members and receive four-fifths of the votes of the entire company.[87] Jones's good fortune was short-lived, however. In a matter of months, he was visiting conscript camps, impressing draftees to fill his company's depleted ranks. In the first months of the war, perhaps, the situation in the military might have only confirmed the social hierarchy of the South. Very quickly, however, the military approached the condition of a democracy.

But to listen to the families back on the plantations, one would have thought that Southern armies were made up entirely of gentlemen. The home folk certainly believed that their class was bearing the brunt of the fighting. A North Carolina woman declared in 1861 that Confederate armies were "composed mainly of gentlemen, the best blood of the South, which will be poured out like water 'ere that rabble shall conquer us!" [88] A Georgian moaned, "Oh, what inroads this horrible war is making in our best population." [89] And another agreed, saying, "Some of the best blood of the country has been spilled. O the horrors of war." [90]

And when a gentleman's blood was actually spilled on the battlefield, he could expect no better social environment in the hospital. Ella Clanton Thomas remarked while visiting the sick in Atlanta, "To a man of refinement and education how horrible the association and proximity of men essentially different from him. No privacy—no seclusion." [91] There was apparently no end to the suffering of the

South's aristocracy. Besides fighting against inferiors, they also had to fight and die alongside them. These were, indeed, children of pride, if not of *hubris*.

The war not only disrupted normal class relations in the military but threatened to disrupt the entire social structure. Planters feared not only that the lower class would rise up but that their own class would slip down. Poverty gnawed at every plantation home, promising a loss of status along with the physical hardship. A year before the war, Vardry McBee, a wealthy North Carolina gentleman, expressed the general attitude toward poverty. He complained of those people who did "nothing whilst able" and who "reconcile themselves under the old saying that poverty is no crime." "It is not a crime punishable by authority in a tribunal," he admitted, "but really it is a disgrace to be very poor." [92]

The disgrace of poverty was something with which many planter families had to contend. A young Georgia girl was ashamed of the new duties which necessity had forced on her. She was busy making her first bedquilt, but the young mistress promised it would be her last. "Only poor white folks made bed quilts," she huffed, "the rich buy blankets." [93] Catherine Edmondston was distressed by the more intimate and long-term results of economic decline. "Ah Poverty!" she rasped, "thy worst evil is the debasing intercourse you force upon your subjects!" While good ancestry was "ennobling" and "exalting," poverty "diluted" the blood. For one who had disdainfully characterized the North as a mongrel nation, the vision of a ruined South was revolting. Southerners railed not only against the "damnyankees" but also against the "vile leveling yankees!" [94]

The early years of the war found white Southerners standing shoulder to shoulder. If the lower classes stood a little closer to the aristocrats than the aristocrats liked, at least they were standing with them. Some planters could not help expressing surprise that the lower classes were holding firm. In January, 1862, the manager of an Alabama plantation reported to the owner that the "laboring *classes* [italics added] were never more comfortable or contented is the remark of *all parties*." [95] The planters particularly scrutinized the behavior of the nonslaveholders when Northern troops approached. "The low white population," a woman remarked in May, 1862, "wonderful to say, commit few excesses even in the presence of the enemy, upon whom they could lay the blame . . . but the indulged negroes . . . are terri-

bly insolent." [96] By continually scanning the horizons for signs of
class eruption, planters revealed their own deep anxieties.

Planters believed that the Yankee invasion would stir most white
Southerners to resist, and they also expressed the belief, or perhaps it
was a hope, that the common experience of suffering would bind the
white South even more tightly together and strengthen its resolve to
win. One Georgia planter thought that "our late disasters are arousing
our country, and making all a *unit*, and inspiring us with a right
spirit." [97] Another Georgian believed that "fellow suffering makes us
all equal & all to feel interested in one another." [98] And a third
Georgia gentleman, speaking after a Northern raiding party had cut
through his neighborhood, said, "These trying times make us all feel a
warm sympathy for each other." [99]

Warm sympathy may have been common in the early months and
years, but as the war lengthened, the darker emotions of envy and
hatred surfaced. Increasing numbers of poor white Southerners came
to see planters as hoarders and speculators, slackers and backsliders.
Didn't slaveholders evade military service, traffic with the enemy,
speculate in food crops, and in general, profit from the misery of
fellow Southerners? The Mobile *News* charged that planters "lowered
the high standards of Southern chivalry . . . and descended from the
most exalted position known on earth—Southern gentlemen—to
become nothing better than common hucksters." [100] Especially annoying to the poor was the planters' insistence on cultivating staples. A
slaveless Mississippian complained to his governor about planters who
sent their slaves into the fields to plant cotton, while in the very sight of
the mansion, "poor soldiers' wives are plowing with *their own* hands to
make a subsistence for themselves and children—while their husbands are suffering bleeding and dying for their country." [101] Planting
cotton was such a blatant affront, such obvious evidence of disregard
for the feelings and needs of poor families, that the average white
Southerner would probably have cheered the *Southern Cultivator's*
declaration that every planter who grew cotton "deserves to be destroyed, or to have all his plantations and negroes ravaged and deso-
lated, and himself fed upon corn cobs as long as he lives." [102]

The reputation of closefistedness was well deserved by some planters. Their vaunted chivalry, paternal feeling, and sense of *noblesse
oblige* toward the lower classes may have been thin to begin with, or
perhaps these individuals sensed betrayal and disrespect and closed off

their hearts and their pocketbooks. Or perhaps they were simply unable to reach beyond their own grim struggle for survival. Whatever the reason, a poor Alabama farmer reported in 1864 that a neighboring planter, when asked if he would help feed several hungry families, had "very indifferently replied that he new meny familys has children war picking Berreys to keep from Starving." A planter's wife refused to help, saying she had "heard a good many famileys was Boilling Potatoes Vines to Subsist on. . . ." [103] But what was perceived as hardheartedness was sometimes insensitivity and ignorance. A daughter-in-law of Howell Cobb's, for instance, claimed that there was more equality than the poor "dream of" between the privations borne by the rich and by the poor. As evidence she offered the fact that "with five plantations we are restricted to the use of the proceeds from only the poorest." [104]

And yet, despite their own struggle, many plantation dwellers expressed a genuine concern for the plight of the poor. Plantation mistress Sallie Hunt was suffering along with the needy when she wrote in October, 1861, "Oh lord pity the poor I pray—when the Rich have many things to fall back on hogs cattle sheep negroes to cut their wood & work." [105] Another woman said in 1862 that "the poor must suffer because everything is so high." [106] Some planters backed their concern with generous assistance. A North Carolina planter, for instance, gave several hundred bushels of salt to the "poorer classes" in his neighborhood, accepting in return only homemade socks, which he donated to the Confederate armies. [107] It appears, however, that the displays of empathy and generosity diminished with each year of the war. In June, 1864, for instance, a Virginian remarked that in his county only he and one other planter had volunteered corn "for soldiers['] families & the Poor." [108]

From the beginning, some planters feared that, despite the Yankee invasion of the homeland and the shared suffering, a long war would mean that white Southerners would become divided among themselves. With their eyes straining to discover signs of class dissension, and with the war producing dissatisfaction among poorer whites, planters inevitably found evidence to support their suspicions. Some saw class warfare presaged by the rising incidence of crime in the Confederacy. Across the South, planters were dismayed by the number of attacks on property, and often interpreted them not as the product of a dislocated and poverty-stricken society but as the expres-

sion of rising class hostility. "I have been informed by gentlemen of
respectability," a planter said in 1863, "that the lower classes in
Mississippi . . . are engaged in robing [sic] and stealing every thing
that comes in their way, and that people of property suffer more from
these wretches than from the Yankees." [109] That same year, a Virginian declared that his greatest worry was that "*want* will drive those who
have not to take from those who have, what their wants require, by
open force." [110] A year later a Georgia overseer explained to his
employer, "Times is hard here and worse is comeing for if the yanks
dont get here our own people is getting so mean that I see no chance to
live among them for they can nearly steal the chew tobacco out of a
mans mouth and him not know it." [111]

   Though they uttered not a word about their tobacco, women in the
Confederacy were worried about being robbed. They also feared that
they were surrounded by traitors. Late in 1862, Catherine Edmondston heard that the people of Chowan and Gates counties in North
Carolina were rampaging and joining the Yankees. She dismissed
them as "the off-scouring of the people and foreigners, people who
can neither read or write and who never had a decent suit of clothes
until they gave it to them, poor ignorant wretches who cannot resist a
fine uniform and the choice of the horses in the country & liberty to
help themselves without check to their rich neighbors['] belongings."
A Virginia plantation woman responded to the news in much the
same manner. "You know the lower classes of the counties of that part
of Carolina have always been very degraded. They could always be
bought, so they have sold themselves to the Yankies. . . ." Edmondston tried to judge them "leniently," but she knew in her heart that
"justice to ourselves demands that we shoot them down like wolves on
sight." [112]

   That lower-class whites would become both thieves and turncoats
disgusted and worried planters, but it did not surprise them. Some had
predicted as much, and others had feared it. Alfred Huger had once
explained, "Those who have *no* property are . . . sufficiently willing
to be the enemies of those *who have*." [113] And by joining the Yankees,
the poorer whites had merely acquired powerful allies in the efforts at
plunder. In the fall of 1861, Southerners discovered that treason and
theft were linked, when rebellions against the Confederacy flared in
the Appalachian Mountains. The Confederate colonel sent to sup-
press the insurrection reported that the prisoners he had captured were

convinced that the Union army "would join them in a few days," and that when it did "the property of Southern men was to be confiscated and divided amongst those who would take up arms for Lincoln." [114]

The Southern gentry had often portrayed the North as a "lower-class nation," and as such, they feared, Northerners were natural allies for poor white Southerners. Northerners were without style and grace, a people of "ditch water blood," who understood neither the "instincts of a gentleman nor the impulses of a freeman." [115] A young Louisiana aristocrat was repulsed by the "vulgar, cunning & ranting Yankee," an individual totally "without manners and without principles." Because the Northerner "knows, feels, & smarts under this inferiority," he harbors "bitter feelings & even cruelty against our best people—against Families of culture and of pride." [116] The North was a society in which liberty had become license, and order, chaos. Under its dominion, neither property nor the propertied class was safe. [117]

Certainly nothing emanated from the North to discourage the opinion that Federal armies were out to cut down the South's aristocracy. Northern propaganda pictured secession as a "slaveholders' rebellion," and portrayed the North as the vanguard against privilege and the aristocratic past. In the Confiscation Acts, Congress displayed its willingness to violate the sanctity of property. One Alabama planter was convinced by 1864 that "an exasperated mob" controlled Northern war policy. "Lincoln does not *lead*," the planter said. "He has been driven . . . & is yet driven on, powerless to direct." [118] And many Republicans clearly wanted the North to go further than it already had. Congressman George Julian of Indiana, for one, said that the war was a struggle "against a rebellious aristocracy founded on the monopoly of land and the ownership of negroes," and he demanded that the plantations be broken up and the lands distributed to persons, white or black, who were loyal to the Union. [119] To some Southerners, he appeared to be inviting not only Unionism, but class and race warfare as well.

Southerners believed that the North was the land of "mob law," and many argued loudly in 1861 that the "law-abiding mass of the American people lies south of the Mason and Dixon's line." [120] Henry Watson, Jr., of Alabama reported that when he received a letter from a Northern friend suggesting that "we are living in terror of our slaves & are not safe from our own poor whites," he could only laugh. He wrote back that he was, indeed, in danger but only from "the heat and drowth." [121]

These particular planters may or may not have been whistling in the dark, but many others became certain that there was a large "Southern element Northernized." [122] The "bread riots" of 1863 convinced Catherine Edmondston. She called the rioters "mobs for plunder" and believed that they were "instigated by the Yankees." They were "low foreigners, Irish, Dutch, and Yankees and in place of wanting bread they threw Rice, flour, etc., in the street and mobbed dry goods and shoe stores!" Obviously, then, it was an "affair for plunder alone." [123] In 1864, a Cobb County, Georgia, planter declared that "the whole country is in a lawless condition, citizens and soldiers of both armies all alike availing themselves of the distracted state of the country, committing all depredations of plundering and murdering." Because of the chaos, "laws are suspended and the evil passions let loose." [124] And by 1865, Ella Clanton Thomas of Augusta believed "the time appears rapidly approaching when we have almost as much to dread from our demoralized mob as from the public enemy." A month later she reported that "the mob rule the hour." [125]

Although the war shook the Southern social order to its roots, it did not transform the members of the South's nonslaveholding class into social revolutionaries. Nonslaveholding white Southerners grew increasingly unresponsive and even hostile to the planter regime and the Southern cause, but the war produced neither a Southern-black nor a poor-white *Jacquerie*. There was a rising feeling among nonslaveholders that they were fighting a rich man's war, but their animosity was probably less often evidence of heightened class awareness than of disaffection with a losing cause and frustration with privation. Instead of picking up either the red or the black flag, they let all flags drop to the ground. They neither approached the planter's mansion with a torch nor confronted him at the ballot box. They simply slipped away from the battlefields and went home. Examples of "revolutionary" activity spied by sharp-eyed planters were usually the foraging expeditions of desperate people. Exhausted, disillusioned, and hungry, most yeoman whites sought peace, not the planters' hides. By 1865, they would probably have accepted a settlement based simply on emancipation and the restoration of the Union. [126]

Perhaps it was this willingness of the poor whites to embrace peace at the expense of slavery that lay behind the planter's deep distrust of the class. That was, in fact, their only truly revolutionary tendency. Catherine Edmondston had entered the war shouting that the non-slaveholders would fight, and fight ferociously, for slavery, and Henry Watson, Jr., had rejected any suggestion that the lower class might betray the slaveholders. By 1864, planters were expressing serious doubts. Watson himself wondered what would happen if the North were actually on the verge of conquering the South. "The *slave-holders*," he reminded a friend, "in all the slave states number but 340,000. When trouble, ruin, starvation & misery come upon our people, will the remaining 5,000,000 hesitate long, on promises of pardon & restoration of their lands & peace, to sacrifice the 340,000 and themselves abolish slavery in the South[?] Between the two, I fear slavery stands a poor chance." [127]

The locus of the Civil War for the Southern planter class was the plantation. The war began when the planters took the South out of the Union rather than risk the destruction of plantation slavery at the hands of a Northern majority. The war was expected to be a demanding but straightforward contest, North against South. But by 1862 plantation dwellers could be heard to pray, "Keep us from internal as well as external foes." [128] Instead of being threatened by a single thrust from the north, the plantation, as viewed from the mansion verandah, appeared to be under siege by forces from all directions. Armies, races, classes, and governments—Northerners, blacks, nonslaveholding white Southerners, and the Confederacy itself—were perceived by planters as clawing at the pillars of Southern civilization. Planters steadily pulled back into their plantations, where they struggled to maintain their mastery over their domains and subjects. But as Alexander Stephens had warned, revolutions are much easier started than controlled, and the men who begin them seldom end them.

# CHAPTER 3

# A Loss of Mastery

"War is father of all and king of all, and some he shows as gods, others as men; some he makes slaves, others free."

HERACLITUS

Because slavery was the planters' touchstone and test of all things, the supreme meaning of the Civil War for the planter class lay in the destruction of slavery. Slavery was embedded in the plantation, and this environment was hammered and battered, disrupted and re-shaped, by the long war. In unexposed parts of the South, slavery was still functioning in early 1865, but in many other areas it had been irretrievably demolished months before. The physical disintegration of slavery exerted enormous pressure on Southern planters to relin-quish their dedication to their peculiar institution and to the ideology which it had spawned. The history of the planter class in the Civil War, however, is the record of a passionate defense of the ideas and ideals they brought to the conflict. Emancipationist sentiment surged in every other segment of the South's population. Slavery was be-trayed, but not by the master class. Slavery's disintegration was not matched by a general falling away from central principles by planters. On the crucial matters of slavery and blacks, Southern agriculture and Southern civilization, planters ended the war much as they began it.

I

Planters had revolted in 1860–61 because they believed "black Republicanism" jeopardized plantation slavery. If the South remained in the Union, they reasoned, abolitionism would surely worm its way into the plantations, undermining the fundamental principles of order and control, without which slavery would crumble. An irony of the war, of course, was that it left planters with little control and the plantations in general disorder. But planters were not content simply to sit back on their verandahs and watch their world disintegrate. They fought to preserve their slave plantations. Their strategy was straightforward and predictable, but in the end their conceptualization of the problem of defense proved naïve and their strategy a failure.

The slave-plantation system stood at the center of the antebellum Southern economy, and at the center of the plantation stood the planter. Before the war, the slaveholder presiding over his isolated estate had been largely free, within only a few broad constraints, to organize, operate, and rule or misrule as he pleased. Almost without outside imposition, he could set his own rules and follow or evade statute law as he pleased. And for very practical reasons he was jealous of his prerogatives. In a forced-labor system, it was imperative that authority remain clearly defined and absolute. Competing centers of power could only disrupt. Order and control demanded that mastership be undivided and complete.

The slave master was an object of fascination among contemporary Americans, but descriptions often clashed. On the eve of the war, one Southern observer, Daniel Hundley, described the planter as an impeccable aristocrat, with a blue-blooded lineage, faultless physique, a well-trained mind, gracious manners and openhanded hospitality, a way with horses, guns, and hounds, and a highly honed sense of honor and duty.[1] But a Northern contemporary, Frederick Law Olmsted, questioned the existence of such a being as the Southern gentleman. He found the planter class to be composed of stupid, uneducated, loutish, vulgar men, who crassly and brutally exploited the lower classes of both colors.[2] Actually, the sprawling plantation country was broad enough to encompass planter personalities of a number of types, from the chivalrous and genteel to the illiterate and tobacco-stained—from the Sartoris to the Sutpen. Some plantations resembled patriarchal families, networks of authority and warm affection, subordination and genuine responsibility, while others were organized in the crudest manner, revolving entirely around profit, with men and beasts treated brutally and considered of equal value.

Despite their enormous differences in refinement and humanity, planters had in common the practical task of managing large numbers of black slaves in the production of staple crops. While slaveholders played many roles, practical economic duty provided an important element of uniformity within the planter class. Tradition commonly portrays the planter as a casual manager, uninterested in production and cost figures, careless about routine and organization, generally slipshod and disorderly in his agricultural operations.[3] Planters bull-headedly clung to some inefficient ways, certainly, but they were often practical-minded men who were decidedly not indifferent to the realities of managing plantation finances and plantation labor. As U. B. Phillips has explained, financial loss endangered more than a planter's bank account. His economic pursuit was often more than a means of maintaining his way of life. It was his life. Nor could slaveholders afford to be careless about their labor force. The situation of Alfred Huger was typical. He said before the war, "I am utterly dependent as to property & as to the safety of my family for peace and tranquility among our Negroes." [4] And tranquil slaves were the product of careful supervision and stern discipline. The most famous antebellum plantations, while hardly modern scientific enterprises, were run in a relatively methodical manner, with planters monitoring both the finances and the labor, seeking to maximize both order and control.

The Civil War threatened to destroy planter control and plantation order by shattering the shield of isolation which protected rural estates. War transformed the Southern countryside from a supportive environment to hostile territory. It ate away at the vital relationships between master and slave and between slave and plantation. It disrupted routine and system and diminished mastery. Before the fighting ended, a score of assailants breached the walls of the plantations. Although none but those who wore blue uniforms were lethal, each inflicted a painful wound on the slave regime.

In the early years of the war, planters seemed to see the protection of slavery largely in terms of controlling slave behavior. Since slaves themselves had always been considered the chief threat to the institution, it was natural that the thinking of planters begin there. Masters constructed a strategy of defense based on the prewar precedent —isolation. Their aim was to keep the slaves in and abolitionist ideas out. If dangerous notions could be kept out of the slave quarters and the slaves kept on the plantations, slavery would be secure. The Reverend C. C. Jones and his son agreed that their "entire social system" depended on their ability to "*seal* by the most rigid police all ingress and egress" to the plantation. They realized, however, that "this is most difficult." [5] Had they been medieval barons, planters would likely have filled their moats to the brim and pulled up their drawbridges until the danger passed.

The worry that the slaves themselves might destroy slavery was as old as the institution itself. It rested in large part on the planters' image of the black personality. This was a dual image, as George Fredrickson has explained, including a "hard" portrait and a "soft" one—painting the black on the one hand as a lower order of human, nearly a beast, and on the other as an immature human, a child. [6] Catherine Edmondston, a long-time observer of life in the slave quarters, believed blacks were a rudimentary type. "I do not think negroes possess natural feelings," she said during the war. In the treatment of their young and their old, they showed none of the "natural sentiments," while in their sexual activity, their feelings were unnaturally heightened. In March, 1862, she witnessed a slave marriage which followed an engagement of one day. "So Cupid gave place to Hymen in a shorter time than usual—primitive customs one will say, but Cuffee strips off the elegancies and refinements of civilization with great ease." [7]

Vying with the image of the black as a lower order of human was the image of the undeveloped and childlike black personality. "I see from your letter, as from many others I receive," Henry Watson, Jr., of Alabama said to a Northern friend on the eve of the war, "that you at the North think we live in perpetual dread of our servants. There could not be possibly a greater mistake. As well might you suppose that we lived in terror of our children." Most slaveholders, he explained, felt "an attachment for the servants similar, in some respects, to that we feel for our children. We feed them, clothe them, nurse them when sick and in all things provide for them. How can we do this and not love them?" As for the slaves, "they too feel an affection for their master, his wife and children and they are proud of his and their success." Watson thought there was a "charm" in the name "Master."

Slaves "look upon and to their master with the same feeling that a
child looks to his father. It is a lovely trait in them. This being the case
how can we fear them?" [8]

Both images existed simultaneously, though uneasily, in most
white Southern minds. A Georgia woman, for instance, called away
from her plantation for a few days, was "perplexed" at having to leave
her "people" without "white protection and control." [9] Whites offered blacks both safety and discipline; they were at once guardians
and jailers of the black child-beast. Regardless of which image dominated in the mind of any particular planter, all agreed that blacks were
inherently inferior. Unequal and thus unfit for freedom, they could
only be enslaved. Either as children or as beasts, they required close
and continuous supervision. Either foolish or irrational, they could
easily be persuaded to flight or worse. Blacks were not an ideal
laboring class, but if isolated from all noxious ideas and kept under the
firm authority of the master, they were capable of steady, even affectionate, service.

Slavery spawned its own defense, and in addition, continuous
abolitionist attack forced Southerners to construct rigorous arguments
in support of their peculiar institution. Southern spokesmen turned to
the Bible, biology, social theory, history, and law for justification.
Theoretically inclined Alfred Huger, for instance, declared that slavery was not merely a "legal interpretation" or a "treaty between men,"
but "a separate and distinct 'institution' ordained by the Almighty!" [10]
More often, however, working planters constructed their defense of
slavery around what they knew best—the everyday, practical circumstances of Southern slaves.

Planters' arguments often took the form of a discussion comparing
the welfare of their slaves with that of free labor. In reply to those who
argued that blacks were savagely treated in the South, plantation
dwellers pointed to the blacks' fate in the North. Planters who visited
the North were often genuinely shocked by what they saw. In 1854, a
Mississippi man wrote home to his sister on the plantation that he was
sickened by the way blacks lived in Philadelphia. "As for the negroes,"
he said, "there is as many as ten or fifteen living in one little hut about
ten feet long and twelve feet wide, with nothing to eate one half of the
time, and I might add nothing to sleepe on. . . ." Some, he declared,
were "actually starving for something to eat." [11]

The defenders of slavery also contrasted the well-being of Southern slaves with the pitiful state of Northern white labor. In 1857, a North Carolina planter—sounding something like a more illustrious Southerner, George Fitzhugh—reported that all of "his people" were "healthy, contented and happy, with plenty to eat" and "well clothed." Each had a house supplied by the owner, "with a pile of wood" and "a nice garden of about half an acre." Negroes had "their supply of meal, pork, molasses and tobacco weekly, with a meeting house to which they resort every Sunday, to sing and pray, and a clergyman to preach . . . and a physician to attend them when sick." When he saw the "comfort" of his slaves, he said, "I sincerely pity the condition of the poor operatives in the northern factories who are turned loose to starve with all the horrors of winter staring them in the face. Without employment, without wages or food, without clothing, without fire, without houses to shelter them, they are turned adrift by their employers. . . ." He could not understand why Northerners, with troubles enough at home, busied themselves "in destroying the peace, confidence, and affection subsisting between the master and his slaves." [12]

Sometimes planters ranged beyond the black and white laboring classes of the North to comparisons on the international level. In 1862 Catherine Edmondston was struck with the bounty and nutritiousness of the slaves' ration, even in the midst of a war. She thought it must be "more than any other laboring class on the globe gets regularly." She made a list: "Think of what the Irish get—'potatoes & porid [sic],' the French—'bread & grapes,' Italiens [sic]—Maccaroni & olive oil, the Spanish—Black bread & garlic, the Swedes—but it is useless to go through the catalogue. The object of their misplaced sympathy, the poor negro, fares better than any of them & has as much freedom." [13] Compared with other members of the same race or class, Southern planters concluded, the slaves were fortunate indeed.

Though they argued that Southern slaves fared better than Northern blacks, Northern white workers, and the world's working class, planters knew that Northerners did not accept this view, and feared that the slaves did not realize their good fortune. And the planters' constant references to it may have revealed their own doubts. But certainly after John Brown's attack at Harpers Ferry, Southerners had little doubt about Northern attitudes. In Southern eyes, the Northern response to this atrocity proved that the North was an abolitionist nation. For decades, Southerners had labored to make the South safe for slavery, smothering debate and insisting on an orthodox proslavery position, but with John Brown's raid their efforts became deadly earnest. In December, 1859, David Gavin of South Carolina was thrilled to hear that so many "abolitionist emissaries have been lynched and expelled from the country." He was dissatisfied, however, with the degree of protection that had been achieved. He thought that "there should be sound and efficient laws passed and a good and sufficient police or number of soldiers enlisted to enforce them, and stringent laws about free negroes, persons of Colour and all white persons who have not a visible means of an honest living." [14]

The secession crisis pushed the South to the edge of frenzy. Rumors of "servile insurrection" raced from Virginia to Texas. Anti-secessionists in the South did their share to feed the panic by arguing that disunion would trigger a massive uprising among the slaves. Abolitionists in the North also promised that the first shot would serve as a signal for the slave revolution. Docility among slaves, planters knew, was not inherent, but the product of careful discipline. Consequently, as one planter noted in the fall of 1860, "A little offense of a negro may cost him his life." [15]

After secession, one of the first orders of business was to tighten controls over slaves and all those who came into contact with them. David Gavin must have been pleased as Southerners put more bite into their laws against "tampering," buttressed their slave patrols and canceled exemptions from duty, called home slaves on hire in the cities, and voided slaves' passes to visit families on other plantations. Individuals also did what they could to tighten security. William Cooper of Mississippi captured four runaways in 1862, and instead of returning all of them to their owners, he returned three and hanged one as a public lesson. [16] Gentlemen in Henry A. Middleton's neighborhood in South Carolina adopted the same punishment but a different mathematics. When they captured six runaways, they returned three and hanged three. "The blacks were encouraged to be present," Middleton reported. "The effect will not soon be forgotten." [17]

But fears of insurrection would not die. Plantation dwellers kept their ears to the ground, listening for rumbles of black revolution. Waves of dread and fear drifted back and forth across the Confederacy. In late 1861, a Mississippi woman heard a rumor that Natchez officials had recently quashed an attempted "servile insurrection" in their city. She told a friend that the revolutionaries "were supposed to come to this co. next [;] they were to kill every Negro that wouldn't join them." [18] More often, letters between planters contained a line or two confirming the fact that their blacks were still quiet. Six weeks after Sumter, William Kirkland let his anxious sister know that the "Negroes here are as subordinate as ever and if properly managed and well treated will I think continue so. . . ." [19] Two years later Fanny I. Erwin remarked that the "negroes too are as quiet & well-contented as they can be, in spite of the fears of a great many who apprehend trouble this winter." [20] The planters repeated descriptions of the slave's docility doubtlessly revealed their nagging fears of his rebelliousness.

Dread reached a crescendo in September, 1862, with Lincoln's Emancipation Proclamation. Planters saw in it the most unprincipled villainy. John Houston Bills of Tennessee thought Lincoln was trying his mightiest to inaugurate "servile War" and feared "a great loss of property and perhaps of life." [21] The young mayor of Savannah looked upon the act "as a direct bid for insurrection," an "infamous attempt to incite flight, murder, and rapine on the part of our slave population." Is it not an effort "to subvert our entire social system, desolate our homes, and convert the quiet, ignorant dependent black son of toil into a savage incendiary and brutal murderer?" he asked his father. His father agreed that Lincoln's message reeked of the "same heartless, cold-blooded, and murderous fanaticism that first began and has marked the war. . . ." [22] When January 1, the day the Proclamation went into effect, came and went quietly, planters breathed a sigh of relief. But as long as slavery existed they were never released from anxiety.

The abolitionist threat was not restricted to speeches and proclamations from Washington. War meant that the South was filled with Yankee soldiers, each of whom, the planters said, was itching to foment rebellion. In Virginia, Thomas Watson declared his "main dread" to be "that the Yankees will attempt to liberate and arm the slaves." [23] The path of Northern armies was marked by the trail of rumors it left behind. Hugh Torrance of Mississippi reported that raiding Yankees had told slaves that to be free "all they would have to do would be to kill their owners & take possession & live as white people." [24] When Federal troops invaded North Carolina, a rumor marched with them that the slaves were only waiting for the signal "to rise up against their masters & strike a blow for Union." [25] Louis Manigault of South Carolina charged that the South was dealing with "an Enemy of no principle whatsoever, whose only aim is . . . to arm our own Negroes against their very Masters; and entice by every means this misguided Race to assist them in their diabolical programme." With "this species of Warfare none of us can boast of our positions," he said, "for never with more truth can it be said None of us can tell 'what a day may bring forth.' " [26]

Yankees, however, were only one source of abolitionist ideas. Some two dozen planters from Marion District, South Carolina, pointed their fingers at another that was closer to home. In a May, 1862, appeal to their governor, they reported that there was in their neighborhood a family of "nonslaveholders" who traded with blacks, who sent no men to serve in the Confederate forces, and whom they believed to be responsible for the burning of several buildings. This family was "dangerous to the Community, subversive of all discipline among our Slaves and hostile to our Government." Soon, the planters declared, these people might even "incite an insurrection among the slaves in the neighborhood." If the government did not act, "we will be compelled for the protection of our families and our property to take the matter in our own hands." [27] Not all nonslaveholders were suspected of being provocateurs, but as a class, they received special scrutiny.

At the beginning of the war, the protection of slavery appeared to planters to be a straightforward if difficult task. The ingredients for slave rebellion were there—3.5 million black slaves, invading Union troops, and home-grown nonslaveholders. Order and control depended, it appeared, upon keeping the different elements from coming together. In the end, no explosion took place. No black insurrection ripped the Southern landscape. But slavery was still not secure. Planters had thought in terms of the wrong metaphor. Slavery did not explode; it disintegrated. The problem of protecting it proved immensely more complicated than planters had expected. Its preservation depended not so much on keeping abolitionist ideas out of the slave quarters as on keeping the disruption and destruction of war away from the plantations.

## II

Slavery eroded, plantation by plantation, often slave by slave, like slabs of earth slipping into a Southern stream. So entangled were slavery and the plantation that a blow to one was felt immediately by the other. Each disruption of the plantation had its greater significance in its impact on slavery. The legal destruction of the South's peculiar institution was the product of presidential proclamation, congressional action, state legislation, and constitutional amendment, but the practical destruction of slavery was the product of war. Between Sumter and Appomattox, enormous changes took place within the institution of slavery. Military defeat finally ended slavery, but vital relationships—that of master to slave and of slave to plantation—were everywhere strained, and sometimes snapped, by the time Federal troops arrived to compel emancipation.

Southern losses during the Civil War were staggering. One historian has estimated that Confederate wealth declined fully 43 per cent during the four war years, excluding the value of property in slaves. In Louisiana, of the more than 1,200 large sugar plantations growing cane at the beginning of the fighting, only 180 still produced sugar in 1865. Production of cotton reached nearly five million bales at the time of Sumter, but by Appomattox it barely measured 10 per cent of that figure.[28] Armies turned plantations into battlefields, hospitals, barracks, headquarters, feed and fuel centers, labor pools, and recreation areas. While either blue- or gray-coated soldiers were stealing animals, fences, crops, or slaves outside, others would help themselves to whatever caught their eye inside. A Georgia planter concluded in 1864, "Wherever the 2 Armies pass, in that vacinity [sic] the foundations of civilized society seem broken up." [29] A Mississippi slaveowner "always dreaded the falling back of our army as much as I did the coming of the Yankees." From bitter experience he knew there was "no such thing as a friendly army on retreat." [30] One observer described the scene near Opelousas, Louisiana, in the summer of 1863. "Some of the plantations are thrown open to the stock, all the fences being destroyed and burned—others, the crops are not planted, and in others, the crops are being destroyed by weeds." Instead of the usual summertime bustle, "no where do we see the plow or hoe at work in the field." In fact, he reported, "I have seen but two plantations retaining their negroes. . . . At other places, we have seen but two or three negroes—at some places not one negro remains." [31] Misery was heaped on misery, and nearly every Southern planter left his own heartsick, detailed description of devastation.

Disruptions of traditional plantation routine resounded in the slave cabins and were often reflected in slave behavior. The impact may have been muted but it was rarely entirely muffled. Almost any change alarmed Southern planters. "I certainly agree with you that the negroes must have meat," Langdon Cheves II told a worried friend. "They have been so regularly accustomed to it that a sudden change would produce great discontent. . . ." [32] But sudden change became commonplace during the war. Two sources of change which promised to be particularly disruptive were the transformation of the agricultural base of the plantations and the government's policy of slave impressment.

Planters were apprehensive about shifting away from staple crops. Staples-slaves-plantations was the traditional pattern, and they feared that the remaining two elements could not withstand the defection of the first. Without a cash crop, how would they maintain their farms? Loss of income was one fear, but they were also worried about how the change would affect the slaves. One argument planters used against a sharp contraction of the cotton acreage was, What would you do with the slaves? The cultivation of staples kept the slaves in the fields for the entire year, providing constant work, known work schedules, and defined tasks. The ruts were deep and therefore safe, stable, and predictable. Food crops, on the other hand, were seasonal, requiring new routines and untried schedules. They made increased supervision necessary just when supervisors were in short supply. Behind the debate on staples versus provisions, then, lurked the older issue of slave discipline.

Only overseers and managers, apparently, were able to see a bright side to the agricultural revolution. Perhaps they were pleased at being relieved of the pressure to produce so many bales to the hand or pounds to the acre. An Alabaman argued that the switch in crops "will change the face of our country very much & is desirable in every view." He explained that "it will rest the lands . . . beautify the whole canebrake with grasses clover stock & other improvements, & perhaps not materially diminish . . . incomes in the end." [33] In answer to a question from the owner about what to do with the slaves when there was so little cotton, an overseer in Mississippi responded, "O, plenty to do, that ought to have been done before, but we were run down after cotton-cotton! We shall have time to ditch, and the plantation needs it much, and long has needed it. We shall fix our fences and hedges; we shall move the negro cabins, and put them up right, and in order, and with brick chimneys. We shall do a heap, that we have heretofore left undone." [34]

The transformation was successful; the South produced enough food, and did it without a slave insurrection. But the transition from cotton to corn was not smooth. It disrupted routine and often affected slave behavior. When slaves were pressed into work that was unfamiliar or outside the old routine, slaveholders often complained of "demoralization," a generic term that referred to every sort of misbehavior from rudeness to rebellion. One Gulf coast planter surveyed his slaves and concluded that he needed to get them back to the discipline and routine of cotton production before they became as useless as the staple they had once produced. [35]

Confederate impressment of slaves was another intrusion that particularly worried planters. They opposed impressments on principle and on practical grounds. When John Houston Bills faced the loss of four of his bondsmen to the military in the fall of 1861, he argued that impressment was unconscionable. "A most villainous call," he cried, one which the government has "no right to make & [which] is the beginning of a despotism worse than any European Monarchy." He reminded the authorities that the South was "fighting for liberty," but he thought "we had more 'Liberty' & prosperity 12 months ago than we shall ever see again. . . ." [36] Toward the end of the war, the Richmond *Examiner* attempted to explain the stubborn refusal of planters to part with their laborers. Planters have been accused of selfishness, the paper pointed out, but their objections were "not so much to the employment of the Negro in itself, as to the shock to the rights of property which is involved." On this one kind of property, the *Examiner* explained, "the South has concentrated all its proprietary feeling, and the man who would submit without a murmur to the impressment of his horses or his crops may very likely shrink back with a species of superstition . . . from the attempt by his own government to deprive him of these very slaves for whom he had already fought a long and desperate war." [37]

The *Examiner* was correct when it argued that encroachments on slavery called forth especially fierce responses for reasons of principle. But very practical considerations also motivated the objections. Planters were naturally reluctant to give up their valuable labor and expensive property, especially after they learned that slaves in government service were often brutally treated and miserably cared for. Also, planters were supposed to receive compensation for the use of the slaves, but payment was erratic. Terms of service were explicit and short, but once the slaves were enrolled they were difficult to get back. And the government had a way of asking for slaves just at harvest time. Howell Cobb declared that planters had a right to expect "reason and common sense in the officials of Government." [38] An objection that was as important as any of the rest was expressed by a Georgia planter in 1862. "If my negroes are carried to Savannah under this order," he declared, "I will abandon them. I do not want them to return to the plantation to demoralize the balance." Removed from their plantation homes and set down in strange and distant places, slaves could develop "dangerous habits" and acquire "foolish ideas." [39] A single infected individual, planters believed, could contaminate an entire slave population.

What was at stake was not only the planter's pride, his prickly individualism, his property, and his liberties, but more than these, the institution of slavery itself. The right to control one's own slaves was paramount. To weaken the authority of the master, to loosen the fetters of slavery, was to tamper with the vital workings of the institution. No wonder, then, that planters failed to respond satisfactorily to the government's call for slave labor. In a report written to explain the shortage of slaves being made available, an official in South Carolina said, "For the end in view, even for what has been accomplished, how trifling has been the sacrifice." In exasperation he explained that "only one month's labor" was being required, but even "that much has not been furnished." In fact, "the greatest complaints . . . have been from those who have furnished least." [40] In Virginia, while slave labor played a crucial role in the state's war effort, planters were less and less willing to serve up their slaves. By 1864, only about 75 per cent of those legally requisitioned by the government were ever provided. [41]

How well slavery functioned on a particular plantation could have been determined, before the war, by a glance at the production figures—the bales of cotton, hogsheads of sugar, pounds of tobacco or rice—but such indicators were useless in the disrupted economy of the Confederacy. One of the crudest ways of keeping track of the situation was simply to list all of one's slaves and then cross out the names of those who ran away to "Lincoln land." Most planters used more subtle methods, however. They scrutinized the behavior of the slaves to see how slavery was withstanding the assault of war. How well did the blacks work in the fields? A bit of hesitancy in the stroke? How did they speak to the white family? A trace of defiance? Planters kept their fingers on the pulse of the plantation for signs of "Yankee fever."

The reaction of slaves to war spanned the widest possible spectrum —from taking up the rifle of a slain master and firing at the vile Yankee to putting on the blue uniform and firing at the vile master. The behavior of most was concentrated in the middle portion of the spectrum, ranging from faithful service throughout the war to slipping away from the plantation at the first opportunity. While the loyal and devoted servant was by no means a myth, he loomed much larger in postwar fiction than he did in wartime reality. Slaves did not often revolt, but they did not remain "loyal" either. Most planters reported more theft and malingering and less diligence and deference. As discipline loosened and routine crumbled, blacks found more and more freedom in the crevices of plantation life.

On one of the South's most famous plantations, Susan Dabney Smedes later remembered, "life went on as usual." If anything, in fact, the servants "went about their duties more conscientiously than before. They seemed to do better when there was trouble in the white family, and they knew there was trouble enough. . . ." [42] Similarly, a South Carolinian reported on Christmas Day of 1864 that his position was "wretched," but, at least, "Our negroes are as orderly as usual. . . . They are anxious about the future & seem to sympathize with us in our distress." [43] Near the end of the war, John Edwin Fripp, owner of two plantations on Saint Helena Island, off the coast of South Carolina, reported that Federals had burned his house and stripped his plantations. "I am happy to say my negroes have acted orderly and well all the time," he announced, "none going off except-ing one or two Boys who accompanied the yanks for plunder but have returned home and appear quite willing to go to work." The others "acted nobly[,] furnishing my family with provisions and return[ing] all they saved by begging the Yankees[.]" [44]

More often, planters were gravely disappointed. In North Carolina,

Catherine Edmondston witnessed the "total demoralization" of her bondsmen. When the war began, her slaves were "diligent and respectful," and she responded as their kindly protector. She recorded that when they learned that "the Yankees were trying to steal them," they "entreated me not to leave them & I have promised to remain at home & take what care I can of them." A month later she noted that slaves on neighboring plantations were behaving badly, but she thought they were "the indulged negroes, servants of widows & single ladies who have not been kept in proper subordination." She was thankful that none of hers thought he was "as good as a Yankee." Shortly afterward, however, she began to be troubled by the behavior of her own slaves. She believed the problem stemmed from her husband's absence and her own frequent trips away from the plantation. "These constant absences . . . are telling on the servants," she declared. "They are getting so awkward, inefficient & even lazy!" By the end of the year, her patience was exhausted. "[A]s to the idea of a *faithful servant, it is all a fiction*," she exclaimed. "I have seen the favorite & most petted negroes the first to leave in every instance." They had changed from dutiful servants to impudent slaves in a few short months, she observed sorrowfully.[45]

When planters spied insubordinate behavior among their slaves, they responded in a variety of ways. James Lusk Alcorn, noticing laziness among his bondsmen, "whipped several in the field" and was pleased with the result.[46] A Georgian promised harsher punishment. After capturing two runaways, he said that if "Jim and Ike tried it again," he would "kill them both." [47] Others sought to maintain control by removing their slaves from proximity to Union troops. The South was filled with masters and slaves searching for a "safe place." The British observer A. J. Fremantle was on hand in 1863 when General Nathaniel Banks marched into Louisiana's Red River valley. "The road today was alive with negroes," he reported. They were "being 'run' into Texas out of Banks' way." [48] Others simply sold their troublemakers. In 1863, a Georgia man reported continual difficulty with a particular slave. At the end of the year he simply noted, "I sold Big Henry for $2400." [49]

Despite the planters' best efforts, however, on some estates power clearly shifted from the "big house" to the slave cabins. Mrs. C. C. Clay, Sr., of Alabama, for instance, was soon forced to rely on "moral suasion" to "get them to do their duty." She noted that her efforts were only occasionally successful. And a year later, her situation had declined to the point where she "begged . . . what little is done." [50] Although the shift was rarely this complete, power did tend to gravitate toward the slave quarters.

Responses of planters to their bondsmen during the war depended a great deal, naturally, on the slaves' behavior. And planters often oscillated between optimism and pessimism as the scene out their front windows changed. But their feelings also depended on their basic assumptions about slaves and slavery. Some felt deep responsibility for and devotion to their slaves. Alfred Huger, for instance, once heard that a cholera epidemic was threatening the Cooper River plantations. If it came to his, he declared, "I shall join my Negroes immediately and shall share their fate." He explained that "the system of slavery is perfectly in keeping with my principles as a Politician & as a Christian, but the Master should in my opinion be the last to run away when danger comes." [51] Others showed a total lack of affection or empathy. An Alabama planter wrote home in 1862 that he "was not very sorry to hear of old Will's demise and if he had only held on until the crop was laid by I could have given him up with all my heart." His wife's news that the slaves were idle did not surprise him, he added. "You must have them whiped [sic] when they need it. You must pay particular attention to the hogs. . . ." The following year, in reply to his wife's inquiry about selling a slave to pay some debts, he said that he "didn't care much" one way or the other, but he certainly did not want her sold at less than "the market price." [52]

Planters sometimes maintained their fondness and concern for their slaves even when their "black family" deserted them. The disloyalty of slaves did not so much shock as sadden them, and they directed their anger at the enticer rather than the enticed. After all, how could whites condemn the Negro for following the dictates of his own immature nature? Planters commonly referred to runaways as "poor deluded wretches" and "poor deluded creatures." A Georgian reported that many of his servants had left, "deserting their best friends, to enjoy the poor Negroes['] idea of freedom, that is perfect idleness, not knowing that God meant all his creatures to work." [53] A South Carolinian said, "Poor fools! how deceived & mistaken they are." He was truly disturbed when he heard that the Federal authorities had taken the men "without regard to family separations and sent [them] any & every where under guards, where they are hard worked & miserably fed." [54] In his eyes at least, slavery had never been so brutal and inhumane. Another planter explained the behavior of runaways in understandable human terms. They fled, he explained, because the "temptation of change, the promise of freedom, and of pay for labor, is more than most can stand." [55] Many planters responded to the plight of the blacks with genuine pity, feeling almost as sorry for them as they felt for themselves.

Many others, however, registered shock, hurt, disillusionment, and rage. They shut off empathy for insubordinate blacks just as they closed off concern for disrespectful poor whites. Many saw themselves as having sacrificed considerable time and effort in training and uplifting *their* "people," only to be betrayed. Louis Manigault was cut deeply by the "ingratitude evinced in the African character." "In too many instances," he said, "those we esteemed the most have been the first to desert us." [56] Catherine Edmondston could neither understand nor forgive and wished "that there was not a negro left in this country." [57] The change of heart was reflected clearly in the nomenclature planters used in referring to their slaves. Before the war, those of the least refinement almost never employed the blunt term "slaves" in speaking of their own bondsmen. They resorted to an abundance of euphemisms, ranging from the plain "servants" and "laborers" to the intimate "my black friends," "my black family," and "my people." In the final years of the war, however, planters commonly spoke of their "slaves" and even of their "niggers." From servant to slave was a long journey. It meant that something had died which would be difficult to resurrect. It marked the early stages of a trend that would lead to disdain and hostility toward blacks during Reconstruction.

Instead of being sympathetic, disappointed, or angry, some planters were simply terrified. For years they had heard orators describe the bloody scenes that would occur if slavery were ever disrupted. And now, all around them, the system was breaking down. Early in 1865, six of South Carolina's most illustrious families—among them the Allstons and the Sparkmans—rushed a petition to the Federal Military Command to plead for protection from the Negroes. Freed by invading Union troops, they were "in the most disorderly & lawless condition, if not savage and barbarous." The petitioners begged in the "name of common humanity & Christian civilization" that the Northern commander send soldiers to save the Pee Dee planters from this "insurrectionary force." [58]

Whatever a planter's feeling toward his slaves, he was bound eventually to agree with the Reverend C. C. Jones that "no reliance can be placed *certainly* upon any." [59] Inevitably, if not his own servant, then the trusted servant of an acquaintance would abscond. But, ironically, just at the moment when planters had the least faith in their bondsmen, they relied most heavily on their loyalty. With the normal supervisors away, blacks were largely on their own on many plantations. Drivers were often pressed into service as overseers. Mary Jones of Georgia explained that one of her plantations was "necessarily left to Andrew's fidelity." [60] When a Mississippi man departed for the army he made his carriage driver foreman of his estate. Realizing that he was asking his slave to assume increased responsibility just when the rewards for disloyalty were highest, he offered him a bribe, telling him that "if the south was successful and he was faithful to his trust," he would "give him his freedom." [61] A promise of personal manumission by a planter was far from the enemy's pledge of general emancipation; still, the very fact that a master felt compelled to match the enemy's offer of freedom with a similar offer of his own meant that the war was turning plantations and slavery upside down.

If the war-storm had not affected slavery, much of the destruction it wrought would have lost its significance. As it was, war sent slavery and plantations into a spiral of disintegration. Distance from the vortex varied, but inevitably the storm arrived, affecting the slaves' conduct and the plantation's functioning. Slave behavior preoccupied planters during the war. They struggled to maintain control over their dominions and their subjects, but they felt their grip weakening. War impinged on vital relationships. By sharply curtailing the production of Southern staples, it removed the slave from his routine activities, suggesting perhaps that such things were not fixed and immutable. By calling the planter away from home to join the military and the slave away to do government labor, it snapped the personal relationship between master and slave. That relationship had always been complex. One was enslaved and the other free, but neither was independent. At the end of the war, bondsmen and aristocrats remained dependent upon one another, but now the planters thought "the negroes free, and master a prisoner." [62]

### III

By gradually crushing the slave-plantation system, the Civil War exerted tremendous pressure on the planters' commitment to their peculiar institution. Although slavery's preservation had been the object of secession, the gentry's attachment to the institution and to the proslavery ideology was sometimes eroded as time passed. War-weariness and anxiety; economic catastrophe; the "demoralization" of the bondsmen; doubt and guilt about slavery; Southern nationalism and American patriotism; the fear of total social collapse—all hammered away at planters' dedication to slavery. Slavery was betrayed —by blacks, by nonslaveholding whites, and even by Confederate officials—and the war threatened to make apostates of planters as well.

Perhaps the single most powerful force tempting planters to acquiesce in the destruction of slavery was the weariness produced by the long, vastly destructive war. Days of worry stretched into months and years. Unrelieved strain sapped energy, health, and confidence. Anxiety—about unpredictable poor whites, untrustworthy blacks, an unreliable government; about where to find food and how to fend off destruction—became the companion of every planter. Other Southerners suffered more, with even fewer cushions, but in the end some planters were brought to their knees, victims of physical and emotional exhaustion. For these, the desire to cease struggling, the need to find a quiet place, became paramount.

War played havoc with the participants' emotions, whipsawing them between grief and rage. Few families escaped the trauma of death. Sometimes it was the loss of a son or husband that touched them first, sometimes the loss of a friend. A Georgia woman who heard of the deaths of several neighbors said, "*Their deaths* have brought the war home to me more forceably than could the deaths of a regiment of soldiers from any other place." [63] While the news of death came suddenly, rage against the enemy built gradually. In 1864, a young planter declared, "Day by day and hour by hour does the deep seated enmity I have always had . . . for the accursed Yankee nation increase & burn higher. . . . they have slaughtered our kindred[,] . . . destroyed our prosperity as a people & filled our whole land with sorrow. . . . I have vowed that if I should have children—the first ingredient of the first principle of their education shall be uncompromising hatred & contempt of the Yankee." [64]

Planters were exhausted by the rush of emotion that flung them from one pole to the other. A Louisiana man thought that constant "excitement is not quite death but pretty near." [65] Ella Clanton

Thomas of Georgia said that a "life of emotion, quick rapid succession of startling events," wore upon "the constitution and weakened the physical nature." Her "nervous organization" was "so completely disorganized" that she needed perfect quiet. "I feel as if I did not have energy to raise my head," she reported. "My mind is sluggish and my will is weak and undecided. I lack energy . . . spiritually, intellectually, & physically. I have been . . . dull inert and desponding." The problem was, she said, that "the human mind is so constituted that it cannot stand a constant pressure" and "the war has been going on for a much longer time than we could have thought." [66] David Gavin hardly understood his problem at all. "I have plenty of provisions," he said, "and yet I am sick, dull and low spirited. . . . sick, sick, heart, soul, mind, body & spirit." [67] Some could not even escape into sleep. In the week the war ended, William Cooper dreamed "of flood & planks to walk on . . . amid mud [and] water—& of my driving [a] wagon amid rain & high water with 2 mules . . . in flight from the enemies." [68]

The unrelieved tension pushed the minds of men and women to the edge of sanity, and sometimes beyond. The British observer A. J. Fremantle recounted the tragedy of a Mississippi planter he met in the summer of 1863. "We had a crazy old planter . . . with us," he recalled. "He insisted upon accompanying the column, mounted on a miserable animal which had been left him by the enemy as not being worth carrying away. The small remains of this poor old man's sense had been shattered by the Yankees a few days ago. They had cleaned him completely out, taking his horses, mules, cows, and pigs, and stealing his clothes and anything they wanted, destroying what they could not carry away." This broken planter, Fremantle said, had "insisted on picking some of the silk of Indian corn, which he requested I would present to Queen Victoria to show her how far advanced the crops were in Mississippi." [69]

By the end of the war anything that promised relief was tempting. In October, 1864, Octavia Otey of Alabama felt "quite desperate . . . like I could struggle no longer." [70] William J. Minor, owner of three plantations in Louisiana, cried out, "Peace—peace —peace—God grant it—and stop this most unnatural & most bloody war." [71] The fiery Southern patriot Ella Clanton Thomas said that "the time and circumstances somehow appears to create a reckless, careless feeling, an impatience to have it over." She craved freedom from war. "At times," she said in March, 1865, "I feel as if I was drifting on, on, ever onward to be at last dashed against some rock and I shut my eyes and almost wish it was over, the shock encountered and I prepared to know what destiny awaits me." She was "tired, oh so tired" and wanted to "breathe free." "I feel the restraint of the blockade and as port after port becomes blockaded I feel shut up, pent up and am irresistably reminded of the old story of the iron shroud contracting more and more each hour. . . ." She thought that someday she might "be glad that I have lived through this war," but "now the height of my ambition is to be *quiet*. . . ." [72] By 1865, peace and quiet had become for some planters the primary object.

Another powerful force operating to detach planters from slavery was the institution's unprofitability in wartime. By 1865 most Southern plantations had become economic burdens rather than financial blessings. Each year of the war, incomes fell off more sharply. Louis Bringier, a large planter in Louisiana, said in December, 1864, "I do not know what we will do with our darkies. They are a great source of annoyance, and but very little profit at the present." He concluded that "they will have to become more profitable or we shall have to give them up in self-defence." [73] Bringier's urge toward voluntary emancipation was only momentary, for in April, 1865, he was willing to take up guerrilla warfare for the Confederate cause. But the fact remains that most planters could not afford to be indifferent to the financial difficulties accompanying slavery in wartime. A few had indicated all along that a handsome profit was their only objective. Before the war, a Virginian had complained that slavery did not pay in his state. "It may be different in Cotton Country," he said, but "it has been a losing business in Virginia." He had decided, therefore, to "clear out every thing but portraits and go right to a city." [74] Planters whose only interest in slavery was profit were sometimes ready and relieved by 1865 to rid themselves of their nonproducing consumers.

An extensive debate grew up among planters about what was the most secure investment during wartime. Until the last year of the war, they engaged in a brisk trade in slaves. But while slave property had always been admired for its liquidity, during the war that characteristic proved a serious problem. Hundreds of thousands of slaves spilled over into the Union lines. Slaveowners sometimes expressed a willingness to sell all their bondsmen if they could find a safer investment. Robert Newell of Louisiana thought "cows and mares" were his best bet,[75] but most planters who sought an alternative to slaves looked to land or Confederate bonds. Henry L. Graves advised his father that "land is the only safe investment now." [76] Another Georgian declared that he would "rather have land than Negroes." [77] If the Federals invaded his Saint Johns River plantation, a Florida man asserted, "I shall take black and white of the family into Georgia and turn the blacks into Confederate Bonds." [78]

Without the income to provide properly for their slaves, sensitive planters found them a heavy emotional burden. John Jones, a minister-planter from Georgia, brooded over his responsibilities. "I am truly tired of my daily cares," he said in 1863, "they are without number. To clothe and shoe and properly feed our Negroes and pay our taxes requires more than we make by planting, especially when debts have to be paid." In his opinion, "the most pressed people in our Confederacy are the owners of slaves who have no way to support them. Sometimes I think that Providence by this cruel war is intruding to make us willing to relinquish slavery by feeling its burdens and cares." [79] Whether they were more sensitive to their own burdens or to those of their slaves, planters could sometimes see in the emancipation of blacks their own personal liberation.

Another force which wore down some planters' dedication to slavery was the slaves' "demoralized" behavior. Insubordination and defection angered many slaveholders. Planters learned how little they knew of their slaves, even their most trusted and "most petted." Shortly after the end of the war, Ella Clanton Thomas learned that "Susan, Kate's nurse, Ma's most trusty servant, her advisor, right hand woman and best liked house servant has left her." [80] They were pained to find that "those we loved best, and who loved us best—as we thought—were the first to leave us." [81] Piqued by their bad behavior, one Virginia planter was for the moment at least genuinely glad that the invading Yankee army had relieved him of "the plague, vexation & expense of so many idle, worthless & ungrateful house servants." [82] Disloyalty among the slaves tended to deaden those warm feelings of paternal responsibility which were a significant buttress, as well as an important reward, of the institution of slavery.

Some plantation dwellers entered the war with doubts about the morality of slavery, and four years of destruction sometimes transformed their doubt into certainty. "Southern women are I believe all at heart abolisionists [sic]," Ella Clanton Thomas of Georgia had said in 1858. The institution, she thought, "degrades the white man more than the Negro and oh exerts a most deleterious effect upon our children." During the war she read proslavery books to convince herself that slavery was right, but she concluded that it was morally indefensible. "This is a subject upon which I do not like to think," she said in 1864, but "taking my stand upon the moral view of the subject, I can but think that to hold men and women in *perpetual* bondage is wrong." [83] Southerners were accustomed to finding the hand of God in all things, and some wondered if the disastrous war was not divine retribution for the sin of slavery. Dolly Burge of Georgia said that she had "never felt that slavery was altogether right for it is abused by many." [84] The wartime movement to humanize the institution of slavery was probably built in part upon doubt and guilt. Despite their efforts, it is likely that some plantation folk saw in the destruction of slavery the fiery cleansing of sin.

In addition, either an indomitable American patriotism or a vibrant Southern nationalism could operate to undermine a planter's attachment to slavery. Although not all Unionists believed their patriotism automatically linked them with the cause of abolition, many persistent Unionists were committed to supporting the Union whatever the cost, even if it meant emancipation. One such Unionist planter claimed after the war that he was "not opposed to secession merely" but even approved "the acts that established the freedom of the slaves." [85] A real, whole-souled devotion to the cause of Confederate independence also could convince a planter that any independence, even one without slavery, was preferable to subjugation and renewed Yankee domination. An exemplar of this viewpoint was Jefferson Davis, that Mississippi slaveholder who as president of the Confederate States of America was willing to sacrifice slavery to win Southern nationhood. Intense patriotism directed to either the United States or the Confederacy, therefore, could diminish a Southerner's attachment to slavery.

By the end of the war, some planters were receiving few financial, political, social, or psychological rewards from slavery. Financially, they considered slavery more a burden than an asset. Politically, they found their views shouldered aside by men with military and diplomatic perspectives. Socially, they recognized that as military and governmental service grew in prestige, slave ownership was no longer the single avenue to status. And psychologically, they received little benefit from plantations filled with restless and footloose slaves. As bad as things were, moreover, they threatened to get worse. By 1865, blacks were moving through the South at will, and nonslaveholding whites were growing increasingly surly and disrespectful. Planters feared a total breakdown of order. Lawlessness and chaos, they thought, were imminent. In a somewhat similar situation in Brazil some twenty years later, slaveholders accepted abolition in order to check further disintegration.[86] It is probable that some planters acquiesced in the final abolition of slavery in 1865 because slavery's rewards had shriveled and its burdens increased. Peace, in some minds, offered the only hope for rest, relief, order, and security.

How the forces generated by war could corrode slavery and an individual's will to maintain it was vividly revealed in the experience of John Houston Bills of Tennessee.[87] Bills owned four plantations—"Cornucopia," "Hickory Valley," "Parron," and "Bonnie Blue"—on the outskirts of Bolivar, about fifty miles east of Memphis. He also had extensive interests in business, merchandising, and real estate. From 1843 until 1871, Bills kept a diary, in which he made staccato entries each day. Before the war, his observations rarely ranged beyond crops, weather, and disease, but with the revolution, he crowded his diary with the events that crowded him.

Lincoln's call for troops in April, 1861, forced Bills to lay aside his American patriotism and reluctantly adopt the cause of Southern independence. "Bad politicians, north and south" had pushed Southerners into their predicament, he thought, but in the end, it was Lincoln's "Abolitionist Crew" with their "unholy prejudices" whom he blamed for destroying the "best government on earth." He could only hope that Southerners could "build up as good upon the ruins." A week after Sumter he subscribed large sums to provide uniforms for Confederate soldiers who would "whip back old Lincoln's Minions of Anti Slavery men." But from Sumter to Appomattox, for Bills it would always be "this terrible and unnatural war."

The conflict quickly impinged upon his affairs. Confederate notes began to circulate in Bolivar in July, and his immediate thought was that "the country is now doomed to a currency as bad as the Old Continental Money." His overseer volunteered for army duty, and Bills was "greatly *nonplussed*," for he knew he would "have to turn overseer" himself. Even more ominous was the fact that the government called up four of his slaves to work on fortifications. He thought it was the grossest hypocrisy for the government to infringe on his liberty in its war for liberty. In May, 1862, Bills could see smoke rising from Corinth, Mississippi, only twenty miles away, as the Confederate troops burned cotton before the advancing Union army.

From the beginning, Bills was pessimistic about the war. The very magnitude of the fighting, he thought, would mean "ruin to both sides." In February, 1862, he attended the Cotton Planters Convention in Memphis and learned that others doubted "success in our *revolution*." In April, his only son fought with the Confederate troops at Shiloh, just a day's ride from Bolivar. Bills left immediately to discover his son's fate. He found him lying wounded in a Federal hospital and was himself taken prisoner. Although he was released in less than a week, Shiloh proved a traumatic experience for the Tennessee planter. He was sickened by the "Waggon loads of Men shot in every Conceivable way," and dumfounded by the mammoth Union army he saw at first hand. His heart sank, he said, "at beholding the immense preparation for the destruction of our people." He thought "it looked as though they had the ability to go where they pleased."

Bills's ordeal began in earnest on June 5, 1862, when General Lew Wallace and his army entered Bolivar, which served as their headquarters for the next twelve months. The disintegration of slave labor became the central theme in his chronicle of his wartime experience. He began a vigil over his slaves as soon as Wallace's troops entered town, reporting thankfully after three days that things were still quiet on his plantations. Two days later, however, the slaves were not working well. That summer he suffered his first runaways, and he lost chickens and pigs, corn and fence rails, to pilfering Federal soldiers. "Gloom and despondency are on the Countenance of all property holders," he reported. Planters feared that the Union army would completely "demoralize" the Negroes. If so, they would be "lost for further use."

During the summer of 1862, Bills began to bend with the most powerful winds. In August, 850 townspeople took the oath of allegiance, while 20 refused and were shipped northward by Federal authorities. Bills took the oath and remained in Bolivar. He learned that living in occupied territory had economic advantages, as well as disadvantages. He sold cotton at twenty-five cents a pound, making eleven thousand dollars on one deal. Two months later he sold more cotton at fifty cents a pound. He also became personal friends with General Lew Wallace.

But any advantage was washed away by a sea of trouble. Three months after the occupation, he reported that the "desolation of Crops, Loss of stock, insubordination of Negroes, runaways—&C Exceed any description. No one knows that he is worth a Cent today." A survey of Tennessee, he said, would show "institutions broken up, Country lawless, blood freely flowing—anarchy generally prevailing—truly a lamentable state of things." Bills was thoroughly "worn out by the War & presence of troops day & night, the rattle of Army Waggons[,] tramping of horses and presence of Common soldiers; with the Evil Counsel upon our Coloured people is unendurable." He was always hurrying from one of his four plantations to the next, locating runaways, repairing damage, noting theft, arguing with Union officers about recompense, attempting to make the slaves work while not driving them off. By the end of 1862 he was "in despair of Saving any thing."

As a result of his troubles, Bills's attitude toward his slaves changed. At first, he reacted to their insubordination tolerantly. He noted that they were not working, but excused it to himself by observing, "Indeed they have a right to feel discouraged as all their labour is lost for the present year" because of thieving Federal soldiers. This statement was remarkable testimony to the stake he believed the slaves had, and recognized, in the system. But in January, 1863, he said, "At times I pity them[;] at others I blame them much." And by 1864, his opinion was unreservedly negative. "The worthlessness & insolence of Negro slaves is most unbearable," he complained. They were "a lazy indolent race," and "not one in a dozen will make a living without the lash or a certainty of it." They wanted "freedom only to loaf and do nothing." Worse, "many of them I think do all they can to have us destroyed & delight in seeing the work of destruction done." In the end, he thought it was "a pity that one of them should ever have been imported from Africa."

"Negro slavery is about played out under 'Yankee' influence," Bills said in 1864, "we being deprived of that Control needful to make them happy and prosperous." Certainly, *he* could not be happy and prosperous with his authority impaired. Slaves continually slipped into the Union camp. Bills claimed that Bolivar residents lost "*half* a million dollars worth of property in one day." In mid-1863, Union soldiers had begun enrolling black troops from among Bolivar's population, and one of Bills's slaves was among the first to join up. A week later, all the male slaves at "Hickory" escaped into the woods because they feared conscription. Bill's situation was not improved, however, when Union troops pulled out of town, for his county became a no man's land, contested by both sides. Waves of blue- and gray-coated soldiers swept back and forth over his plantations. The "scenes of Missouri are upon us," Bills moaned, "the fruits of an ill-advised war."

Bills's plantations were ground to powder. His normal cotton crop exceeded a hundred bales, but the combined crop of 1863 and 1864 barely reached seventeen bales. He considered not planting at all. Even if the slaves would tend the crop, soldiers would take it, he reasoned. But "if we do not[,] *Want* will soon be upon us," and he planted once again. By mid-1863 only twenty-two of his original several score of slaves remained with him. They worked his crops, but only after they had finished cultivating their own. In early January, 1865, he recorded, "Nothing doing, but Setting [*sic*] by the fire & Eating up our little remaining substance." And a week later, "Matters truly discouraging—Negro slavery of no Value, but much Expense." Finally, on May 11, he heard his first good news. "The war is over," he cheered. "God be praised." On May 29, a Union officer arrived to announce to the slaves that they were free. That same day, Bills met with his former bondsmen to tell them that he accepted their freedom and was willing to write contracts with them for cultivation of the present crops on a share basis.

War devastated the social environment which had nurtured slavery. It gnawed away at the planters' attachment to the slave system. In some, the commitment to slavery proved to be a perfect reflection of the health of the institution. Each step in the deterioration of slavery was matched by an equal decline in support. But in a far greater number of planters, the commitment to slavery survived the actual destruction of the institution. Individuals are not independent of their society, but neither are they identical with it. Ideologies derive in part from the immediate social context, but they do not correspond to it totally or respond to changes in a one-to-one fashion. When slavery and the war ended, a substantial majority of the Southern gentry continued to display a passionate fidelity to slavery and to their proslavery beliefs.

## IV

Like a blackened chimney standing amidst charred ruins, the proslavery ideology survived the destruction of the institution of slavery. Total continuity, like total change, does not occur in history, but this time, in the interplay between inertia and flux, clearly the traditional orthodoxies prevailed. Planters' basic ideas about slavery, blacks, agriculture, and Southern civilization revealed a remarkable resistance to change. Slaveholders had led the South into secession because they could not conceive of their social order without their peculiar labor system. When the war ended, they still were unable to imagine a decent and enduring Southern civilization without slavery.

Because ideological revolutions are rarely synchronized with social revolutions, dominant ideas can easily be out of phase with rapidly changing social environments. In the midst of disequilibrated systems, men and women often continue to operate within the confines of traditional ideas, though not without intense personal strain and tension.[88] The anxiety which planters experienced during the war probably stemmed in part from their own private struggle to retain a set of ideas in the face of the destruction of the institution which had produced those ideas. Planters had little opportunity in the midst of war to construct an alternative ideology. Rather, their energies were consumed in a military struggle to preserve their peculiar society against an ideologically opposed enemy. They sought to deny the reality of the emerging, and still quite inconceivable, post-slavery world. Their Northern conquerors did not and really could not provide them with a convincing alternative ideology which would allow them to face their particular free-labor situation with any degree of confidence.[89]

A large part of what planters witnessed during the war, moreover, served only to re-emphasize the essential validity of their traditional assumptions. While a number of powerful forces were working to erode the planters' commitment to the slave-labor system, most of these could also have the reverse effect. War sometimes intensifed doubt and guilt about slavery, for instance, but more often it operated to strengthen convictions about slavery's justice and utility. Direct contact with Northern soldiers convinced many planters of what they had always suspected. Despite their pieties, Yankees hated blacks, and the blacks' only salvation lay with protective Southerners. A Cobb County, Georgia, planter was appalled to hear a Union soldier say he was "willing the war should continue for 7 years longer if only to kill the Negroes off." [90] Another Georgian declared, "If we are to judge of the future welfare of the colored race by what they have already experienced from the tender mercies of the Yankies, we cannot see that emancipation will be a blessing to them." [91] Even Ella Clanton Thomas, who at the beginning of the war believed slavery was morally wrong, became "convinced the Negro *as a race* is better off with us as he has been than if he were made free. . . ." [92]

While the "demoralization" of the slave population disillusioned some planters and soured them on slavery, black insubordination more often supplied planters with concrete, empirical evidence for slavery's indispensability. As their authority waned, planters learned that blacks often interpreted their new freedom as an opportunity to stop work and to look beyond the boundaries of the plantation. Planters could see that emancipation would mean the creation of millions of "shiftless black vagabonds" roaming the South. The lessons were all too clear—without subordination, blacks were irresponsible and destructive, and without coercion they would not work. When his slaves deserted, Louis Manigault cried out, "For my own part I am more than ever convinced that the only suitable occupation for the Negro is to be a Laborer of the Earth, and to work as a field hand upon a well ordered plantation." [93]

War spawned reform movements to alleviate the worst aspects of slavery, but those efforts were rarely sponsored by the plantation gentry. Churchmen called for reform; plantation men demanded stricter slave codes. Planters pointed out that those gentlemen who had run the most permissive operations were the first to have trouble. One South Carolinian, for instance, said that it "has now been proven that those Planters who were the most indulgent to their Negroes when we were at peace, have since the commencement of the war encountered the greatest trouble in the management of this species of property." [94] In the planters' eyes, mounting evidence pointed to the necessity for stricter laws, more rigid discipline, and less "petting," not a more humane slavery system. And certainly it was the planters and not the clergy who had their way during the war.

Moreover, churchmen themselves rarely had doubts about the essential justice of slavery, only about its practice. They were probably among the most ardent supporters of the Southern cause. They did, of course, have to deal with the problem of explaining how Southerners, a God-fearing people, could be getting whipped by those godless and sinful Yankees. And they found explanations that did not shake Southerners' faith in the cause. Clergymen could argue that the latest military defeat was but a temporary setback, that, as with Job, God was merely testing and tempering his people, or simply that the Almighty moved in mysterious ways.[95] Some slaveholders, however, found their own answer to the puzzle. Dolly Burge, a slaveholder who had doubts about slavery, simply decided to put the entire question of right or wrong out of her mind and into God's hands. If the South was right, God would give it victory; if slavery was wrong, "I trust that He will show it unto us." [96]

The nature of the evidence precludes a definitive answer to the question of whether the South was guilt-ridden over slavery, but my reading of it indicates that no more than a small fraction of Southern slaveholders felt even twinges of doubt and guilt. Most of those who did were women, who had a special perspective just because of their position as women in a slave society. They may have had special empathy for slaves because they subconsciously recognized the parallels between their positions, one as slave and the other as "Southern lady." [97] More concretely, the existence of miscegenation undermined their faith in the institution. One woman thought that if the South were to lose the war, Southern women would have their revenge when Northern soldiers took the "bitter cup" of miscegenation back home.[98] Their dedication to the institution was also challenged by the fact that as plantation mistresses they felt the burdens of slavery but few of the rewards. "I have never ceased to work," Dolly Burge declared, and "many a northern housekeeper has a much easier time than a Southern matron with her hundred slaves." [99]

The vast majority of plantation men, and probably most plantation women, had no doubt about the morality and absolute necessity of slavery. Kenneth Stampp's assertion that one of the reasons the South lost the Civil War was that many Southerners were tormented by a moral crisis over slavery and saw in defeat a way of ridding themselves of a moral burden does not hold true for the planter class. As part of his evidence he points to the unwillingness of many Southerners to subordinate personal interests to the success of the Confederacy, and argues that had they seen the consequences of defeat as unbearable, they would have sacrificed more for victory.[100] But planters had never been model citizens. A rural class, intensely individual and local in outlook, jealous of any intrusion into plantation affairs, planters had always tended to think of themselves as individual sovereigns who happened to give sustenance to the state. And in wartime, failure to give their all to the government in Richmond grew in part from the conviction that Richmond had proven almost as unfaithful to slavery as Washington. For four full years, by word and deed, the planter class proved that the slave-plantation system received their primary allegiance, and that its preservation was their first priority.

Other forces which worked to dissipate Southern attachment to slavery were localized or checked by more powerful counterthrusts. American patriotism and Southern nationalism were potent sentiments in the South, but they rarely dislodged planters from their primary commitment to slavery. Few planters ever entirely suppressed their national patriotism, but it was usually conditional, in 1865 as much as in 1861. If anything, war dampened warm feelings for the Union; it rarely fanned them. And Confederate policy, particularly where it touched slavery, undermined planters' allegiance to their government in Richmond. In addition, while slavery certainly grew less profitable, most planters ended the war still owning slaves, and most would have preferred to keep them. There was a substantial increase in cotton planting in the spring of 1865, and although slavery had not paid during the war, peace promised to end those conditions which had made it unprofitable.

It was probably the unusual combination of powerful forces and special circumstances that so completely shattered John Houston Bills's commitment to maintain slavery. First, this Tennessean was an ardent nationalist and a very reluctant Southern revolutionary. Second, living in a border state easily penetrated by Federal troops, he faced occupation earlier than most planters and endured the disruption of his plantations longer. Third, his plantations became definite economic liabilities, and his slaves grew particularly insubordinate. Fourth, unlike General Benjamin F. Butler and General Nathaniel Banks in Louisiana, General Lew Wallace did not demand *de facto* emancipation, and consequently, Bills lived with a malfunctioning slave system for three full years. Fifth, he had extensive business interests outside the South and was not totally dependent on slavery. Sixth, very early in the war, Bills came face to face with the reality of Northern power. And finally, he lived in an area in which significant numbers of people were reacting just as he was. Farther south, people looked more unfavorably upon taking loyalty oaths and fraternizing with the enemy.

For the majority of the planter class, the war served to re-emphasize, not undermine, the validity of traditional beliefs. War-time experiences were even powerful enough to transform the fundamental ideas of those who had earlier denied the logic of the proslavery argument. The metamorphosis of John Hartwell Cocke is a dramatic case in point. Clement Eaton describes this Virginian as one of the leading examples of liberalism in the antebellum South. Although he owned more than a hundred slaves, Cocke had called slavery "a curse on the land" and the proslavery argument "monstrous." He had been consistently willing to lay the blame for black backwardness on whites, arguing that slavery itself was the true cause of black inferiority. He had purchased two plantations in Alabama expressly to train and prepare his slaves for emancipation and freedom in Liberia. By the 1850s, Cocke was weakening in his conviction that slavery was an unmitigated evil, but still, on the eve of the war, he stood apart from his class, a lonely Jeffersonian in the age of Calhoun, a believer in the doctrines of equality and natural rights, an opponent of slavery, and an admirer of many things Yankee.[101]

For John Hartwell Cocke, the war became revelation. Unfortunately, we do not know how he arrived at his conclusions, but we do have a remarkable journal written in 1863 and 1864, in which he revealed that for him the war was a pilgrimage to slavery. He was struck, he said, with "the new light shed . . . over the Southern mind by the events of this war," and more pointedly, he declared that "the events of this war have developed the subject of slavery in a new light. . . ." Now he understood that "the institution of slavery [was] established by God himself" and had "been recognized & provided for by his Providential Government [in] every age down to the present time. . . ." From his fresh perspective, he could see that "the distinctions of colour" and "the different degrees of intelligence among men . . . stand as living monuments to the falsity of the modern doctrine that men are born equal." In truth, he declared, "God has made his creatures unequal—and fitted them to fill unequal lots—the madness of the French revolution and the puritanical fanaticism of the Yankees to the contrary notwithstanding." The "Golden Rule of God," he now believed, was "Subordination & Submission to Authority."

He was not willing to claim that all slavery was a positive good, but he did argue that what determined whether slavery was "a Blessing or a Curse" was "the characters of the heads of the tribes or families making up the Social Community." An "unregenerate master," he admitted, could be a "most prolific source of crime and wickedness," but "Human ingenuity may be challenged to conceive a more perfect & happy community than one made up of families" governed "by true Christian patriarchs." Wherever a master had received the grace of God, he argued, "the condition of the slaveholder on a Southern estate approaches more nearly to the covenant which God established with his servant Abraham than that of any other community." For on that plantation one could see the fulfillment of God's design—"the power of the Husband over his wife; the power of parents over their children; and . . . the power of Masters over their Slaves. . . ." [102] After a lifetime of opposition, therefore, and ironically just as slavery was failing, this old Jeffersonian capitulated. He no longer stood apart from his class but accepted its fundamental social beliefs—in the divine sanction of slavery, natural inequality, the immutability of conservative, hierarchical principles, and the failure of an egalitarian Northern society.

But to talk in terms of either total continuity or absolute rupture in the planter mind is too neat and tidy. Most usual were intermediary positions characterized by confusion and tentativeness. The changes that swept the South were sometimes bewildering. "This is a strange world, anyway," Henry L. Graves said early in the war, "and these are strange times. One does not know what to beleive [sic], or what to think; things have all got into a sort of whirl wind, and are whirling and kicking & jumping around at such a rate, that half the time, a man hardly knows whether he is standing on his head or his feet. He does not know whether to laugh or cry." [103] Rapid change was disorienting. "I feel as tho I held in my hands only broken threads, thwarted plans," Catherine Edmondston said. "My time seems like the fragments of a broken mirror. . . ." [104] At the end of the war, a Virginia military hero explained that he felt "as does a soldier after a great battle or the explosion of a mine." [105]

Despite some transformation and disorientation, however, plantation dwellers displayed a remarkable adherence to basic principles. The fundamental premises which underlay the proslavery ideology stood firm in the face of the deterioration and then the destruction of the peculiar institution itself. Blacks were inferior beings, planters agreed. Because they were not fit for free labor, it was both necessary and proper that they be kept in slavery. Only there would they remain productive and subordinate to whites. Slavery was, indeed, the sole solution to the problem posed by the massive presence of blacks and the enormous labor requirements of the South's vast plantations. Without slavery, the Charleston *Mercury* asserted in January, 1865, the South would become a *"most magnificent jungle."* Emancipation would mean that "our great productions, cotton, rice, and sugar, the basis upon which rest all other forms of industry in the Cotton States, must quickly be swept away." And the destruction of plantation agriculture would mean the obliteration of Southern "civilization, society and government." [106] Although the Confederacy was quickly passing into history, its ideological cornerstone had clearly survived. In 1861, Alexander Stephens had declared that slavery was the "natural and normal" condition for blacks, and four years and a war later Robert Barnwell Rhett, Sr., asserted that "it is absurd to suppose that the African will work under a system of voluntary labor. . . . the labor of the negro must be compulsory—he must be a slave." [107]

The clearest and most graphic demonstration of the planters' loyalty to slavery was found in the final months of the war when the Confederate Congress debated a proposal to arm and free three hundred thousand Southern slaves. With Federal armies squeezing the life out of the Confederacy, President Jefferson Davis concluded that the South would probably have to sacrifice its peculiar institution in order to achieve independence. He proposed the beginning of emancipation as a means of gaining both manpower for the army and recognition by England and France. From the early months of the war, slaves had been used as government laborers, and free blacks had been enrolled as militia; and in February, 1864, the Confederate Congress had authorized the impressment of free blacks and slaves for noncombatant military roles. But in November, 1864, Davis proposed that the government commit itself to the gradual emancipation and military use of blacks, declaring to the Congress that if Southerners had to choose between "subjugation or . . . the employment of the slave as soldier, there seems no reason to doubt what should be our decision." [108]

The proposal to free and arm slaves provoked an immediate reaction from planters and their spokesmen. Clearly, it was a major step in the destruction of slavery, one they refused to take. In July, 1864, Jefferson Davis had told a newspaper reporter, "We are not fighting for slavery. We are fighting for independence." [109] But in the spring of

1865, the Charleston *Mercury* declared, *"We want no Confederate Government without our institutions."* Robert Barnwell Rhett, Sr., asked who gave Richmond the right "to destroy that which it was created to protect and perpetuate." [110] Opponents in the Congress offered resolutions declaring the proposal unconstitutional, hazardous, and in violation of property rights and the Southern social system. Robert M. T. Hunter, a Confederate senator and prominent Virginia planter who had been a consistent supporter of the administration, broke with Davis on this issue. It was the "most pernicious idea that had been suggested since the war began," he declared. He reminded his fellow senators that the Confederacy had been born because Southerners feared that the Republican party "would emancipate the negroes in defiance of the constitution." "And now," he asserted, "it would be said that we had done the very thing . . . without any more constitutional rights." [111] Representative James T. Leach of North Carolina, owner of nearly fifty slaves, was dumbfounded that any white Southerner would advocate putting guns into the hands of slaves and predicted that they would turn their weapons on their masters. [112] A Mississippi planter-politician declared flatly that the idea was nothing less than a "proposition to subvert the labor system, the social system and the political system of our country." [113]

Working planters reacted with almost universal horror. In January, 1865, Charles Ellis of Virginia reported that "public opinion is largely opposed to making any such concession to Yankee power and Yankee fanaticism, independent of the fact that such a measure plainly means the emancipation of every slave in the South." [114] Planters recognized that the program contradicted fundamental principles. Crenshaw Hall of Alabama said in March, 1865, "many are bitterly, fiercely opposed to it—some from principle, others from meaner motives. It is argued that we yield in this great principle. . . ." [115] And Catherine Edmondston of North Carolina was certain what that principle was. By offering emancipation as a reward, she explained, the South was giving up everything, for Southerners had "hitherto contended that Slavery was Cuffee's normal condition, the very best position he could occupy, the one of all others in which he was the happiest, & to take him from that & give him what we think misery in the place of it, is to put ourselves in the wrong essentially." "No!" she cried, "freedom for whites, slavery for negroes, God has so ordained it!" [116] Howell Cobb proclaimed the same message more succinctly.

"If slaves will make good soldiers," he said, "our whole theory of slavery is wrong—but they won't make good soldiers." [117]

In March, 1865, just weeks before the end of the war, the Confederate Congress authorized the president to enroll slaves in whatever military capacity he directed, but instead of calling for emancipation, it left ownership in the hands of the masters. Despite this touch of conservatism, the program was a radical one—to arm slaves. How could the Richmond government, once almost the agent of the planter class, have accepted a policy toward which planters were so hostile? Charged with the survival of the new nation, the Confederate Congress had from the beginning been compelled to adopt whatever means appeared necessary for victory. When pressed by an increasingly desperate military situation, the Congress had even been forced to rethink the issues of slavery and independence. The ultimate decision to arm slaves was also made easier by internal changes in the Congress. The elections of 1863 generally returned congressmen having less wealth and fewer slaves than their predecessors. Men who owned fewer than twenty slaves, for example, had made up less than half the first Congress but constituted more than half of the second. Even more important according to a recent analysis of the Confederate Congress was the fact that by November, 1864, a majority of congressmen came from areas occupied by Federal troops. Because any commitments called for by the Confederate Congress would be exacted only from those within the Confederacy's reach, the "external" members and their constituents were immune to the consequences of their own legislation. They were therefore more willing to sacrifice slavery.[118] Even then, the Senate passed the bill by a bare majority, nine to eight; only one of the six planter-senators voluntarily supported the proposal, and he represented a district in occupied Mississippi. Congressional opposition was concentrated in those seaboard states where slavery still functioned, however poorly.[119] In the end, of course, before slave soldiers could go into action, the war ended in a thumping Southern defeat.

Northern victory meant the final destruction of slavery. But emancipation was not always immediate. Planters occasionally released their slaves as soon as the news drifted to their estates, but just as often they refused to accept the verdict and sought to conceal the knowledge from their slaves. More than three months after Appomattox, a Terrell County, Georgia, planter wrote his wife that he was staying on the plantation, watching "the place and negroes," but expected to see her in the fall "if I can sell this place with *all* of them." [120] The decision about when to free one's "freedmen" was often not a simple matter. Catherine Edmondston's family argued the issue at length. When she heard in May that her father planned to emancipate his slaves, she "could not understand it." "It seemed inexplicable to me," she said, "& suicidal in the last degree." She and her husband discussed emancipation late into the night, "viewing it in every point of view, as it bears upon our future life, upon our plans, & our property & talking over our fears for the terrible days which seem to be coming upon us. . . ." A week later they announced emancipation in the "slave quarters." [121] It was often the arrival of Federal troops with the official proclamation that ended such debates. With only an occasional exception, by the beginning of summer even the most stubborn knew that slavery was dead.

The reactions of slaveholders to the final collapse of slavery are not as easily ascertained as might be thought. For Appomattox marked the end of slavery, the end of the Confederacy, and the end of the war. Planters' responses to one of these events were intertwined with their responses to the others. Joy that the war was over can easily be mistaken for relief that slavery was gone, for instance. Those few who had expressed doubts about slavery during the war, of course, did feel genuine relief in 1865. Ella Clanton Thomas, for one, disliked "the loss of so much property" but concluded that abolition was to "some degree a great relief." Curiously, though, this woman who had once owned ninety slaves discovered different emotions by October. "I alone know the effect the abolition of slavery has had upon me," she said. "I did not know . . . how intimately my faith in revolution and faith in the institution of slavery had been woven together." That she actually suffered a loss of religious faith bears out her impression of slavery's hold on her. [122]

Even the planters' direct statements about their reactions to emancipation can be misleading. A substantial proportion of those who expressed themselves on the subject after April, 1865, declared their satisfaction that slavery was gone. Scarcely a single memoir or autobiography written after the war defended slavery, except perhaps as a boon to blacks. Planters often said they welcomed the institution's destruction because of its heavy burdens. Joseph Buckner Killebrew of Tennessee went further to declare that "slavery was a great curse." He rejoiced that this "relic of barbarism" had been crushed.[123]

Often, in fact, planters even denied that slavery had ever been central to Southern history. Thomas Watson had spoken for his class when he declared in June, 1864, "It was to save that Institution that we seceded, and braved the fanaticism of our northern foes. Our political organism is based on slavery." [124] But after the war, planters could often be heard to argue that the Confederacy was founded on other principles—liberty, independence, and especially states' rights. One old planter remembered years later that "contrary to the opinions of many," the Confederacy "had for its origin other aims & objects than to sustain a system of slavery." Rather, it was an example of the fealty of the "English race to constitutional liberty." [125] The most striking recantation, however, was that of Alexander Stephens, who had once asserted that slavery was the cornerstone of the Confederacy, and who after the war declared that it "was not a contest between the advocates or opponents of that Peculiar Institution." [126]

Kenneth Stampp has argued that the speed with which white Southerners dissociated themselves from slavery is an indication of how great a burden it had been for them before emancipation.[127] More likely, it is evidence of a nearly universal desire to escape the ignominy attached to slavery in the postwar period. Certainly Stampp's thesis is rarely corroborated by evidence from the years *before* emancipation. Planters had not been elusive or ambiguous about the principles of the Confederacy during the secession debates, and the inescapable fact is that they engaged in one of the bloodiest wars of the century to protect their institutions. Most relinquished their bondsmen not with just perfunctory resistance, but only when Federal soldiers appeared at the gates of their plantations.

Our clearest evidence of how planters felt in 1865 about emancipation is found in their visions of the future. There were some, of course, who readily accepted the end of slavery and who were sanguine about the future of the South after the triumph of free labor. In June, a Georgian wrote to his sister to encourage her to continue to plant. He was confident that she had "the tact and ability for the Emergency," and was certain that she could "make money with free labor." The trick was simple: "Let the women and children go," and "Hire only those who are able bodied." "It is all over," he said pragmatically, "and we must make the best of it." [128]

More representative, however, was the opinion of an Alabama

gentleman. He had lost his masterhood, but he could not relinquish the attendant social perspective. "The Yankees have declared the Negroes all free," he began his report to his absent partner. "We have no authority to control them in any way, or even to defend ourselves except by military law." He predicted that murder and rapine would soon prevail. "Our country and town are filled with idle negroes, crops abandoned in many cases. On some plantations *all* the negroes have left. . . . The result will be that our whole country north and south will be impovished [sic] and ruined. Our situation will soon be like that of Jamaica." Try as he might, he could not find a single bright spot on the horizon. "In all our material interests, we are hopelessly ruined. The loss of our slaves, to a very great extent destroys the value of all other property, credits, etc." Everyone, he said, was trying to sell, but "no one wishes to buy. No one has money to buy with. All wish to sell and get out of the country. Many expect to go to South America, others will go to Misouri [sic] & Iowa. Many to Texas. The idea is to get away from the free Negro." What else was there to do? he asked. "Most of our people are entirely satisfied that they can not control the labour of the free negro." [129]

Southern planters entered the Civil War convinced that plantations and slavery were one. Plantations would not have developed except for slavery, and without slavery they would die. The growers of sugar, rice, and cotton agreed that "this country without slave labor would be wholly worthless, a barren waste and desolate plain." [130] Emancipation would mean not only that grass would envelop proud plantations but that it would grow in the streets of every Southern city as well. Without slavery, they believed, the South would experience racial warfare, social anarchy, and economic collapse. Because they identified their entire society with their labor system, they concluded that emancipation would mean the end of everything decent in Southern life.

In 1865 as much as in 1860, planters believed slavery provided the only effective method of controlling black labor and securing racial adjustment and social order. That judgment proved false, of course. The labor of blacks was not lost after emancipation, and the bottom rung did not replace the top in the South's racial hierarchy. Inventive Southerners discovered effective alternatives to slavery—other forms of binding blacks to the soil and other means of keeping blacks at the bottom of Southern society. But planters were not prescient. They could not look ahead to liens and debt-peonage, Jim Crow and the Ku Klux Klan. Planters had to deal with the rush of events as it came, and that experience did not invalidate their basic ideas.

Planters clung to their proslavery beliefs even when there were facts to the contrary because the stakes involved in abandoning them were too high. They could not reject or even compromise their central myths, for to do so would mean condemning a whole culture as a lie. Their basic premises did not automatically seem false simply because slavery had been destroyed. Planters often reminded one another that although they had been whipped, might did not necessarily make right. Wartime experiences, in fact, often served to underscore the continued need for slavery. In their minds, the war had provided evidence that blacks were innately and immutably inferior, that without total subordination they were dangerous and destructive, and that without coercion they would not work. War had taught planters that free blacks would be vagrants, robbers, and idlers. Free-labor experiments under Federal supervision in Louisiana and Mississippi ended miserably, and successful efforts like those in the Sea Islands were either unknown or unacknowledged. From the planters' point of view, even a fool could see that the disintegration of Southern society had been paced by emancipation.

Southern planters were particularly ill prepared for the revolution of emancipation. Abolition in the United States was lightning-fast when compared with abolition in other countries; it came as the result of civil war and was imposed from without; and it was not preceded by a pre-emancipation, prerevolutionary era in which slaveholders could gradually adjust to new dispensations. As it was, when abolition arrived, planters were engaged in both an intellectual and a military defense of their slave-plantation system. War destroyed slavery, but it did not provide masters with a common, workable set of ideas to replace their old beliefs. The North's own free-labor economy seemed an inappropriate model since it rested on white labor, and free black labor remained unimaginable, not because it had been tried and failed, but because it contradicted fundamental assumptions. Arguments supporting the practicality of free black labor were dismissed as the naïve and foolish prattle of an alien and inferior Northern culture.

Ideologies, once constructed, have lives of their own. Any evidence which might have contradicted the planters' basic beliefs faced an *a priori* denial.[131] Consequently, emancipation confronted planters with a problem their deepest convictions told them was impossible to resolve—the management of staple-producing plantations employing free black labor.

# PART III

# AFTERMATH

# CHAPTER 4

# Bricks without Straw

"And Pharaoh commanded the same day the taskmasters of the people, and their officers, saying, Ye shall no more give the people straw to make brick, as heretofore: let them go and gather straw for themselves."

EXODUS 5:6–7

Emancipation was a rolling barrage that enveloped every plantation by 1865. For the planter class, slavery's destruction became the central experience of the Civil War. It confronted each planter with problems his most deeply held assumptions told him were insoluble. Not only did he believe that a decent Southern society required the labor and race controls only slavery provided, but he was also still wedded to the notion that it was impossible to manage successfully a staple-producing plantation using free black labor. Unable to imagine a South without slavery or making cotton without coercion, some refused to try. They escaped the problem, by one means or another. But the majority saw no choice but to remain and go on planting, and the search for a system to replace slavery became the central concern of their economic lives. For at least two years, however, their actions lacked the conviction, or indeed any expectation, of success. They worked with a form of labor they assumed would fail.

I

Because the free-labor revolution rode on Yankee bayonets, the new regime actually began to emerge even before the old was defeated. Emancipation sometimes came early and abruptly, as when Federal troops swooped down upon the Sea Islands only seven months after Fort Sumter. Willie Lee Rose eloquently describes the transition of the islands from slavery to freedom. The Port Royal experiment, she demonstrates, was a rehearsal for Reconstruction, a preview in miniature of the revolution that would sweep the south.[1] And yet, the Port Royal experiment was in one important way unique. Because Beaufort District slaveowners fled when the first Northern soldiers came ashore, the transition from slave to free labor was made without the presence of the masters. The Sea Island episode dramatically revealed Northern intentions and black desires, but by its nature, it could not suggest the planters' response.

More indicative was the drama taking place in another Southern theater. In most of the Federally controlled portions of Louisiana, Mississippi, Arkansas, and Tennessee, a contract-labor system replaced the legal institution of slavery. All the major actors were present—Federal authorities, blacks, and planters—as well as a supporting cast of philanthropists, scoundrels, and sightseers. When the curtain rang down on the first act in 1865, planters unanimously agreed that they were performing in a tragedy.

The Mississippi River, life line of valley planters before the war, became a highway for Federal invasion after 1861. New Orleans fell to sea-borne forces in April, 1862, and Union troops under the command of General Benjamin F. Butler occupied the city. Farther north, after General Ulysses S. Grant's capture of strategic Confederate positions in western Tennessee, Union armies began working their way down the river, and they did not stop until the summer of 1863, when their capture of Vicksburg placed the entire Mississippi River in Federal hands.

Slavery had begun to come apart even before Union troops arrived. Up and down the river, slaves began to stir. The mere rumor of a Federal advance precipitated an unprecedented strike by blacks in southern Louisiana. At "Magnolia," the slaves of Henry Effingham Lawrence were in "a state of mutiny," and he was forced to bribe them to keep them in the fields.[2] In Bayou Lafourche, Franklin Pugh observed that news that Northern troops were near caused "a perfect stampede of the negroes on some places."[3] Even more threatening than strikes and runaways was the sharp increase in black violence. While there were no major insurrections, small rebellions became common as blacks asserted their independence.[4] At "Energy," when sugar planter David Pugh and his overseer attempted to whip one obstinate slave, they were beaten, tied up, and carried off to Thibodaux by his comrades.[5]

With actual invasion, plantations often became military battle-grounds. Disputed areas were ravaged by warring soldiers, and ruin came in both blue and gray. A Bayou Teche plantation was stripped by Confederate troops, who hauled away "nearly every resource for living from day to day."[6] A Mississippi planter declared that Union cavalry "were feeding on me every time they come to Holly Springs, and they made 72 raids there."[7] From New Orleans to Memphis, the banks of the Mississippi River were a monotonous spectacle of ruined and abandoned plantations. "The whole country here . . . is a perfect waste," a planter in Port Gibson, Mississippi, declared in December, 1863, "not a[n] ear of corn scarcely to be found & most of the population are receiving provisions from the Yankees. . . . The negroes that remain are in a most demoralized condition & are really of but little use."[8]

Federal occupation accelerated the process of disintegration. Rather than witness the slow death of slavery, some planters fled. They took their slaves and streamed into Texas and Alabama. Most stayed, however, determined to battle for their estates.[9] But the mistress of the McCollam plantation in Terrebonne Parish reported in 1863 that nearly all of their slaves had deserted. Even those who remained, she said sadly, "were not more faithful than many who went off but staid out of a policy to see how the thing would turn out." Her hope was that they could get through the season without total collapse.[10] William J. Minor, a Natchez resident who owned three Louisiana sugar plantations, complained of "troubles and difficulties" without number. No sooner would he overcome one problem, he said, "than a new one arises & I do not feel competent to contend successfully against them all." By January, 1863, his slaves were "completely demoralized . . . going, coming & working when they please & as they please." He saw "the handwriting on the wall." If the war continued for twelve more months, he said, "all negro men of any value will be taken, the women & children will be left for their masters to maintain, which they cannot do." The landowners "will make nothing, the lands will be sold for taxes, & bot. [bought] by northern men & the original owners will be made beggars." [11]

Federal military authorities in Louisiana were unwilling to give slavery another twelve months. Although slavery was still legally intact, in the summer of 1862 General Butler began substituting a system of compensated labor. And even after the Emancipation Proclamation went into effect on January 1, 1863, specifically exempting from its provisions loyal areas under Federal occupation, General Nathaniel Banks, Butler's successor, continued and extended the new labor system. The Butler and Banks plan was embodied in a detailed code that regulated all aspects of the employment and treatment of black labor. In its final form, the code required planters to enter into contracts with their laborers and to compensate them with rations, housing, medical care, garden plots, and wages or shares of the crop. Flogging and other forms of physical punishment were outlawed. Laborers, for their part, were required to work in the fields or face harsh alternatives. Once they signed their contracts, they had to remain for the entire season. Feigned sickness could lead to a forfeiture of pay or rations. Insolence or disobedience would be punished by local military authorities. Parish provost marshals assumed final authority to settle disputes between planters and their laborers. In time, the new labor code spread from southern Louisiana throughout most of the Mississippi valley. [12]

The Union program was in many ways not a dramatic break with slavery. Union officials shared important ideas with planters about the proper role of blacks. Occupying Northerners believed, like planters, that blacks should remain on plantations, labor diligently, and continue to be subordinate and obedient. They had no intention of fomenting social revolution. In fact, the new regulations were intended to maintain control over blacks and to stabilize plantation agriculture. Essentially, Union officials created a system of forced free labor, for blacks with neither homes nor jobs were sent to plantations to work under contract. [13]

The immediate response of planters to the new regulations varied. Some die-hard Confederates refused to co-operate at all, and either fled or quit planting entirely. But most planters grudgingly participated, seeking to mold the new labor program to their specifications. Consequently, when Union officials called local meetings to elicit Southern opinion, planters attended, eager to express their views of the new system. And many regularly took advantage of whatever services the Union army could provide. Depending on the local provost marshal, the services could be considerable. One planter was encouraged when he heard in 1863 that the authorities in his neighborhood "have sent word to the planters to come and get their negro women and children," for he was certain that the army would soon return the men.[14] Planters regularly engaged in "politicking" at the local heardquarters, hoping to wangle favors. Like many others, William Minor succeeded on several occasions in having Federal soldiers visit his plantations to intimidate fractious black workers.[15]

And yet it would be wrong to assume that the Union army and the planters were allies, that their differences were insignificant, and that the planters were content with the army's substitute for slavery.[16] The participation of planters in the new system did not automatically imply their surrender of any right of property in slaves. Nor did participation assure their approval of the final program. Most planters admitted that they had been heard, but most were also convinced that their advice had not been heeded. They realized that despite all its solicitude, the occupying army had ended slavery. While Union troops had put blacks back on plantations, they had not, the planters maintained, put them back to work. Planters were forced to pay wages or shares; they were officially forbidden to whip; and blacks could theoretically change employers every year at contract time.[17] The Union army certainly wanted to keep blacks in the fields, but it also clearly sought to guarantee that they were compensated and that they were not brutalized and re-enslaved. Planters could not join with the army in celebration of the new labor system, despite an abolitionist's charge that the scheme was tantamount to the "reestablishment of slavery." [18] It may have been no more than a single step toward freedom, but in planters' eyes it was one step too many.

It was a system of "practically free labor," planters cried, and they predicted unequivocally that it would ruin them all. "Our negroes will soon be ashes in our hands," James Lusk Alcorn of Mississippi declared, "our lands valueless without them." [19] The essence of the planters' argument was expressed in the summer of 1863 when a provost marshal asked William W. Pugh for his opinion of the new labor system. This prominent Assumption Parish sugar planter declared that he expected a total breakdown when it came time to harvest the sugar cane and carry it to the mills. Then, he said, the press of hard work would reveal the error of the new system's central assumption. It would prove that, contrary to Northern opinion, Negroes could not "be transformed by proclamation." Successful planting required "thorough control of ample and continuous labor," Pugh explained, but under new regulations, Negroes "are expected to perform their new obligations without coercion, & without the fear of punishment which is essential to stimulate the idle and correct the vicious." Without "the right to punish (however moderately)," he argued, the new labor system must fail, for blacks could not "be induced to work by persuasion." [20]

The fact that plantation agriculture along the Mississippi was rapidly falling apart was undeniable. Planters invariably blamed free labor. A Louisiana gentleman complained that because there were "no police, no watch, no guards to arrest them," Negroes moved at will, often "travelling all night." Another asserted that the entire plantation country was infected with "a spirit of destruction and semi-barbarism." One old man explained in detail how free labor had dragged him down. For thirty-seven years, he said, he had been a sugar grower, employing an average of seventy-five hands a season. Before the war his crop averaged more than eight hundred hogsheads of sugar. Under the wage system in 1863, he had made only forty. His crop would have reached his prewar average, he explained, but for the defection of his hands at cutting and boiling time. Without slavery, he could not exercise compulsion at the crucial moments of the season. Under the government's revised wage schedule, adopted in 1864 to stimulate black labor, he did no better. "High wages will not make the Negro industrious," he asserted. The "nature of the negro cannot be changed. . . . all he desires is to eat, drink and sleep, and perform the least possible amount of labor." Free labor meant that everything was "fast passing to destruction." [21]

Only rarely did planters acquiesce in the labor revolution. More often, if they accepted it at all, they did so reluctantly and solely because the power of the Union army of occupation gave them no alternative. They sought to evade its requirements whenever possible. [22] Planters moved quietly to re-establish the compulsions of slavery. William Minor explained to his overseer that the Negroes "must be got back to the old way of doing business by degrees. Everything must be done to encourage & make them work before resorting to corporeal punishment." But if they would not work without the lash, he made clear, "it must be resorted to & inflicted in a proper manner." [23] And in the summer of 1864, Augustin Pugh left little doubt about what he meant when he recorded that his overseer had given one "unruly" slave "a good punishing." [24] But with the provost marshal just down the road, blacks usually had some redress, and planters like William Minor and Augustin Pugh spent many days arguing before Federal authorities.

Planters sought to defend their interests wherever they could, including the political front. In 1863, many of those sugar and cotton growers who had managed to survive the Federal invasions of Louisiana formed the conservative wing of a group which was attempting to restore the state to the Union and re-establish home rule. Unlike the Free State forces, however, they were, as one observer noted, the "party that has learned nothing and forgotten nothing," for they sought to keep "slavery on its ancient throne." But in December, 1863, President Lincoln cut short the planters' effort when he declared that the acceptance of emancipation would be the first prerequisite to restoration. Consequently, planters were largely absent when a convention met in April, 1864, to draw up a new state constitution. Still, spokesmen for the old order defended the theory of slave labor and called for continuing the constitution of 1852, which by apportioning representation according to total population (including slaves) had assured the dominance of the plantation parishes. The majority of the delegates, however, denounced slavery, rebellion, and black-belt dominance, and strongly intimated that planters had gotten just what they deserved. There would be a resurgence of reactionary forces after the war, but for the moment it appeared to planters that their counterrevolution had failed, both on the plantations and at the capital. [25]

Southerners were neither the only ones participating in early Reconstruction farming in the lower Mississippi valley nor the only ones disheartened with free black labor. A small band of Northern civilians had followed in the wake of the Union armies, eager to become managers of the abandoned plantations the Federal government inherited. Contemporaries generally believed Northern lessees were more interested in fortunes than in freedmen. The superintendent of freedmen in the Natchez district, for instance, denounced these Northerners as men whose "highest thought is a greenback, whose God is a cotten bale, and whose devil is a guerilla." [26]

Occasionally, however, a different sort found his way into plantation country. In February, 1864, Isaac Shoemaker took charge of a cotton plantation near Warrenton, Mississippi. He became a "Yankee planter," he explained in his diary, because he wanted "to give labor to the Freedmen, and endeavor to learn them how to appreciate their new condition, and to enable them as soon as possible to take care of themselves, and lighten the expense the Govt is now burdened with on their account. . . ." [27] Even admitting the possibility of a degree of self-deception, Shoemaker was certainly no carpetbagging gambler.

The young Northerner's idealism was quickly put to the test. He knew that slavery was a hideous institution and was prepared to find that it had left its mark on the bondsmen, but he was shocked to discover how deeply it had cut. Troublesome habits and attitudes proved entirely resistant to his ministrations. He complained that the freedmen were forever "timid and doubtful of everything." He found that he could place "little dependence" on their "word." They were just "like careless children, dropping everything just where they last used it." He thought they were "governed by any whim." And their continual stealing "certainly lessens one's interest and sympathy." After only two months on the plantation, he concluded sadly that "it will take many years to get them systematized, and without that, they can never thrive themselves." In the meanwhile, firm discipline was required, for "they have been so long used to obedience to positive command, that the change must be gradual and in proportion to their education in their new sphere." Rebel raiders cut short Shoemaker's experiment in planting, and in May, 1864, he packed his bags and headed north. [28]

Shoemaker's experience in Mississippi is revealing in that it shows how an outsider's ideas could quickly begin to take on the coloration of the ideas of an average Southern planter. That so sanguine a person could so rapidly become discouraged with free black labor helps explain why planters faced the future with so little hope. Even more important in Shoemaker's reaction to his experience, however, are the clear limits to his acceptance of the planter perspective. While his faith in the freedmen had been sorely tested, he stopped short of adopting the theory that slavery was a positive good. He retained his belief that blacks could *eventually* become self-reliant citizens, and he steadfastly focused on the deficiencies of slavery, not the deficiencies of blacks. He realized that in the freedmen he encountered social, not racial, characteristics. From his perspective the difficulties were remediable, whereas from the planters' they clearly were not.

What Shoemaker had learned was that slavery was sometimes a poor seedbed for the Protestant work ethic, that the habits and values spawned were not always immediately functional in a wage-labor system. He was disillusioned because he could not in a single season imbue in a premodern work force values and attitudes that had often taken a generation to develop in the North and a century or more in England. Elsewhere in the South, however, other Northerners found that when freedmen were treated fairly they often worked without coercion. Blacks did not object to work but to the attempt by planters to continue forms and conditions of work which were only slavery by another name. An observer was essentially correct in his emphasis when he concluded, "The difficulty is not with the emancipated slave, but with the old master." [29]

By the close of the war, agriculture in the lower Mississippi River valley was prostrate. Neither planters nor provost marshals, singly or together, were able to sustain the antebellum plantation economy under Federal occupation. Complete control, the planters' dream and sometimes their achievement, had evaporated. As plantation discipline eroded, blacks resisted the continuation of the old ways and production suffered enormously. The sugar harvest of 1865 was a pitiful 3 per cent of that of 1861. Land that had sold for a hundred dollars an acre went begging at five dollars. Attrition among planters was astounding. One estimate was that in the sugar country not more then one in seven kept going. [30]

Even the chief architect of the new system, General Banks, had to admit that his experiment was in serious difficulty. In November, 1864, he solicited advice from planters about how to revive plantation agriculture. A committee of Terrebonne planters, including Andrew McCollam, William Minor, and Tobias Gibson, met personally with Banks. They requested enactment of a long list of new laws emphasizing increased controls on labor. One proposal would have prohibited black ownership of livestock, another would have made workers financially responsible for teams and equipment, and another would have reinstated the old pass and curfew system to regulate the movement of blacks. They based their requests, Minor remembered, on their "experience in regard to the character of negroes and their management." [31]

But General Banks rejected their proposals. Planters, he declared, "were full of theories, prejudices, & opinions based on the old system." Banks advised them to "look to the new state of things, to the future and not to the past," for their "future steps were not to be guided by the lights of past experience." But the planters' past experience with slavery and their recent experience with free black labor provided the only light available. And in their eyes, while slavery had succeeded, Banks's system had "proved a complete failure." [32]

Slavery's spokesmen had for decades promised that abolition would spell disaster, and by 1865, planters were surrounded by debris. "The wish of the Negro is now the white man's law," William Minor asserted bitterly. "A man had as well be in purgatory as attempt to work a sugar plantation under existing circumstances." [33] The wartime response of Mississippi valley planters to the free-labor revolution was but a preview of the larger performance which would take place across the South after Appomattox.

## II

In April, 1865, planters' dreams of perpetuating slavery in an independent republic vanished, and they awakened to defeat and ruin. Their revolution had cost the South a quarter of a million men dead, two billions in slave property lost, and three and a half million black laborers freed. Hundreds of plantations had been devastated, and dozens of towns and cities were in ashes. Yet despite the physical and human destruction of the South, the planters' basic assumptions were intact. "Nothing could overcome this rooted idea," a visiting newspaperman noted, "that the negro was worthless, except under the lash." [34] Predictably, therefore, when the war ended and it was time to begin putting the pieces together again, some did not even try.

The most extreme individual symbol of resistance to Appomattox was Edmund Ruffin. An eccentric Virginia planter and agricultural reformer, he was the ultimate irreconcilable. For more than a decade before the war, Ruffin had labored furiously to light the fires of Southern nationalism, and finally, with Fort Sumter, years of disappointment were swept away. But his celebration quickly turned to frustration as Jefferson Davis proved ineffectual and Confederate armies failed to strike the decisive blow. When Yankee troopers overran his son's plantation, burning his house and driving away his slaves, frustration became bitterness. He cried out for a strategy of "revenge" and scorched earth. In 1865, Appomattox lay like ashes in his mouth. His personal world was in shambles, and his beloved Southern nation was lifeless. Weary, sick at heart, confronted with the sight of Northerners and blacks freely swarming over his homeland, he decided upon the act of supreme intransigence. In his final entry in his diary, he said, "And now with my latest writing and utterance, and with what will be near my latest breath, I here repeat and would willingly proclaim my unmitigated hatred to Yankee rule—to all political, social and business connections with Yankees, and the perfidious, malignant and vile Yankee race." Unable to free the South, he chose to free himself. On June 17, 1865, he fired one last and literal volley of defiance, and with it he ended his own life.[35]

Many other Southerners were also determined to resist defeat and its consequences but chose less extreme avenues of resistance. Thousands, perhaps as many as ten thousand, quite literally turned their backs on the catastrophe and left the South. As one emigré later remembered, Southerners had either "to turn the sword into the ploughshare . . . or to emigrate." [36] Despite pleas from Robert E. Lee and other Confederate heroes to stay and rebuild, many could not contemplate farming in the postwar South. Some left when they heard the news of Lee's surrender. Others spent months in "meditation, deliberation, and preparation." [37] Some were attracted to the prosperous cities of the North and to the rich farmlands of the Plains and the West. Others left for Europe, usually settling in England or France. And still others chose destinations in Latin America. Emigration cut across class lines, but Southern planters, including the most prominent, were heavily represented in the exodus.

For every planter who actually packed his bags and left the South, there were several others who longed to join him. Many had "the inclination," a Mississippi woman observed in January, 1866, but "they have not the means." [38] In Charleston, William H. Heyward expressed both the circumstances and the aspirations of many of his

class when he said, "I hope the day is near when we may be able to sell
our land, the only property we now have, and that we may realize
sufficient from it to enable us to turn our back on this accursed
government and people." [39] Planters with limited finances would
sometimes pool resources to send out an advance agent to scout
locations. One Louisianan claimed he represented six hundred fellow
planters when he sailed for Mexico. [40] In time, reports from scouts and
early emigrés began to drift back to the South, and while the stories
occasionally glowed, more often they told of hardship and disappointment. The Federal Government also erected road blocks to
emigration. In 1866, it prohibited emigration to Mexico and arrested
agents of Mexican colonization schemes operating in the South. [41]
Obstacles of every description kept plantation families at home. Had
the desire to leave been the only determinant, however, the small
stream of emigrés would surely have been a flood.

That so many planters actually left—ripping families from their
homes and neighborhoods, selling or giving away whatever had been
saved from the war, risking a dangerous, expensive journey, often to
an unknown, alien land—was dramatic evidence of the terror of their
vision of the postwar South. Emigration has traditionally been the
product of both a push and a pull, an unpleasant immediate circumstance and a promise of a better life elsewhere, but in the planters'
case, the push was immeasurably more potent than the pull. They left
not merely to better themselves in a new land but to escape destruction
at home. While there was no "exile mind," emigrés did share a mental
picture of a devastated, degraded, and uninhabitable South. And
given their estimation of their prospects under Northern rule, with
free black labor, their decision to leave was fully rational.

The restoration of "Yankee" government drove many from the
country. One Virginia woman found it "so humiliating to be under
Yankee domination after all our hard fighting" that she was "nearly
crazy to go to Europe." [42] In May, 1865, another Virginian began
preparing "for a new life in South America" because he could not
"live in peace under Yankee rule." [43] Similarly, a Mississippian
earlier sought "some other country" because he could not "live in
southern Yankeedom." [44] And a Louisianan, John Perkins, was so
nauseated by the South's subjugation that he personally put the torch
to his own plantation before fleeing to Mexico. [45]

The practical consequences of Northern power were frequently crucial in planters' calculations. Prominent Confederates often fled in fear of their lives, especially after witnessing the treatment the North accorded Jefferson Davis. Robert Toombs, for instance, headed for Havana to escape being "imprisoned and treated with indignity." [46] William H. B. Richardson of South Carolina believed Northern confiscation of plantations was "inevitable." He reasoned, therefore, that one could abandon everything and not suffer any greater loss than if one stayed.[47] And the events of Reconstruction provided planters with additional stimuli. An Alabama planter who worked as an agent for a Brazilian colonization organization reported in October, 1867, that "military despotism" and the "enfranchisement of the negroes," as well as a drop in cotton prices, had convinced many more planters "to abandon the country." [48]

Emancipation, however, was the crucial factor in many decisions to emigrate. Major Joseph Abney, a former slaveowner and president of a colonization company, explained that planters believed that because they could not make "the negro to labor without coercion," the South's future was "poverty, decay, and bankruptcy." To emancipate the slaves with "one fell dash of the pen, to set free the negroes who constituted three fourths of all the property that remained us, and nearly the whole of the laboring power of the country, and quarter them among us, where they will defy our authority, remain a subject of continual agitation for fanatics . . . and discourage and utterly hinder the introduction here of a better class of laborers, is enough . . . to drive any people into despair and desperation." A "deeper degree of destruction and want is inevitable," Abney predicted, "and as the negro will not work, and must eat, hunger and starvation, and madness and crime will run riot through our borders and there is no earthly power that can interpose to save us and our children. . . ." [49] Emancipation had severed the taproot of Southern society, and the South's collapse was but a matter of time.

The desire to escape from free blacks was almost universal among plantation emigrés. "To live in a Land where Free Negroes make the majority of the inhabitants," a relative of William Porcher Miles said in 1867, "is to me revolting." In South Carolina, he complained, "Every mulattoe is your equal & every 'Nigger' is your superior & you haven't even a country." It was inconceivable that anyone would remain who could "possibly get away." Only his health and age prevented him from fleeing to England, where Negroes could not "offend yr nostrils as in these USA." He could foresee no future for his children "different from what they would have if they were in Jamaica," and he asked Miles if he did not agree that their only hope was "that the Blacks will die out so that they will interfere with us as little as they do in N York or Paris?" [50] Two years later, a gentleman suggested emigration to another South Carolinian, James Sparkman. "*You* and *I* may not be able to profit much by it," Sparkman's old friend told him, but for the children's sake, he thanked God that there were still some places "beyond Negro rule." [51] Free blacks not only offended planters' sensibilities, but some believed they also threatened planters' lives. Lucy Judkins Durr remembered that her family's departure from Alabama was prompted by fear of the freedman, "an idle menace—the man without a hoe." [52] In 1867, Henry L. Graves made plans to move his family from Georgia to Honduras. "I think it will be unsafe for families of ladies, especially those so fully identified with rebellion as we are, to remain in the country this fall and winter," he declared. "I am no alarmist," Graves said, "but I think an outbreak among the negroes will be inevitable." [53]

Scores of plantation families chose to leave the South, therefore, rather than suffer its final destruction. But however eager they were to escape, they rarely fled blindly. Because planters chose their destinations with some care, the locations of their new homes provide clues to their motivations and goals. Those who headed for New York, London, or Paris were obviously not hoping to reconstruct their lives according to the old pattern, but those who sailed for Latin America often were. Latin America had fascinated Southern slaveholders for decades, and after 1865 the basis of their interest shifted from curiosity to urgent necessity. Every country south of the border attracted Southerners, but by far the most popular were Mexico and Brazil.

Mexico and Brazil resembled one another in many respects and often attracted Southern planters for the same reasons. Both countries offered huge expanses of fertile land easily adapted to familiar plantation crops, attractive social institutions, and large reservoirs of cheap labor. The rulers of both countries, Maximilian and Dom Pedro II, personally encouraged Southerners to come to settle and gave them warm welcomes. That both states were monarchies apparently bothered almost no one, though emigrés often expressed anxiety about the governments' stability. Some planters openly admitted their relief at leaving the "mobocracy" behind, and looked forward to life under an enlightened monarch. [54]

Most fundamentally, both Mexico and Brazil appeared to offer planters the possibility of resurrecting antebellum Southern society. On the plains near Veracruz and in the river valleys beyond São Paulo, planters dreamed of establishing insulated colonies where they would be free to rebuild the familiar plantation life. They had no intention of assimilating into Mexican or Brazilian society. One emigré remembered that Southerners in Brazil were "tenacious of their ideas, manners, & religion" and laughed "with scorn" at their "adopted land." They were "egotistical," suffused with pride, and had to be "*masters.*" [55] The Mexican experiment collapsed in 1866 when Maximilian fell, but had it survived, it is likely that the plains of Carlota would have resounded with the shouts of young Southerners jousting in chivalric tournaments, just as did the back country of Brazil.[56]

Despite their similarities, Mexico and Brazil did differ strikingly in one respect. As one emigrant observed, while neither country had "Yankees," only Brazil had "slaves." [57] Planters were very much aware of the differences between the labor systems of the two, and many chose Brazil precisely "because it was the last resting place of slavery." [58] Henry M. Price of Virginia, for example, who said after the war that his "belief in the orthodoxy of Slavery is as firmly fixed as my belief in [the] Bible," decided on Brazil because of its dazzling resources, its rich soil, and the presence there of slavery.[59] On the other hand, Matthew Fontaine Maury, who became the Imperial Commissioner of Colonization for Mexico, decided against Brazil because of its slave-labor system. His most fervent wish was to rebuild antebellum Southern society abroad, but he concluded that Brazil was unsuitable because it "was a slave society, and for the Southern people to go there, would simply be 'leaping from the fire back into the frying pan' again." Another emancipation would simply be too much to bear.[60]

On the whole, however, the differences between the two labor systems only slightly affected emigration. Southern planters assumed that both the Mexican and Brazilian labor arrangements would support their colonies. It is true that in the early days of emigration to Mexico, planters sometimes brought in their former slaves under the guise of servants, but from the beginning they fully expected to build their plantations upon "the gentle and docile race" of Mexican peasants. Planters assumed that the peasants were inherently tractable, steady, and compliant, unlike blacks, and that, therefore, they would not need the coercions of slavery.[61] Because of the racial composition of the labor forces in Mexico and Brazil, therefore, most Southerners were confident that they could build their plantations equally well in either country.

And yet, Southern emigration to Brazil presents a paradox. A dominant motive for emigration was the desire to escape free blacks, but Brazil was the home of millions of blacks who were freer than those the planters had left in the South. The key to the paradox apparently lies in the planters' ignorance of the Brazilian social order. In 1865, Southern newspapers were jammed with tales of the paradise which lay below the Amazon. Planters learned of Brazil's fabulous resources, its sympathetic government, and its flourishing system of slavery. But they did not read about its social relations, and early emigrés expressed no reservations about what they expected to find. If they thought at all about the race relations and free blacks they would encounter in Brazil, they probably imagined them in terms of their own antebellum experience. Free blacks had certainly been a nuisance, and hostility had mounted in the decade before the war, but in the South they had represented less than 3 per cent of the free population, and their behavior, like the behavior of most blacks in the region, had usually befitted their station in society.[62]

Firsthand experience with Brazilian life, however, usually shocked and appalled Southern planters. A member of a colony in the Amazon valley reported angrily that several of their band had recently left "in disgust with colored equality." She took sardonic pleasure in the thought that they were returning to *"negro superiority."* [63] And by 1867, the truth about Brazil was out. An organizer for Brazilian emigration reported that planters still expressed a desire to leave the South, but were rejecting Brazil because of "its remoteness, different language, religion, and social ideas." But the declining interest in Brazil was not merely a reflection of that country's changing image, for as the organizer further observed, many planters were now attempting "to go to the non-negro districts of the United States." [64] Less than three years after the end of the war, planters themselves were beginning to change. Many were no longer seeking a racial master-slave hierarchy; instead, they now sought a free-labor society with as few blacks as possible.

In the immediate postwar years, however, Brazil did attract plantation families from the South. And from the beginning their responses to what they found differed sharply, as evidenced by the experiences of Colonel Charles G. Gunter of Marengo County, Alabama, and Andrew McCollam of Terrebonne Parish, Louisiana. During the summer of 1865, the entire Gunter family, with the exception of one son, sailed for South America. In December, Gunter wrote back that he liked the climate, people, land, and government, and expected to buy a plantation with fifty to a hundred slaves soon.[65] Eight months later, he could not praise his new home lavishly enough. "Dispose of, give away and settle my affairs as if I were dead to the U.S. I shall never go there again," he told his son. He now owned six thousand acres and "enough negroes to work it," and grew not just cotton or tobacco or sugar but all three! He was busy organizing a massive colonization scheme in the Doce River region, about three hundred miles northeast of Rio de Janeiro, and asked his son to send him all the young planters he could find. He concluded confidently, "We shall be rich here." [66]

Harris Gunter, a son who accompanied the family to Brazil, said, "Father thinks he has struck the place intended for him by Providence." And, indeed, Harris agreed that their only worries were "ants and a spirit of democracy among the people—no great evils in comparison with free negro labor, radicalism and taxes." [67] The entire family campaigned to convince the lone holdout to join them in Brazil. "I think you will get tired of living in any sort of connection with Yankeys," the father predicted. "I would rather have my children here naked than with 10,000$ apiece in any part of the U.S." Face facts, he told his son. "There is no possibility of peace, comfort or a fixed government in the South for the next twenty years." [68] And, in a very short time, "we will have enough Southerners around us to furnish good society." [69]

The Southern community did not materialize, at least not permanently, but Charles G. Gunter went on to achieve remarkable success and wide acclaim as a planter in Brazil.[70] While the father found almost everything he had hoped for, his son Harris did not. At the end of 1866, he was still advising his brother in Alabama to emigrate, but not to Brazil. His choice now was Argentina, for unlike Brazil, "they are free from the darkey element and from emancipation in the Future." If not to Argentina, he and his brother could go to "Chile or Oregon or Canada," for "now that we have become thoroughly uprooted in Alabama I am willing [to] try any country and to see as much of the world as possible." [71] The father had learned to live with Brazilian ways and was prospering on the land, but the son had no passion to plant and only wanted to put space between himself and blacks.

Andrew McCollam of Louisiana was also drawn southward after the war. In May, 1866, he placed his two sons in charge of "Ellendale," armed himself with twenty letters of introduction to "the most considerable planters in the country," and sailed for Brazil. [72] He went to determine the possibility of planting sugar with slave labor. Accompanied by his brother and several neighborhood planters, he arrived in Rio de Janeiro in late June. McCollam had not idled away the hours on the long cruise. He had scrutinized the social and economic conditions of every port of call. At Saint Thomas, for example, he found "free Negroes lounging on all quarters. . . . The island is not cultivated[;] fredom [sic] destroyed all agriculture[;] at best it is but a rock." By the time he reached Rio, he had not seen a single place that was "worth a cent."

He began his investigation of the Brazilian plantation country on July 4, and almost immediately decided that "all is not gold that glitters here." While he felt "more independent . . . with an Imperial flag . . . floating over me than I could in my native land under the miserable tyriny [sic] now prevailing," he was depressed to find everywhere "the finger of decay." The soil was exhausted, the agriculture primitive, and the people backward, he concluded. He made an intensive analysis of farming methods and production rates at each plantation he visited, and at first thought the deterioration could be reversed by hard labor and skilled management, of the sort American planters could provide. He was certain that he "could do more work with the same number of hands than was being done." The endless ceremony and celebration at each stop exasperated him. "Trifling away the time of business men will impoverish any Country that lives by honest industry," he declared. He saw "more idlers and idleness" in a few weeks in Brazil than he had seen in his entire life in Louisiana. He discovered that "to a man that has been in the habite of makeing things move with some vim the motions of the people are vexatius in the extreme." [73]

Even more disturbing than the decay, inefficiency, and pace of life was the state of race relations and slavery. McCollam thought social arrangements were "sickening." A sense of white mastery was missing, and everywhere he looked he found "white men & negro women all

together." In his opinion, "the negroes were the better of the two."
And incredibly, the "ludest conduct is no bar to a mans entree into
society such as it is." Neither race nor conduct seemed to count, he
said disgustedly; only wealth mattered.[74] But in the end, McCollam
rejected Brazil as a new home because of the shaky status of slavery.
Throughout the back country of Rio de Janeiro province he heard talk
of emancipation. One wealthy planter he met had yielded "to the
prevailing impression that slavery would be abolished in less than 20
years[,] perhaps . . . in ten years." And McCollam had not the
slightest doubt that with "slavery abolished in this Empire it will be the
poorest country on the face of the Earth."

Even without legal emancipation, McCollam concluded, slavery
in Brazil was doomed. He noted that the native planters constantly
complained that the Negroes were "passing away." One planter told
McCollam that there were only half as many slaves in the country as
there had been in the early 1850s, when the slave trade was abolished.
The Brazilian believed disease was responsible. He had begun with
five hundred slaves, he explained, but despite additional purchases,
only two hundred remained. McCollam thought the "rapid decline in
the number of slaves" was due "chiefly to deaths being more frequent
than births," but he also recognized that the small number of females
made it difficult for slaves to reproduce their own numbers. The
Louisianan thought the evidence was conclusive that "the black race
will all disappear on this continent" in three or four generations,
"even without emancipation."

McCollam was captivated by Brazil's physical beauty and would
have liked to have stayed. "The Parahiba [Paraíba] resembles the
Mississippi river so much that without any great flight of fancy one
. . . might think . . . that he was on the great river of the north." If
only a hundred "families from Louisiana could be located here and
the institution of slavery insured I should think I had found a new land
of promise," he said wistfully. But because slavery was crumbling, he
did not have "the courage to settle." He had, in fact, even "less
confidence in the future of this Country than at home." Returning to
Rio, he declared angrily that the entire country ought "to be put in a
bag and all thrown into the sea for the lies about Brazil." With that, he
boarded a steamer and headed back to Louisiana, where he immediately fired off letters to several newspapers exploding the
"Brazilian myth."

Had McCollam surveyed the new coffee lands west of São Paulo, he would have found less racial mixture, better prospects for economic growth, and a slave population that was increasing, not decreasing. But even there, it is unlikely that he could have competed successfully with the enterprising native coffee planters.[75] One colony, organized by a Texas planter who demanded evidence that applicants were "Southern in feeling, pro-slavery in sentiment, and that they have maintained the reputation of honorable men," was established in the interior, northwest of São Paulo. But a variety of factors, including inadequate transportation and capital, resulted in its failure.[76] Only at a small colony in Santa Barbara, which survived on cotton and then on the unlikely crop of watermelons, was there even the semblance of success and an indication of the planters' ability to maintain in Brazil a group identity as conservative Southerners.[77]

One other slave society was to be found in the Western hemisphere, in Cuba, but probably because it was much better known than Brazil, Cuba received much less attention from Southern planters. Andrew McCollam, however, persistent in his search for a new plantation home, visited the Spanish island less than a year after his ill-fated Brazilian adventure. "If it were not for the doubt that hangs over the future of this fine island," he concluded after a short stay, "I would be a citizen of free happy and enlightened Spain before another year." But again, because slavery was so fragile there, he would not risk emigrating.[78] Another Southerner who spent time in Cuba also thought it was "very fertile and Boundless in wealth, with slave labor." But "without it," Robert Toombs declared, "its history is already written in that of Jamaica and Hayti." And in his opinion, slavery was "doomed." England and the United States would "force Spain into the policy of emancipation."[79] A Northern newspaperman confirmed the two Southerners' suspicions. On his swing around the South after the war, Whitelaw Reid took a short side trip to Cuba, where he found that "the whole slave community is said to be fermenting with ideas engendered by American emancipation." He agreed that slavery was "doomed."[80] Very few Southerners, therefore, seriously considered Cuba as their new homeland.

In the end, Southern planters failed to recreate antebellum plantation society overseas. No foreign country really provided the proper materials, and the planters themselves were not particularly well suited for the effort. Though often planned as joint endeavors, Southern colonies tended to founder on what one disappointed emigré described as "*individualism* utterly opposed to any concerted common action." [81] Grand communal efforts were nearly as alien to planters as the new environments in which they labored. After a time, most expatriates began to look toward home. The lack of economic success prompted many to return, as did the fact that time had put to rest the worst fears which had originally spurred emigration. It is also likely that planters abroad had themselves started to change. The postwar South began to appear tolerable, not because the alterations in it had actually been insignificant, but because planters could now begin to believe that the transition from slave to free labor had not been fatal to their basic values. By 1870, most planter emigrés had found their way back to the South. Only a small remnant remained abroad, forever alienated and unreconstructed.

In planters' eyes, Appomattox meant political subjugation, social upheaval, and economic ruin. Rather than face the consequences of their loss, a considerable number fled the region. Shamed by defeat and disgusted with free blacks, they decided the South had no future, only a past. Many of those who sailed for Latin America hoped to rebuild the antebellum society which was now only a memory. But except for an occasional individual victory, the quest was marked by failure, and eventually most wandered back to the South. There they joined the majority who had stayed behind, living in the new world.

## III

The first summer of peace found most Southern planters back on their plantations, face to face with what one gentleman called the "emancipation trails." [82] However much they may have wished to flee the South, they stayed, having no realistic alternative. As a planter remarked, returning to his cotton fields, "I am obliged to try. . . . I have no other way to make money." [83] But disasters sometimes impose new ways of life as the price for survival. And in the ruptured plantation economy of the postwar South, the price of survival for former masters was adjustment to former slaves. The dominant theme in planters' lives became the search for a substitute for slavery. But they began their quest with no more than a glimmer of hope. "How does 'Freedom' work with you?" asked one worried Georgia planter of another in October, 1865. "It runs badly down this way for all parties," he added quickly. "No human wisdom can foresee the

issue—we are working without data—sailing on an unknown sea
—without chart or compass." In his opinion and in the opinion of his
class, "It is all experiment." [84]

The South after Appomattox was a giant kaleidoscope of emotions.
Lee's surrender was "a great shock mentally and morally," one young
planter remembered. "Terror, indifference, recklessness, hope and
despair" intermingled in the "agitated mind of the people." [85] Some
of the plantation gentry were stunned and immobilized. "We are
almost paralyzed here," a Georgian reported.[86] "I don't think I fully
realize my situation yet," an Alabama woman declared eight months
after the war. "I am almost tempted to doubt my self sometimes and
ask if this is really I, to doubt my own identity." [87] And another
plantation mistress said she felt as if "I had lost a part of myself in losing
my country." [88] Occasionally, a planter displayed amazing ability to
absorb completely the impact of defeat. James Lusk Alcorn, for
instance, perceived enormous opportunity in the postwar landscape
and eagerly anticipated his chances.[89] But the ravages of war and the
shock of defeat were collective experiences which very few planters
escaped. A majority were neither traumatized nor galvanized, but
rather, exhausted by the four-year ordeal and sick at heart at their
failure.

It was not simply their memory of the war that depressed them.
There was also the war's grim aftermath and a frightening future. The
wretchedness of the South in 1865 was itself enough to demoralize
and confuse strong men, as evidenced by the experience of Henry
Watson, Jr. In November, 1865, Watson returned to his Alabama
plantation after four years in Europe. He had not left the South in
1861 because he lacked sympathy with its cause. He had been accustomed to escaping the pestilential summers of Alabama by traveling to
the seaside in Massachusetts, but after war broke out, he had not
wanted to go north, and believing he could not safely remain in the
torrid South, he had sailed for Europe. From the Continent he
scrutinized every scrap of war news and fed information and advice
back to his Southern friends. He proved an exceptionally intelligent
and clear-eyed observer who constantly urged Alabamans to "take
*facts* as they are." [90] From his vantage point beyond the storm,
Watson was truly a voice of reason.

He remained in Europe for a few months after the war ended and continued to send his neighbors in Alabama advice, this time about how to deal with defeat. He attacked their gloom and denounced the recalcitrance of Southern politicians. "Facts are facts," Watson said again. "When a tornado has destroyed one['s] crops, forests, houses, outhouses, & fences, it is the height of absurdity to sit down & lament, blame Heaven for it & assert that should not have been." The "only course," he told them, "is not to groan but to go to work at once to rebuild, plant, make anew." The South risked all on the war. "It has lost," he said. "The only thing now is to admit the failure, take things *as they are*, not as they should be, and set about repairing the mischief." Southerners should think "*practically*" and salvage what they could. Put the farms back into operation, he declared. Let slavery go, for it was "*lost*" in the war. Take the amnesty oaths and apply for pardons. Work with the moderates in the North, lest the radicals gain ground. "Go back into the Union," for without representation "we shall not get rid of military rule, shall not be permitted to control our negro population." [91] Confident and enthusiastic, Watson boldly outlined a plan of salvation and then in November, 1865, headed for Alabama.

Back on his plantation, Watson's cool confidence and impressive logic deserted him. He almost wished he had remained in Europe, where he had been "so free from excitement, care and anxiety." Thrust into the environment Southerners had endured for four years, he became confused and indecisive. His friends "daily asked for advice as to what they had better do about this or that, should they sell, should they rent, what is their property worth, what do I think & would advise about selling cotton, what about the currency, what about the political prospects, etc., etc.," but he discovered that he no longer knew what to tell them. Everything was "in such a disorganized, uncertain condition here that no one knows what to do," he said. "I have been in many troubles in the course of my life," he declared only three weeks after his return, "but I never before was in one in which I did not see, or think that I saw, some way to get out. . . . I am completely at a loss now. I am completely at sea." [92] Calm and resolute when an outsider, Watson was bewildered by his plunge back into the post-Appomattox South.

However, the profound pessimism and anxiety which gripped

Southern planters did not usually result in drift or paralysis. Howell Cobb, for example, could say in September, "The present is as
blank and the future as full of doubts and perplexities as our worst
enemy could desire it to be." But at the same time, he was unwilling
merely to wander about aimlessly. He would, at least, seek some path
through the difficulties. "I have advised my friends," Cobb replied to
an inquiry from another Georgia planter, "to yield to our destiny with
the best possible grace—recognize as a fixed fact the abolition of
slavery—conform in all respects to the new state of things—cooperate
in the early restoration of our state to civil government. . . . take the
amnesty oath when permitted to do it. . . . apply for special
pardons. . . . and make up their minds to live out their future days in
the Old Union." [93] That the majority of the South's planters adopted
Cobb's strategy—submitting to defeat, putting the issues of the war
behind them, and responding practically to realities—was clear to
most contemporaries. [94]

The small knot of planters who refused to recognize the new order
were enraged by the majority who had. In the eyes of these unreconstructed rebels, an acceptance of unalterable reality was a betrayal of
old trusts. They had no intention of adapting to the New South. There
was only one proper stance—faithful allegiance to slavery and steadfast resistance to Yankees. A Georgian who refused to give up his
slaves throughout the summer of 1865 declared that Southerners were
"pusilanimous wretches," who acted the part of "the whipt Spaniel[,]
Kissing the hand that smits them . . . bowing at the footstool of
power . . . singing hosannas to the union." [95] A recalcitrant Virginian railed against those who had "fallen down in adoration of the
'golden calf.' " He complained that planters were rushing "to save
property and person," scrambling to "take oaths and secure pardon,"
willing to acknowledge anything, whether they were "traitors or devils." Rather than "hugging the chains" that bound the South, he
would resist. "I will not lie & say that the north had a lawful right to
take my slaves," he shouted. "It was unconstitutional confiscation." [96] Most planters would have agreed that might did not
necessarily make right, but they also understood that the military
might of the North had established the parameters of the possible in
the postwar South.

Willingness to adjust to radically changed circumstances did not
mean planters had abandoned their traditional views. Nor did their

attitude spring from an optimistic appraisal of their chances of restoring their plantations with free black labor. Planters openly admitted that they were grasping at straws. Many feared that they were merely postponing inevitable collapse. Even though they had consistently equated plantations with slavery, the Southern gentry could not acquiesce in the final destruction of the plantations now that slavery was gone. Preservation of their plantations had dictated their behavior for decades, and most were flexible and resilient enough in 1865 to make yet another effort. As grim as the thought was, they had to contemplate plantation agriculture without slavery.

Emancipation so disrupted the plantation South that planters found themselves in ambivalent relationships not only with blacks but also with one another. Before the war, planters had been bound together by their class interests and by the problems common to all slaveholders. But in the postwar years, relations became strained —co-operative and competitive at the same time. On the one hand, they all faced the same series of difficulties in seeking to restore their plantations, and few were confident enough to go entirely their own way. Even before the war ended, planters in Amite County, Mississippi, began meeting together to discuss how to handle freedmen "so as to have order." [97] After Appomattox, planters often organized in county associations, hoping their unity on wage scales and share arrangements would undermine the bargaining power of blacks. [98] Individual planters continued to seek out others for advice and instruction. One week before hiring time, a Virginian prepared for a trip to the Albemarle and Louisa county courthouses, where he intended to talk with other planters about how they "manage this business," about "how they determine prices, time, etcetera." [99] William H. Heyward of Charleston burrowed into works on European political economy in his search for solutions to Southern agricultural problems, but he also carried on an extensive correspondence with "practical gentlemen." [100]

But while planters sometimes moved co-operatively, they were also caught up in fierce competition. Polite conventions were stripped away as they battled one another for scarce resources, human and material. Slavery had united the gentry, but free labor threatened to splinter them. "The *competition* is frightful & the planters are literally cutting one another's throats," one South Carolinian reported in 1866. [101] A Louisiana sugar grower complained that cotton planters from Mississippi had swept through his neighborhood seeking to woo freedmen away with extravagant promises. "I am afraid that if cotton planters are successful," he said, "sugar planters will not be able to get hands next year." [102] An Alabaman concluded that the "more like a negro the Employer is the greater has been his success in getting hands." According to his experience, the "best masters have made the greatest failures and an impossible fellow with a bottle of whiskey and liberal promises can entice all labor from any one of them." [103] The problem was severe enough for several states to include penalties for "enticing" in the so-called Black Codes, which began to be introduced toward the end of 1865, but competition for workers continued.

Competition not only made it difficult to get and keep labor, but also, many claimed, ruined what labor was obtainable. "Negroes doing generally badly," a Texas planter noted in September, 1866. "High wages offered by *asses* has turned their heads." Moreover, competition between planters seemed to destroy community standards for labor. The Texan complained that he could not get his field hands to pick "clean cotton." They know other freedmen pick "trash," he explained, and "think I am hard to please." [104] A similar report came from a young rice planter in South Carolina. "The negroes do pretty much as they please," he said, "and laugh at threats of dismissal as there are any number of places where they can go and do as they please." [105]

Whether they acted collectively to meet the black challenge or separately in private searches for black labor, planters faced similar problems in reorganizing their plantations and resuming staple production. On one level, the preservation of the plantation in the postwar South depended, as it always had, on the successful application of management skills to land, labor, and capital. But the typical planter emerged from the war in control of only one of this triad. He could say with John S. Dobbins of Georgia, "I have got little left now, only my land." [106] And throughout the South, land values had declined sharply. In addition, the land had frequently been devastated. The bayou country of Louisiana was "ruined almost entirely," one planter reported. In his neighborhood there was "not a house, fence or even vestage [sic] of Civilization." [107] Worse off still were those few who returned home to find that they had lost even their land. The Freedmen's Bureau, established in March, 1865, to help the freedmen move from slavery to freedom, seized some plantations as "abandoned lands." The government sequestered others under the Confiscation Acts or for nonpayment of taxes. And even planters who managed to hold on to their lands were anxious because of the rumor that Congress was about to give each freedman forty acres and a mule. They knew full well that if this occurred, at least the forty acres would be cut from their property.

Staple production required substantial amounts of capital, but as Henry L. Graves said, "The smash up left every body in this country flat." [108] Thomas T. Munford returned to his Virginia plantation "without a cent," and once there, "found nothing to sell." [109] Planters needed cash for immediate necessities, as well as for unpaid taxes, debts, and interest. The McBee family of North Carolina, for example, emerged from the war with more than twenty thousand dollars in debts, stretching back to antebellum slave purchases. [110] John Berkley Grimball owed more than ten thousand dollars in accumulated interest alone. [111] Those few planters who had successfully hidden cotton were in fine shape, for when Southern ports were thrown open, they made fortunes. A. H. Boykin of South Carolina sent a whopping 460 bales of cotton to his Charleston factor, who sold it for an average of fifty cents a pound. [112] Others had nonagricultural investments they could draw on. Lewis Thompson of North Carolina sold bonds worth twenty-one thousand dollars to put his plantations back into running order. [113] But most Southern planters had far more debts and Confederate currency than cotton and bonds, and the summer of 1865 saw a mad scramble for credit.

Moreover, planters at this time often found labor as scarce as capital. Freedmen everywhere had greeted emancipation by abandoning their slave cabins and taking to the roads, escaping former masters, seeking families, or merely experiencing the feel of freedom under their feet. On some places not a single black remained. A Louisianan said in September, 1865, that there were "*immense* tracts of the most valuable land vacant in consequence of the disappearance of the negroes. . . ." [114] And even when blacks stayed on, planters discovered, they tested their freedom by getting out to the fields hours late, by refusing to work on Saturdays, and in scores of other ways. George W. Munford of Virginia reported that he was using "all sorts of expedients" to "seduce" work from his laborers but that they were "without the activity to jump Jim Crow." [115] Few would have disputed G. E. Manigault's declaration that the "system of labor on plantations is completely disorganized." [116]

While the task facing the planters was familiar in one way, it was radically different in another. Emancipation had introduced a new factor, the freedman. Planters agreed that the future of the South's plantations rested upon the behavior of free black labor, and, universally, they referred to free labor as "the experiment." There were several shades of opinion in 1865 about its chances of success. Here and there a maverick optimist could be found. "In casting ahead in thought for future employment I see nothing more profitable or agreeable than farming," Everard Green Baker of Mississippi declared that summer. When he bought a second plantation in September, he said forthrightly that it was "an experiment in freed labor," but admitted that "all seem to think I have done wrong & that it will prove a failure." [117]

Certainly, as the Mississippian realized, the bulk of planter opinion was negative. "No planter sees any way by the present lights to make usefull [sic] laborers out of free negroes," an informed Alabaman reported in July, 1865, although, he added, "prices of cotton may tempt the experiment." [118] The pessimism of planters reached its most dismal level among the many who believed that blacks would not even exist in the South much longer. Without the paternal protection of slavery, they could not survive, much less work. "Where shall Othello go?" asked one planter. "Poor elk—poor bufaloe—poor Indian—poor Nigger—this is indeed a white man country." [119] Would blacks labor without the lash? Could they even avert extinction without masters? These questions were on planters' lips in 1865. Although their answers were usually in the negative, even the most despairing were rarely free to act upon their fears. Buyers of ramshackle estates were scarce, crops were already in the ground by summer, and planters could only hope to hold on to whatever labor they had.

The Federal Government, too, was eager to keep the freedmen on the plantations. There, at least, they would be fed and housed and off the government's relief rolls. The task of supervising the transition from one labor system to another in the South fell to the Freedmen's Bureau. Building upon the labor program developed during the war by the Federal military, the Bureau launched a vigorous campaign in the summer of 1865 to bind black laborers and planters by contracts which would cover the remainder of the season. [120]

Planters signed the contracts in 1865, but they rarely expressed confidence that the agreements would resolve their labor problem. The Bureau did in fact provide planters with important services, just as had the Federal army during early Reconstruction in the Mississippi valley, and contracts did prove the steppingstone to renewed planter authority over labor. But in 1865 the Bureau's services were only recognized as valuable by planters who had faith in the new labor system. Those still rooted in the master-slave relationship, those still seeking the prerogatives of masterhood, did not regard the Bureau as offering any vital service. In the immediate postwar years, most planters viewed contracts as the measure of the revolution that emancipation had brought to the South. Contracts represented the consummation of the blacks' transformation from slaves to freedmen.[121]

Planters believed that contracts impinged more on them than on blacks. The Bureau's regulations in Alabama, for instance, required employers to put away the whip and to provide food, clothing, shelter, and medical care, in addition to wages or shares.[122] Contracts actually made enormous demands upon blacks, but planters responded that the labor provisions were only as good as their enforcement. Blacks could not be expected to voluntarily fulfill the agreements, they reasoned, and real authority was now vested in the Freedmen's Bureau. And most doubted that the Bureau would actually compel freedmen to labor. In his county, a Texan said in 1867, the Bureau was "totally inefficient." For blacks "to violate a contract now is no offence," he declared.[123] Many saw the Bureau as meddlesome and dangerous. In March, 1866, another Texan cheered President Andrew Johnson's veto of "that most rascally Freedman's Bureau Bill." In his opinion, the Bureau was "the abolitionists' programme to drive the white men of the South into open antagonism with the Negro. . . ."[124] Many planters believed that the officers of the Bureau were actually Negrophiles. "The negro is a sacred animal," Samuel Andrew Agnew of Mississippi said in disgust. "The Yankees are about negroes like the Egyptians were about cats."[125]

What planters believed they needed to insure black performance was not a Freedmen's Bureau but a comprehensive labor code, molded to their needs. Without bold state legislation, Robert Toombs declared from his exile in Havana, the South "must abandon the application of capital to agriculture except on two hundred acre (or less) holdings. That is, we must come to the tenant system of

Europe." [126] "Unless Southerners are permitted to enact stringent apprenticeship acts which will be rigidly carried out," Frederick G. Skinner of Virginia asserted, "we will find ourselves saddled with four millions of paupers[,] vagrants and rogues." [127] Striking a more benevolent tone, another Virginian demanded "some system by which the poor creatures can be kept from the sad fate which must be theirs if left to their resources for livelihood and employment." [128] Southerners had always believed that labor and race relations were too important to be left to individuals, and in 1865 they began to devise a new system, put into effect through the so-called Black Codes.

That autumn, Southern legislatures started adopting detailed codes regulating labor in their states. Officially, the aim of the codes was to "guard them [blacks] and the State against any evils that may arise from their sudden emancipation," a goal consistent with the antebellum image of blacks as both immature and primitive. The immediate effect of the codes, however, was to channel blacks back to the plantations, and, once they were there, to coerce labor from them. Regulations varied from state to state, but most made vagrancy a criminal offense. South Carolina went further, prohibiting blacks from working outside domestic service and agriculture and making the violation of a labor contract a serious criminal act. Charles Sumner thought the codes were a blatant attempt at "semi-peonage," but planters believed they were absolutely necessary. In the behavior of blacks, they said, lay the key to the future of the South. [129]

The efforts of the Freedmen's Bureau, state legislatures, and planters, in conjunction with the freedmen's own miseries, succeeded in driving most blacks off the roads and back into plantation cabins by 1866. But the flurry of activity had not created a permanent new labor system. Federal officials soon disallowed the Black Codes, and in 1866 only the roughest outline of a new labor arrangement was apparent. The critical interior lines of the system would have to be drawn in on thousands of separate plantations across the South. Planters felt they had no pertinent experience, no usable past, to draw upon. They had only a set of assumptions about blacks and agriculture. They were convinced that blacks did not respond to the same inducements as whites. Blacks were like children—improvident, oblivious to the future, unable to appreciate the obligations of a contract, incapable of accepting the responsibilities freedom had bestowed upon them. The quest for the restoration of prosperity and order on the plantations had many facets, but the dominant concern was the freedman.

## IV

Intent on holding their plantations together but not sure how to accomplish it, planters set about experimenting with new arrangements, moving ahead by trial and error, hoping to find a system that worked. "All the traditions and habits of both races had been suddenly overthrown," a Tennessee planter remembered, "and neither knew just what to do, or how to accommodate themselves to the new situation." [130] Planters were no longer free to organize plantations as they wished, for now the desires of freedmen and of the Federal Government entered the equation. With traditional relationships all askew, the restoration and rehabilitation of the plantation proved almost as much a social as an economic problem. After more than two years of effort, however, the vast majority of planters believed they had been unsuccessful in their search for an adequate substitute for slavery. Planters and freedmen were still floundering about in 1867, and the rural South remained disordered, unstable, and poor. In most planters' minds, free black labor had proven a failure.

Self-interest demanded that planters do everything they could to make the new labor system work, and most threw themselves into the task with feverish intensity. They sought to be realistic and practical, but their early efforts clearly reflected their continued faith in slavery. As Cary Charles Cocke of Virginia remarked in August, 1867, planters' ideas were still the product of "observation & practice under the old system of cultivation." [131] Their inability to give up their preference for compulsory service meant that they strove to reinstitute their authority in the freedmen's lives and labor. Rebuilding plantations along familiar lines required the continuation of work gangs, white supervision, task systems, clustered cabins, and minimal personal freedom for blacks. Subservience and regimentation were the planters' goals. Unable to accept the implications of emancipation, they sought to keep blacks as nearly slaves as possible.

There could be no return to the old plantation, however. For one thing, the Freedmen's Bureau was there to guard against black re-enslavement. For another, blacks themselves now sought to supply more than muscle in the reconstruction of Southern agriculture. In thousands of separate plantation arenas, landowners without laborers confronted laborers without land. Blacks and planters were in a constant tug of war over the freedmen's responsibilities. "Pa wants his hirelings to do anything he wants," Samuel Andrew Agnew of Mississippi reported in November, 1865, but "George wants to hire to make a crop only." [132] In the opinion of a bitter South Carolinian, freedmen had acquired "the notion that they are part proprietors." [133] Blacks were determined to remove the vestiges of slavery. If they could not yet legally share the land, they wanted at least to share in decisions about how they would farm the land. They objected to the continuation of gang and task labor and to planters' involvement in their personal lives. They demanded to work independently and to be free from constant white supervision. They demanded, in other words, that planters accept emancipation and trust in free black labor. [134]

Planters were determined to keep their plantations from breaking up, and almost no one would sell land to blacks. Many even refused to rent. Renting to Negroes was "very injurious to the best interests of the community," a Georgian claimed. [135] Planters had no desire to further economic democracy, white or black, and no confidence that freedmen could farm successfully independent of whites. A survey of Cooper River, South Carolina, planters in February, 1866, revealed that a majority had managed to retain slave-style gang labor and were giving shares of the crop as compensation. As one Cooper River gentleman explained, planters adopted the practice of paying in shares because they were short of cash with which to pay wages and also because they hoped an interest in the crop would make for a steadier, livelier work force. [136] The share system was widespread in the South in 1865 and 1866, but it was unstable. Freedmen sought independence, not gang labor and shares. If they could not own land, then they wanted to rent land, and if they could not rent, then they hoped to sharecrop.

Although wage labor survived in the cotton South, sharecropping gradually came to dominate. It proved the primary means of bringing together landowners without capital and laborers without land. Sharecropping was a compromise, and it satisfied neither planters nor freedmen. It offered blacks more freedom than the labor gangs, but less than owning land or renting; it offered planters a means of resuming production and of exercising some supervision, but less leverage over labor than they desired or believed necessary. Forces were at work which would eventually produce a degree of uniformity in the cotton South, but for a number of years labor arrangements continued to resemble the region's well-known patchwork quilts—a display of almost infinite variety. "On twenty plantations around me," an Arkansas gentleman observed a year after the war, "there are ten different styles of contracts." [137] While sharecropping presaged the future, planters were unable to recognize any permanence. They perceived only confusion and flux in early Reconstruction agriculture and were convinced that nothing they saw could restore the grandeur of the plantations.

The search for a replacement for slavery involved more than comparing the profits and losses of various economic arrangements. Slavery had defined both economic and social systems, and the introduction of free labor meant that both labor and race relationships had to be redrawn. "Old owners and overseers have much to learn," and Negroes "have as much to learn before they can understand their new positions," an Alabaman observed in December, 1865. [138] Individuals accustomed to dealing successfully with blacks as slaves often found themselves unable to deal with them as freedmen. "I am not fit to manage negroes now, at least hired servants," a woman in Alabama declared. "They, nor I either, are prepared for the changes in our situation." [139] A North Carolinian agreed. "I have done many disagreable [sic] things in my life but very few more so than to hire *Freedmen*," he said. "They ask so many questions." [140]

Extensive experience in the old regime did tend to make adaptation to the new regime more difficult. Older planters by the score washed their hands of plantation management, turning over administrative duties to younger men. James Baker of Florida made his son manager of his plantation, reasoning that the younger Baker held "his temper and gets along better with the freedmen." [141] A planter in Greensboro, Alabama, wrote his nephew that cotton plantations could be had there on advantageous terms. "Most of the old planters are disposed to abandon the business in part at least," he reported. "That is they are turning over their lands, teams, provisions, etc. to young men & receive a share of the crop by way of rent." [142]

The shock of black freedom affected young and old alike, however. As a Georgian observed in August, 1865, the "dark, dissolving, disquieting wave of emancipation" succeeded in "withering and

deadening the best sensibilities of master and servant." [143] Embittered
by the results of the war, soured by insubordinate black behavior, or
merely quick to take advantage of new economic opportunity, planters
often displayed a callous disregard for the welfare of former bondsmen
in the reorganization of their plantations. Of course, the economic
realities of participation in the world's commercial market place had
always threatened the realization of the Southern ideal of a patriarchal
and paternalistic master. The result had been, in Eugene Genovese's
words, a "bastard slavery," a hybrid of paternalism and crass economic
exploitation. [144] Yet, as antebellum planters had realized, paternalism
and profit-seeking were not mutually exclusive. Paternalistic behavior
was sometimes encouraged by rational economic motives. It made
economic sense to be personally involved in the care of scarce and
valuable black labor/capital. It made sense to encourage vigorous
work through rewards and positive incentives. It made sense to seek to
minimize problems of labor control by encouraging black gratitude
for planters' kindnesses. Of course, some planters never behaved
paternalistically. Others, having acquired paternalistic sensibilities,
never lost them. But for the majority, while paternalism had once
been an important element in the treatment of black labor, after 1865
it decayed, sometimes to the point of utter insignificance in plantation
life.

The effort to adjust from the paternalistic relationships associated
with slavery to the purely contractual relationships associated with
compensated labor became a dominant theme in the reorganization
of plantation agriculture after the war. The realities of the economic
world pushed especially hard; and without the restraints bred of
ownership of labor, without the façade of black subservience and
affection, without the advantages of black production, paternalism
had few buttresses. Under the radically altered circumstances, in fact,
profit-seeking apparently did not even allow, much less encourage,
paternalistic concern for black welfare. Lacking recourse to corporal
punishment or stringent state labor codes, planters had no choice but
to rely upon the coercions of the market place to motivate black labor.
The harshness of the competitive free market—with its ultimate sanction of starvation—was the only leverage available. Benevolent behavior toward blacks could no longer encourage productivity or increase control. Planters believed that it could only insulate freedmen
from the consequences of economic irresponsibility and encourage
their natural proclivity to indolence.

The behavior of considerable numbers of planters demonstrated that they believed that the law which freed the slaves also freed the masters. For them, all obligations deriving from the relationship of master and slave had ceased to exist. Henceforth, their relationships with freedmen would be determined by the letter of the labor contract. Tough-mindedness about labor matters was a necessity, a young South Carolinian declared, "if the plantation is to be money making and not a charitable institution." The place to begin, he suggested, was in "culling" the labor force. [145] That some planters were following that policy was clear to another South Carolinian, who observed that his neighbors were "hauling them out below here & putting them down in the Road—bad weather for outdoor living." [146] Expelling the old and sick, underpaying or totally refusing to pay the young and able—this did not become everyone's new standard, but it did become common.

Because the "illegal abolition" of slavery was forced on the South "by the strong hand of military power," reasoned a Virginia planter two months after Appomattox, Southerners were "in no wise responsible for it." Absolved from responsibility for emancipation, Southerners were also absolved from responsibility for the consequences of emancipation. "All feeling must be discarded," he argued. "Our own interests, although it result in [the freedmen's] total ruin and annihilation, must alone dictate the course for us to pursue." Survival in this hostile, unwanted world required "a judicious & thorough reorganization of the slaves [*sic*] upon the plantations, selecting those best calculated & qualified to promote our own & their own interests by affording a steady & reliable supply of labour & discarding all who do not come up to these requirements." Even then, he was not optimistic. Because the minds of blacks were filled with "visions that money will come to them without working . . . nothing short of [the] starvation of many of them & their families will ever open their eyes to truths. . . ." And the survivors might still be "more trouble than their services are worth, if some compulsion of some kind is not brought to bear, besides the tenure we now have over them." He suspected that the final consequence of emancipation would be "the substitution of white instead of black labor." [147]

Adopting a similar logic, a Mississippi planter declared in the summer of 1865 that his aim was to make his former bondsmen "wholly self-sustaining." The freedman would have to learn the lesson of hard work, he said. "If he does not, he cannot eat *my* bread and meat or wear *my* clothes . . . a proper allowance should be made for house rent, garden space, wood, milk and butter and feeding his poultry from *my* corn crib . . . in the amount of money wages paid to him." Having read blacks out of the plantation family and denied the paternalistic tradition, he had apparently moved to full acceptance of the principles of contractual free labor. But as in many of his colleagues, his conversion to laissez-faire capitalism was incomplete. Actually, he had little faith in the effectiveness of the market place in making blacks work. In his opinion, planters still required the master's power of coercion. The best means of assuring planters that authority, he believed, was for the state government to designate each plantation a separate town and each planter "a judge of police, with power to sentence and inflict." [148]

Because emancipation altered drastically the economic relationships on Southern plantations, it impinged on paternalism. Paternalistic sensibilities were also challenged by rapidly changing black behavior. Planters now usually perceived not what they considered good and faithful service, but instead insubordination and ungratefulness. "They are obviously changing in character every day," William Henry Stiles of Georgia observed in September, 1865. [149] And as black behavior evolved, white attitudes kept pace. In the early summer, Catherine Edmondston of North Carolina expressed pity for her former bondsmen and spoke warmly of their "affectionate cheerful simplicity of manner and speech." But a few weeks later the freedmen had become "discontented and moody." Soon they were "ceaselessly trying their new chains, seeing how little work they can accomplish & yet be fed and endeavoring to be both slave & free at the same moment—a slave on the food, shelter, & clothing question but free where labour is concerned." Simple freedom no longer satisfied them, she declared, for now they wanted "their master's land." "Red Republicanism" had finally linked arms with "Black Republicanism." [150] Freedom, quite simply, had ruined good Negroes, and for bad Negroes she had little sympathy.

The metamorphosis of Mary Jones of Liberty County, Georgia, took considerably longer. Like her late husband, the Reverend C. C. Jones, who was known as the "Apostle to the Blacks" because of his evangelical work among slaves, Mrs. Jones displayed a deep concern for the welfare of the black people on her three plantations. She consistently went beyond what was required of her in the labor contracts, providing freedmen with free milk, meat, and syrup, and sometimes even cooking things for them in her own kitchen. But eventually, she encountered behavior she considered outrageous. Disrespectful language, impertinent gestures, and inadequate labor all began to erode her sympathy. Finally, in May, 1866, two black laborers had her hauled before the Freedmen's Bureau, where they accused her of trickery in labor contracts. She won her case, and returning to the plantation, she promptly called all the freedmen together. As she remembered, "I told the people that in doubting my word they offered me the greatest insult I ever received in my life; that I have considered them friends and treated them as such . . . but now they were only laborers under contract, and only the law would rule between us, and I would require every one of them to come up to the mark in their duty on the plantation." [151]

Paternalism declined but by no means entirely disappeared in the early Reconstruction years. A sense of obligation sometimes outlasted the shock of emancipation. "What I shall do with mine is a question that troubles me day & night," Dolly Burge of Georgia declared in May, 1865. "It is my last thought at night & the first in the morning," she said. "I told them several days ago that they were free to do as they liked, but it is my duty to make some provisions for them. . . . They are old & young[,] not profitable to hire[,] & what provision shall I make for them[?]" [152] Some planters continued to pride themselves on the benevolent and self-sacrificing care they extended to blacks. In November, 1866, S. Porcher Gaillard of South Carolina allowed two elderly blacks, both former slaves of his, to move into a cabin on his plantation. He did it against his better judgment, for he knew that a neighbor had run them off his property for failing to fulfill their labor contracts. [153] As the planters' struggles to maintain status, wealth, and pride intensified, the pressures on paternalism grew.

Whatever their attitudes toward the freedmen, planters agreed that their primary task was extracting labor from them. Strategies differed widely. William Cooper of Mississippi had never shirked violence in dealing with slaves, and he continued after emancipation to whip blacks in his cotton fields. [154] An overseer for the Howell Cobb family believed a slightly less violent method might succeed. "I think I will get Som of them by not feeding them which proses is now going on though tha is rather two mutch fruit and green corn to have good effect." [155] Andrew McCollam of Louisiana used food more positively. He directed his son to plant several acres of turnips, reasoning that no Negro would leave the place with one of his favorite foods ripening before his eyes.[156] A Georgian suggested another tactic. "What we have to do is, as far as practicable, to make the Negroes content and happy, and induce them in the present change in their status to realize the obligations devolved upon them." [157] Because planters believed making blacks work was a difficult problem, they expended enormous energy seeking a solution.

Regardless of how ruthlessly or benevolently they treated their labor, planters were rarely able to overcome all the obstacles that stood between them and renewed prosperity. While taxes and interest rates rose, land values and cotton prices plummeted. In addition to the Federal tax on cotton which remained in effect until 1868, new state taxes were a heavy and unprecedented burden. Credit was both scarce and expensive. From southern Georgia came the report that planters there were abandoning their places because they could not find credit enough to buy provisions for another year's farming.[158] Those fortunate enough to secure credit sometimes paid charges as high as 3 percent a month, despite legal ceilings on interest rates. Land values, upon which planters relied for mortgages and credit, slid downward almost as relentlessly as the price of cotton. Nature also got in its blows. Floods and storms demolished healthy cane and cotton crops in both 1866 and 1867. The backdrop for the entire effort in agriculture, moreover, was the political confusion of early Reconstruction. As long as politicians continued to move the pieces around, planters found it difficult to put them back together. And, of course, there was the planters' own inability or unwillingness to fully accept free black labor. Their expectations of failure could hardly have increased the new labor system's chances of success.

Wealth had not entirely deserted the Southern countryside, of course, but tales of success were as rare as pairs of matched mules.[159] As one gentleman remarked, "Old Mother Fortune is a sad old bitch; blindfolded indeed, nothing blindfolded could make such sure licks." [160] A visitor to Natchez observed that the nabobs were now "not worth a cent." They "hold proud heads tho', and the ladies look lovely, and the men drink whiskey, same as before." But "all of them talk, even smell, of 'burnt cotton.' " [161] And soon legend would outstrip the reality of poverty. Many young Southerners would grow up hearing tales of those dark days: of white women who did their own washing in the attic and never hung their clothes outside for fear of being seen working; of old families entertaining guests and assigning one of the daughters to blacken her face and hands to serve the food; of prominent people calling on their neighbors on some pretext just at mealtime and graciously accepting their hospitality; of gentlemen who did not know how to work and were too proud to learn. [162]

Hard times did indeed force a number of planters out of the managerial class and into the ranks of labor. John C. Calhoun had once declared, "No Southern man, not even the poorest, will, under any circumstances, submit to perform menial labor. . . . He has too much pride for that." [163] During the war, however, the *Southern Cultivator* had predicted that the time would come "when it will no longer be a disgrace for a rich man's son to be seen in his shirt sleeves, and the sweat from honest, hard work pouring down his face." [164] And after Appomattox, soft-handed sons, and even their fathers, did sometimes find themselves trudging along behind broken-down mules. One woman expressed surprise when she heard that her cousin had become "*a plough boy*," but then added that she ought to have known better than doubt "anything that speaks of the poverty of the *Southern aristocrat*." [165] The most prominent names in the South were included among the manual laborers. A former mayor of Savannah, his wife reported, was "hard at work" with "his hands hard and burnt like a common laborer's." [166] A former Secretary of the Commonwealth of Virginia worked on his plantation in the "triple capacity of gentleman, overseer, and Cuffee Freedman." At sixty-three years of age, he said, he was "just in the full tide of the experiment whether I can compete with Cuffee as a day Laborer or not." [167]

Plantation mistresses had never led very leisurely lives, and after emancipation their days were often filled with heavy physical labor. Because house servants were usually the first to leave and the last to return, housework fell to the white woman. "Pa was out today hunting a cook and washer but had no success," a young Mississippian reported in January, 1866. Negroes considered the position of servant "a servile one," he said, and "we must do our own work as we have been doing now for some time." [168] "When I get through with the day's work," one plantation woman declared in June, 1866, "I am tired enough to enjoy the bed." [169] After a few months without servants, a West Virginia woman moaned, "I am broken down now. . . . my life is one of incessant toil." [170] Masters and mistresses alike would have agreed with the woman who said in 1866, "The war was truly a time of plenty in comparaison [*sic*] to this," [171] and with the man who declared in 1867, "The time is at hand here when every fellow has to root mighty hard for his provisions." [172]

Rooting was not pleasant, certainly, but planters at first actually prided themselves in their ability to meet the challenge. However, poverty and physical labor were difficult for people conditioned to wealth and ease. The physical tasks were exhausting and the social consequences galling. Despite drastic social dislocation the stigma of poverty and manual work had not entirely disappeared. Godfrey Barnsley, a down-and-out planter from Georgia, revealed his fears when he explained how difficult it was "to economize to the utmost extent" and "at the same time keep up appearance." [173] An Alabaman estimated that nearly all of his state's aristocracy were "uncomfortably embarrassed" and would be "unable to conceal this much longer." [174] One new recruit to field work explained its consequences. "I take the hoe & work all day, & as the weather has been hot . . . the exposure to the sun on my neck has blistered it smartly." [175] Poverty was, then, quite literally making planters into red necks. But it was the long-term social effects of poverty, the social sunburn, that more deeply disturbed the gentry.

When John G. Guignard's wife presented him with a new son in 1867, he noted that the youngster "promises to suite the times, haveing [sic] remarkably large hands as if he might one day be able to hold plough handles." [176] He almost certainly meant the remark sarcastically, for all across the South, planters were casting about for means by which their sons could escape agriculture. Before the war, James H. Hammond had said, "Planting in this country is the only independent and really honorable occupation." [177] White Southerners had whistled a little jingle:

> All I want in this creation
> Is a pretty little wife and a big plantation.

Planting was more than a vocation; it provided status. But after Appomattox what a man needed was a job. "Owning a handsome blue grass farm—a rich inheritance—turns out to be like owning so much blue sky," young Randall Lee Gibson complained in February, 1867.[178] Often it was more like having a millstone around the neck. James M. Willcox even asserted that "the more land one holds the worse off he is." [179] It was in their consideration of their sons' futures that Southern planters displayed their deepest misgivings about the future of plantation agriculture.

Fathers began actively seeking positions for their sons outside the world of the plantation. The professions had always been honorable, but now the list of acceptable positions lengthened considerably. Henry Watson, Jr., was on the lookout for a place for his eldest son, something "where he will make a business man." [180] "What to do with a host of boys is a source of anxiety indeed," a Virginian declared. "None of my boys care[s] for books—and what trade to put them at is difficult to decide. . . ." [181] John Berkley Grimball of South Carolina sent inquiries to a London mercantile house. "I dont know if John would like Mercantile life," he admitted, "but I think he will require some means of support." The elders resisted some occupations, but their resistance crumbled rather easily. When another of Grimball's sons decided to open a country store and become a furnishing agent for a large plantation, his father was upset, but he realized that "he had better do this than be completely idle." [182] When John G. Guignard's son informed him that he was going to become a traveling salesman, his father objected because "the business of drumming" was so "demoralizing." In the end, however, he let his son go because "the business will be so remunerating to him." [183]

The sons, too, were eager to carve out a niche for themselves in the postwar economy. They were enthusiastic, but not about Southern agriculture. After only a few months of what seemed to him hopeless struggle on his late father's Georgia plantation, John Floyd King dropped everything and headed for New York. "One thing only is before me," he said in anticipation, "labor and success." [184] In June, 1867, Thomas Barrow announced to his father, who had once owned three hundred slaves, that he was going into the commission business in Savannah. "*I think that I see money in it,*" he exclaimed. [185] When William Minor's son returned to Louisiana after the war, he was "anxious to get to work at something in which there is no need of negroes." [186] Some youths jettisoned their lifelong ambitions. "The plan of life I have chalked out for myself is the independent, innocent one of *planter*," Henry L. Graves had written home in 1862 from a Confederate army camp. "I want to be entirely independent of all persons," he explained, "free to go & come when I wish, subject to no man's or community of men's caprices." He returned to Georgia after the war to take charge of his family's estates, but by January, 1866, he was desperate to get out of the plantation and into the practice of law. He felt "chained hand & feet by the management of the estate," he confided to his sister.[187] The life of a postwar planter had not fulfilled his dreams; it was not even tolerable.

The elders themselves did not always turn a blind eye to the business world. For many, business had never been an alien concern, but rather had occupied a minor and subordinate position. Antebellum planters had engaged in a variety of entrepreneurial activities, and many could be described as hyphenates—planter-lawyers, planter-merchants, planter–land speculators. After the war, as their agricultural endeavors grew less rewarding—materially, psychologically, and socially—a considerable number moved into towns to give increased attention to their more remunerative interests. Agricultural poverty left them little choice but to redirect some of their energies. "Farming is pleasant enough with money to keep the wheels greased," George W. Munford explained after the war, "but when they creak & squeal it is a confounded jarring & grating sensation." [188]

While many expressed a desire to escape the plantations, relatively few succeeded. Often untrained for anything else, with nothing but their land and their agricultural experience, they for the most part remained on the land. There, despite their best efforts, they usually failed to restore the antebellum standard of prosperity. The causes of economic failure were complex—war had devastated the economy, emancipation had destroyed the labor system, Reconstruction churned the political waters—but planters almost to a man had a single simple explanation of what had gone wrong. Very early on they had established their position. "This year will test whether they can be relied upon as Laborers," a Florida planter said in 1866.[189] A Texas planter tagged 1866 "the test year." [190] By regarding their efforts to restore the plantation economy as resting entirely on what they called the "experiment" of free labor, planters provided themselves with a handy yardstick with which to evaluate the results. When production lagged and plantations failed to return much profit, they could only conclude, as they had anticipated, that free black labor was a failure.

Planters grumbled about taxes and cotton prices, government interference and military oppression, but their discussions always returned to the inability of black people to respond to anything less than the coercions of slavery. "The true cause of the shortage of the cotton crop is the inefficiency of the labor & the impossibility of managing it," an Alabaman declared in December, 1867.[191] In the opinion of a Georgian, planting had become a "very hazardous business because of the difficulty of finding laborers, the expense of free labor," and "the uncertainty of being able to control & make them work."[192] A South Carolinian whose lands had been caught up in the Port Royal experiment thought it "took 3 to do the labor of one before the war."[193] Another planter was hardly more generous in estimating that blacks accomplished only "two-fifths of what they did under the old system."[194] In June, 1867, a Tennessee man concluded that blacks were "a trifling set of lazy devils who will never make a living without Masters."[195]

While they themselves retained their monopoly of land, planters were aware only of the freedmen's near monopoly of labor. "The darkies have the long end of the pole," a Virginian declared in June, 1867, "for we cant supply their places, that I know of."[196] And without the prerogatives of mastery, planters believed, they and the freedmen were not evenly matched. "The negro can never be made to work as when a slave," a bitter South Carolinian asserted in January, 1868, "and the wear and tear on those who have to follow them will in time kill many of our young men or drive them to other pursuits."[197] Many, in fact, promised never to drive another plow into the ground if they could sell their lands. In September, 1867, a Virginia aristocrat explained the mood in his neighborhood. "The Harrisons, Hobsons, Bollings, Galts, Cockes, Cabells, and others with whom I have associated—first rate James River farmers—owners of fine estates and of every thing upon them except their former slaves—are restless, despondent, almost despairing." To a man they agreed that their difficulties grew chiefly "out of the changed condition of labor." They were "barely making expenses" and what little they made came "at the expense of feeling, and almost of self-respect, very trying to them." Many were "endeavoring to sell their estates, others to lease. . . ."[198]

After two years, sentiment against free black labor was almost universal. Demurrers were heard occasionally, of course, but optimism was almost always a springtime flower. By summer, it had usually withered. The criticisms of free black labor were more than just expressions of employers' dissatisfaction with the performance of their labor force. Planters predicted not merely continued difficulty but often disaster. Abolition would "be the end of what has been the most splendid [of] agricultural countries in the world," concluded a planter in Louisiana.[199] In Texas, another declared, "Cotton cannot be grown to any great & successful extent by free negro labor." [200] In the judgment of a Chickasawhatchee, Mississippi, man, "Cotton has got its doom stamped upon it." [201] And "freedmen won't do to tie to" was the terse conclusion of a Virginian.[202] Almost any planter would have gladly paid more than the reward offered in the *Southern Cultivator* in 1868 by a gentleman who promised fifty dollars to anyone who would show him how to make a living with "free negro labor." [203]

Northerners were sending Southerners a different message about the value of a free-labor economy, of course, but how could planters accept the basic economic principles of the damned Yankee culture? Northern ideas seemed naïve and ignorant, or at the very least, irrelevant. A year after the war, a South Carolinian reported that the Northerner who headed the Freedmen's Bureau in Charleston was committed to "fair play for both sides," but he added that this attitude was precisely the difficulty. "The fairest minded of all these officials," he explained, "seemed not to be able [to] comprehend the difference between the 'nigger' freedman and the white northern laborer." [204] Another planter visiting New York in 1866 on business wrote home that people there "think that the negroes will naturally—must inevitably—work with a better will, with more spirit & vim if they have a prospect of receiving wages, *paid to themselves*[,] than they would, could, or *did* under the former system." As a Southern planter, however, he was "just as positive that they do not & never will." [205]

Rather than eroding old prejudices, therefore, two years' experience with free labor reinforced planters' suspicions. In much the same way that the war had buttressed antebellum beliefs, the immediate postwar years continued to provide support for old assumptions. But in 1865, the basis for pessimism had still been largely theoretical. By 1867, planters believed they had seen the future fail with their own eyes. Howell Cobb, for one, moved from a position of skepticism to outright gloom. In June, 1865, he had reaffirmed his belief that slavery provided "the best system of labor that could be devised for the negro race," but he had also urged Southerners "to recognize that slavery had passed away." He understood that it would "tax the abilities of the best and wisest statesmen to provide a substitute for it," but he implored planters to accept the challenge.[206] Only a year and a half later, Cobb was ready to admit defeat. "The truth is," he explained, "I am thoroughly disgusted with free negro labor, and am determined that the next year shall close my planting operations with them." [207]

By 1867, Southern planters were hardly closer, intellectually, to accepting free black labor than they had been in 1863, when they first encountered it in the Mississippi valley. Cotton was not being produced without slaves—not profitably, at least—and the future seemed to offer little relief. Rather than launch a quixotic campaign to reinstitute legal slavery, planters strove in practical ways to channel rural life back into the well-beaten paths of the plantation past. But without slavery, life was unalterably and fundamentally transformed. It is hardly surprising that a central theme in planters' early postwar lives was a sense of powerlessness. We do not need to accept the assertion of a South Carolina planter that emancipation had made "the planter a slave, far worse than his slaves use to be." [208] But judged by their standards, standards established in an earlier regime, they were enfeebled. Perhaps a Virginian did articulate a widespread if unexpressed desire in 1867 when he said, "All those people who say they would not take back their slaves if they could are near of kin to Baron Munchausen. I am no kith & want mine." [209]

# CHAPTER 5

# "The Soul Is Fled"

"... from that Old World to this New one, through the war-Storm."

SIDNEY LANIER
*May 12, 1866*

Little more than a decade after Appomattox, a visitor to the rural South would have viewed a landscape reminiscent of antebellum days. Blacks were back in the cotton fields and kitchens, cotton had resumed its throne, plantations still dominated the countryside, and white Southerners again controlled the fields and the courthouses. As in the years before Fort Sumter, the lives of planters seemed hardly touched by external events, but responded to the everyday imperatives of crops, weather, blacks, disease, salvation, and family. Apparently, the planter regime had survived the revolution—shaken perhaps but essentially unchanged.

And yet, the image of continuity would have been as much illusory as real. Planters and plantations did continue to dominate the rural landscape, but slavery had perished, and with it much that was once considered fundamental. On the eve of the war, Southern planters had justified slavery as a moral right and secession as a legal one. They

156

had pictured plantation society as organic and conservative, hierarchical and chivalric, while portraying Northern society as chaotic and cancerous. A decade later, slavery was gone and secession lay buried at Gettysburg. Industrial capitalism had triumphed over the political economy of slavery. With the North's victory, new systems of labor and race relationships marched south. In fundamental ways, the South was nothing less than a world turned upside down.

Antebellum planters had proven shrewd judges of the essentials of their world. They had steadfastly declared that slavery was indispensable, and indeed, emancipation had resulted in the death of a distinctive society. Their bright, satisfying world of masters and slaves had given way to the dull, disquieting reality of employers and employees, of landlords and tenants. The journey from slave to free labor, from lord to landlord, was arduous. Change was sometimes concrete and readily apparent, as in planters' economic and political lives. At other times, as in their mental habits and social relations, change was subtle and intangible but even more fundmental. Planters' days continued to revolve around cotton, blacks, and plantations, but as one observer noted, they had passed "from that Old World to this New one, through the war-Storm." [1]

I

Planters had identified their entire society with slavery, but after Appomattox economic survival forced all of them to grapple with emancipation at its most immediate and practical level—that is, as the loss of their labor system. To make the black work became their central imperative. Survival required that they find their way through a maze of practical economic difficulties, but it also demanded that they put behind them notions about the indispensability of slavery. So tenacious was the old allegiance that many nevertheless sustained their proslavery orthodoxy for years after the defeat. After 1867, however, restatements of the old arguments declined. Assertions that emancipation meant imminent and inevitable collapse diminished. Increasing numbers came to accept the new economic system as permanent and workable. Some turned into such celebrants of competitve free labor as to become thoroughly unrecognizable. And yet, most planters were never so completely divorced from their antebellum selves as to learn to greet free black labor with complete optimism and confidence. Just as the emerging system produced only partial freedom for black workers, it received only partial and incomplete acceptance from white planters.

In one sense, of course, planters had accepted free black labor almost immediately upon defeat. By the autumn of 1865, almost every planter had shifted from slave labor to some sort of compensated labor. Practical adjustment was a necessity, compelled by Federal troops and by the absence of any alternative. Within five years, moreover, the plantation system of the cotton South had settled into a pattern of share tenancy which would vary little until well into the twentieth century. On an intellectual level, however, planters often believed that the new postwar arrangements were makeshifts, mere pauses on the road to total collapse. The proslavery ideology had decreed that destruction was the unalterable consequence of emancipation, and although they hardly had their hearts set on ruin, planters found it difficult to shed old ideas.

Eventually, almost inevitably, planters' assumptions did begin to achieve a degree of harmony with everyday, row by row plantation reality. Millions of sweating black field workers could not be ignored forever. Grudgingly and haltingly, planters moved toward recognition of the permanence and utility of the new system of free black labor. From the earliest moment of emancipation, of course, a few planters had argued for acceptance. Everard Green Baker, for instance, had transcended the slavery ideology and predicted that freedmen would respond to the same inducements that spurred white labor.[2] But he and others like him were unconvincing and were shouted down by planters who claimed to know their Negroes. Time, experience, and new circumstances proved more potent agents of change.

Competing with the idea that free black labor was an unpromising "experiment" was another notion—that the immediate postwar years were a time of "transition." Viewed as a moment of transition, the period could be considered either a brief hesitation before final collapse or an interval of only temporary chaos before better days. Emancipation had been so "marked and violent," declared Charles C. Jones, Jr., in May, 1866, that it was to be expected that the Negro "does not at once adapt himself rationally and intelligently to the change." He was, after all, only "a child in intellect." "Time alone can impart the necessary intelligence," the young Georgian explained. With time, "fear of the law, as well as kindness and instruction," could unite "in compelling an appreciation and discharge of the novel duties and responsibilities resting upon him." [3] A South Carolinian who was still "experimenting" with various methods of free black labor was less analytic but also cautiously optimistic. "I have an abiding hope that every thing will work out all right yet," he said in 1868, "but think that it will require much more time than most persons are disposed to give it." [4]

Time did work its changes on freedmen. Immobilized by share tenancy, terrorized by the Ku Klux Klan, dispirited by the failure of Reconstruction, blacks gradually settled back into behavior which whites found more acceptable. In 1866, *De Bow's Review* had printed a letter from an irate planter who complained that the hope for land of their own had produced "discontent, impatience, and insubordination" among freedmen. [5] But land was denied them, and the keys to the corncrib and smokehouse remained in planters' hands. As the grandson of John C. Calhoun said years later, blacks "realized their true condition" and went to work. [6] From her Virginia plantation, Ann Hairston reported in 1870, "I never saw even in the days of slavery as little passing about and what few I see look as humble as any slave I ever noticed." A neighbor, she added, had told her that "they are much more manageable than he has ever noticed them." [7] The more the freedmen resumed the habits and postures of slaves, the better the planters were able to accept the new system.

Planters' growing acceptance of the new system, however, was not primarily a function of modifications in black behavior. Their rejection of the system had never rested on the freedmen's refusal to work, but rather had sprung from the proslavery assumptions which survived the war. Changes in black performance could ease planter adjustment, but more important were changes in the norms and standards whites used to judge black performance. Behavior viewed as insurrectionary in 1865, they learned to accept as conventional in the 1870s. Events had so altered plantations that old ideas were increasingly awkward and inappropriate for evaluating new agricultural realities. Detached from the actuality of slavery, the norms and standards slavery had produced grew dim. As planters edged toward adaptation, moreover, they grew increasingly less aware of the revolutionary gulf which separated them from their former selves.

Furthermore, time disproved certain of the planters' predictions. A central premise of antebellum thought had been that the black was a natural slave, unable to function successfully outside the master-slave relationship. Because planters believed that the bondsman was a child-beast, they had predicted quite logically that with emancipation he would either meet extinction or revert to savagery. But blacks did not oblige. They neither died out without the master's care nor slid into barbarism without his control. Even the most jaundiced planter had to admit that blacks had not gone the way of the "Indian" and the "bufaloe" or of their "savage ancestors." Despite emancipation, those particular nightmares had not become a reality.

Almost from the moment of emancipation, planters' predictions of catastrophe had often clashed with the actual behavior of freedmen. Letters and diaries are a curious amalgam of expectations and actual experience. Apocalyptic prophecies mixed with plantation realities. A New Iberia, Louisiana, planter complained in October, 1866, that freedmen were "so much elated with Freedom that most of them have the strangest inclination to run all about and not labor," but he admitted that in his parish "they have been peaceable and obedient with few exceptions." [8] A Brunswick County, Virginia, man prayed in 1866 that he could "get good white labor before long," but added that his black workers were "doing quite well." [9] James Baker of Florida doubted that free blacks would do field work but reported that his former slaves had "gone to work rather better than I hoped." [10] A woman in Norfolk, Virginia, noted that the city was alive with blacks, who would "no doubt give us much trouble," but that thus far they had "behaved better than we expected." [11] And a young rice planter in South Carolina observed in October, 1868, that "the negroes on the plantation are orderly enough just now," but he added, "they are very treacherous and only await their opportunity." [12]

Sometimes the inconsistencies were astounding. In July, 1866, a Greensboro, Alabama, planter predicted a cotton crop only a quarter as large as usual. He carefully noted that the "very unfavorable season has done more to produce this result than the want of energy in the part of Americans of African descent." In fact, "the negroes have generally done fair-work." But he followed this evenhanded observation with the thought that the season would not be a total loss because it would at least "show to the whole *world* the difference between the two systems of labor." [13] In February, 1868, a South Carolinian complained of back-to-back crop failures. One year had been too dry and the next too wet, he explained. "I must confess however," he added, "that the present system of labor had much to do with the failures each year, as no such thing had ever occurred before. . . ." [14] Planters could even hold freedmen responsible for unco-operative weather! They were caught between their assumptions on the one hand and the actual behavior of blacks on the other. Inevitably, however, reality impinged upon old ideas.

Planters had a saying that the Negro was what the white man made him. Because the free-labor experiment was conducted during Reconstruction, some planters were able to transfer responsibility for any failures to Northerners instead of resting the blame solely on the blacks. Increasingly, planters argued that their labor difficulties stemmed from the Yankee presence. In December, 1865, Henry Watson, Jr., declared that the "great problem and uncertainty" was the Union soldiers who "poison the mind of our negroes." [15] The freedmen "are working tolerably well here and I believe the generality of them are disposed to work and to do well if they were only let alone by those miserable and designing radicals," declared Kimbrough Jones in the summer of 1867. [16] A Mississippi man agreed, pointing out that the "Freedman works vary [sic] well until they commence getting up these radical meetings." [17] Another Mississippian, who had lost everything in the "revolution," went so far as to declare, "I feel satisfied that if the Freedmen[']s Bureau and military men were all removed from our midst and we be allowed to organize our system of free labor as free men, black and white, the abolitionment of slavery would not only not operate seriously in our injury, but in a short time prove decidedly beneficial." [18]

The withdrawal of Federal soldiers was expected to return effective control of the labor system to white Southerners. Few planters believed that postwar laws could fully restore the efficiencies of slavery, but they welcomed the discipline and constraint imposed by law as preferable to the more anarchic results of slavery's downfall. The wife of a stubborn Georgia planter had sought in the summer of 1865 to convince her husband to give up his slaves by arguing that whites could reassert authority through state laws. [19] William H. Heyward of South Carolina even maintained that the civil and criminal codes could make blacks more completely slaves after emancipation than they had been before. [20] Many expected that even if freedom did not become a mere formality, with the end of Yankee tampering blacks would inevitably and naturally resume their dependent and subservient relationships with their betters. Had not that leading antebellum spokesman for the slavery interests John C. Calhoun declared, "No people, indeed, can long enjoy more liberty than that to which their situation and advanced intelligence and morals fairly entitle them"? [21] With the removal of Northerners, therefore, authority would revert to the capable, and blacks would return to their natural station.

Moreover, plantations here and there began showing a profit with free black labor. These functioned as early demonstration farms, testifying to the possibility of making money under the new system. Sometimes successful planters went further and became energetic spokesmen for postwar plantation agriculture. In frequent letters to the *Southern Cultivator*, David Dickson opposed Southern emigration, condemned the importation of immigrants as an alternate labor force, shouted the advantages of scientific agriculture, and argued that cotton, properly cultivated with a well-trained and carefully directed black labor force, was the most profitable crop for the lower South. He claimed, furthermore, that a general acceptance of his "System" would restore the planter class to power in a "counter-revolution" and reinstitute "diversity of condition and distinction of class based upon a landed proprietorship." Planters could again become "the light and life of society." Dickson broadcast his message for twenty years and was doubtless successful in rallying some farmers. [22]

Eventually, therefore, with modifications in their circumstances, assumptions, and expectations, significant numbers of planters made peace with free black labor. "The planters, without exception, so far as I have heard them speak, are thoroughly satisfied with the colored man as a laborer," reported the Northern visitor Charles Nordhoff in 1875. They found some fault, he admitted, "but they say that the negroes are orderly, docile, faithful to their engagements, steady laborers in the field, readily submitting to directions and instructions, and easily managed and made contented." Across the South, he declared, he heard planters say, "We have the best laboring class in the world." [23] According to this observer, therefore, Southern planters were at least as satisfied with freedmen as they had once been with slaves.

Doubtless there was an element of truth in Nordhoff's account. He was an able, even scholarly, reporter, and Southern planters had indeed come a long way since the dark days of 1865. But Nordhoff was also sympathetic to the South and eager to see Reconstruction end. He may have been influenced by the desire to soothe Northern anxieties about the fate of blacks if they were left in white Southern hands.[24] For while some planters were sanguine enough in 1875 to celebrate the new labor system, others continued to find it barely tolerable. Probably a majority of planters were dissatisfied to some degree with slavery's replacement. Planters had never viewed black slaves as perfect workers, of course, and they had frequently described them as lethargic, careless, and wasteful. Nevertheless, slavery had usually satisfied, while its substitute often did not.

Unreserved acceptance of the new system had from the beginning faced serious obstacles. Two were crucial. First, there was the planters' racism. Emancipation had freed the blacks, but it had not freed planters from their racist assumptions about black character. Because of the blacks' natural instincts, planters continued to reason, they required large doses of externally imposed discipline and constraint, not easily administered under the new system. Still, emancipation did effect a change in planters' attitudes and expectations about racial patterns on the plantations. Emancipation meant the shift from a desire, based on paternalism, for intimate white supervision of black slaves to a desire to avoid personal contact with free blacks while profiting from their labor. Thus, a transformation of the white antebellum plantation mentality allowed planters, despite their racism, to move toward an acceptance of the postbellum free-labor plantation. Nevertheless, to have reconciled themselves entirely with the imposed order, planters would have had to transcend racism of every stripe.

The second obstacle to unqualified approval of free black labor lay in the unhappy economic realities of postwar Southern agriculture. The patchwork of share tenancy perpetuated many of the inefficiencies of the old system, with few of its economic benefits, while adding new burdens of its own. Judged by the most direct standard —profits—free labor could often be considered a failure. General prosperity would have offered convincing proof that free labor was successful; poverty, widespread if relative, was often taken as a concrete demonstration of its bankruptcy. To have gained complete acceptance, free black labor would have had to overcome both white racism and Southern poverty, neither of which could be surmounted in the nineteenth-century South.

The Reconstruction years are jammed with complaints against the new system. Clearly, not every planter forgot the old antebellum standards. A Texan grumbled in 1866 that his hands were picking very poorly. "Oh, for one of the days of '60," he cried wistfully. "To this place it would be worth 25 bales of cotton." [25] Keating Simons Ball of South Carolina declared that his principal difficulty was "to get the Labor done." It required from "two to three hands to do per dium what one hand used to do for a day's work in former years." [26] Another South Carolinian complained in 1870 that his laborers were not working, "from no cause at all except that they are free." Seven years later he asserted that it would be impossible ever again to make "old time crops" without "old time facilities of labor." [27] George W. Munford, who farmed near the coast of Virginia, complained that blacks would sign contracts on shares, occupy a cabin, use wood, plant private gardens, but only put in a small crop and then let that go to grass while they went to the ocean to harvest oysters. Surely, he grumbled, with black labor "the sharing system is a *shearing system*." [28]

Nor did dissatisfaction cease with the end of Reconstruction. Home rule solved some problems, but it did not cure the planters' ills. It could not touch difficulties still perceived as inherent in free black labor. A Virginian who had owned 225 slaves complained constantly in 1879 about "idle, vagrant negroes." He had once enjoyed agricultural life, he said, but now "the labor, i.e. the negro, is hard to regulate." [29] In 1882, a rice grower from the Cape Fear region of North Carolina claimed that "since the emancipation of the slaves, the cost of agricultural labor in the South has increased by more than one-hundred percent. . . ." Workers "openly refused to undertake tasks, easy under a sterner system," he said. [30] From Tennessee came the prediction that prosperity would return only when planters accepted "smaller farms carried on by the skill and labor of intelligent white men." In this planter's opinion, "No reliance can be placed in the disposition of the negroes to fulfill their contracts." [31] More than three decades after the last Federal occupation forces had withdrawn from the South, a traveler reported that he had discovered throughout the plantation country widespread discontent with black workers. Negroes, planters had told the visitor, were indifferent, inefficient, and simply unreliable. [32]

Sometimes dissatisfaction took more concrete forms. Planters' anxieties led them to participate in two postwar campaigns which revealed that they were less than content with the quality of their labor force. Planters led a widespread and concerted effort to attract white immigrants to the South, and also showed considerable interest in schemes to deport and colonize blacks outside the United States. Although both movements were products of complex mixtures of forces, an unfavorable estimation of the free black laborer was an important element in each.

Emancipation caused planters to reverse their traditional position on the advisability of attracting immigrants to the South. Edmund Ruffin had expressed the general feeling of planters before the war. "One of the greatest benefits of the institution of African slavery to the Southern states," he said, "is its effect in keeping away from our territory, and directing to the north and northwest, the hordes of immigrants now flowing from Europe." [33] Immigrants would bring strange customs, alien faiths, and—especially worrisome—unorthodox views of slavery. But the guns had barely cooled when planters began to cast about for new sources of labor. Louisiana planters were "determined to exhaust every effort to procure white laborers rather than depend on Cuffy," a Baton Rouge newspaper reported in January, 1866. [34] Even earlier, a young Virginian declared that he intended to grow wheat, using white labor exclusively. He would tap the local labor market first, he explained, but he thought he would eventually have to go to the streets of New York City. [35]

The interest in immigration stemmed from perceptions of a black work force as inefficient, perhaps useless, and also scarce, perhaps on the road to extinction. Planters agreed that free blacks were lazy and shiftless and likely to remain that way. At the same time, they faced an immediate labor shortage. Emancipation had meant that many black women and children had deserted the fields for family cabins and schools. In addition, it appeared to planters that the entire region had been tipped westward and that much of what little black labor there was had slid to Texas. On a trip from Louisiana to Virginia in 1869, a young member of the McCollam family found that planters all along his route were complaining about their lack of field hands and were surprised to learn that plantations to the west of them were also shorthanded. [36] Free black labor, therefore, posed both a qualitative and a quantitative problem. Planters who had black laborers did not like them, and those who did not have them wished they did.

Individual efforts to attract immigrants were quickly superseded by

organized, even public, programs. Local agricultural societies everywhere endorsed resolutions favoring the importation of nonblack
labor. In 1866, South Carolina established a commission of immigration, and other states quickly followed suit. The immigration movement received enthusiastic support from varied, often incongruous,
groups. Opponents of plantation agriculture, such as James D. B. De
Bow and the Granger leaders, hoped that European immigrants, with
backgrounds in intensive and diversified farming, would replace black
labor and free the South from its dependence on staples. Industry-
minded New South spokesmen hoped to build a pool of factory
laborers. But the movement was led by plantation owners. Planters
did not want the land divided among small farmers, or the immigrants
channeled into industrial work. They wanted white labor for their
plantations. The British consul at New Orleans reported in 1872 that
to planters "a labourer is a labourer . . . whether he be French or
German, Italian or Norwegian, British or Chinese, he is to be housed,
fed, and treated just as the black race used to be." [37]

At first, planters sometimes viewed the importation of immigrants
as a means of disciplining and controlling black workers. Orientals
were brought into Louisiana in 1866, for example, primarily to
confront blacks with the choice of working or starving. But in a short
time, even in Louisiana, immigrants were seen as permanent replacements. Godfrey Barnsley, formerly a Georgia planter but now a
New Orleans factor, was in a position to know the trends among
Mississippi valley planters. In September, 1869, he predicted that
unless "prevented by Northern radicals," valley planters would bring
in "large numbers of Chinese to take the place of negroes as they are
said to be better laborers[,] more intelligent and can be had for $12 or
$13 per month and rations." [38]

South Carolinians were among the most vigorous proponents of
immigrant labor. "If these plantations are to keep up," the young
manager of Henry A. Middleton's plantations said unequivocally in
1871, "it will have to be by coolie labor." [39] William M. Lawton,
chairman of the Committee on Chinese Immigrants for the South
Carolina Agricultural and Mechanical Society, explained the crisis.
"I look upon the introduction of Chinese on our Rice lands, &
especially on the unhealthy cotton lands," he said, "as new and
essential machines in the room of others that have been destroyed [or

are] wearing out, year by year." "Evil disposed & Misguided men" had first freed and then tried to control "a race of whom they had no *experience or conception* of their characteristics." Negro labor was "gradually dwindling away[,] *dying out,* and becoming year by year, less efficient & reliable." [40] Thus, while the interest of New South industrialists in immigrant labor was fed by optimism about the South's future, planters turned to immigrants in a desperate effort to stave off the final destruction of the plantations.

Southerners had little success in luring immigrants to their region. The new arrivals consistently chose the cities and farm lands of the prosperous North over those of the poverty-stricken South. The few who came were rarely content to remain plantation laborers. In 1866, an ambitious son of a Georgia planter brought in a hundred German immigrants to work on plantations along the Mississippi River. In a matter of weeks, thirty-five had deserted. Even those who stayed had their faults. The young man claimed that in comparison with blacks, the immigrant "is much more expensive to feed and keep, and at present is ignorant of the manner in which the plant is made to grow." [41]

Despite the poor results of the immigrant campaign, planters continued to support the program well after the end of Reconstruction. Time, obviously, was unable to erase entirely the planters' discontent. In 1879, a Natchez planter explained his decision to join an association whose aim was "to import Chinese or foreign labor." He was satisfied, he said, that "sooner or later we shall be forced to abandon negro labor. . . ." [42] In 1885, Alfred Holt Stone successfully used Italians on his Coahoma County, Mississippi, plantation. Twenty years later, he published an article predicting that immigrant labor would drive blacks from the cotton fields. Negro "shiftlessness and improvidence," he declared, had created a "spectacle of broken-down fences, patchwork outhouses, half-cultivated fields, and garden spots rank with weeds." [43] Another Southern critic, historian Walter L. Fleming, concluded in 1905 that "free negro agricultural labor has in most places, except in the Yazoo Delta, proved a failure; the fertile lands of the black belt have never again reached the production of 1860; the better wages paid to the negro have simply enabled him to work less—three days a week instead of four." Southern agricultural development in the black belt was at a standstill, he concluded, "because of the worthlessness of the black and the difficulty of getting more white labor." [44]

Planters' dissatisfaction with free black labor was reflected not only in the campaign to attract whites to the South but also in their interest in the movement to deport blacks from the South. Since the 1820s, sentiment for the colonization of blacks outside the United States had been primarily Northern. Antebellum Southerners had increasingly looked upon colonization as a long-range threat to slavery. With the outbreak of the Civil War, the deportation movement took on new life, as President Abraham Lincoln and other powerful Republicans sought to combine emancipation with colonization. But after 1863, support for colonization declined rapidly in the North. At the same time, it began to develop in the South. [45]

White Southerners had always tended to regard free blacks as superfluous, dangerous, and detestable people, and with emancipation the number of free blacks rose to nearly four million. The automatic response of some planters was to wish for space between themselves and freedmen. "I am utterly disgusted with the race," a South Carolinian declared, "and trust that I may some day be in a land that is purged of them." [46] Some demanded that the freedmen all be pushed into west Texas or New Mexico. Others proposed isolating them in a few counties in each state. [47] And still others envisioned even more distant destinations. "The nigger wont work," one elderly planter said in 1866, "he will be a free nigger as free niggers always have been—they will worry us until we will be forced to run them off to Yankee land for sympathy, and then will come colonization and the white man's government." [48]

Colonization was out of the question as long as Republican regimes held power in the South, but with the return of home rule, deportation schemes revived. Despite the restoration of Southern white supremacy and the rosy pronouncements of New South spokesmen, many Southerners denied that blacks had made progress since emancipation, and argued rather that they were showing steady decline. In 1889, Philip Alexander Bruce, whose father had once owned five hundred slaves, suggested in his widely read book *The Plantation Negro as a Freedman* that the "withdrawing" of the South's Negro population would be desirable. [49] At about the same time, Senators John T. Morgan of Alabama and M. C. Butler of South Carolina introduced bills in Congress to foster black emigration from the

South. Henry Shelton Sanford, diplomat, entrepreneur, and owner of a vast Florida citrus estate, hoped the creation of King Leopold's Congo Free State in 1885 would serve as "another Canaan for our modern Israelites," discharging the "black cloud" that hung over the South.[50] Randall Lee Gibson, Louisiana planter and senator, applauded Sanford's idea, as did Senator Morgan. Gibson believed that the "exodus of our African population is inevitable."[51] Morgan thought it necessary, as white Southerners had "failed to remove the negro race from the plane which they appear to have selected for their pursuit of happiness, in accordance with natural laws."[52]

Interest in colonization was relatively minor even in the postwar South, and more a product of a deteriorating racial and political situation than a response to free black labor. But a low conception of black workers after emancipation doubtless played a part. In the end, of course, Southern whites did not deport Southern blacks. Colonization was totally impractical, and—as important—Southerners were never really willing to dispense with their large, experienced, and inexpensive work force. But the ambivalence of one community was apparent in the report of a Virginia woman that her neighborhood's blacks were flocking to the cotton states. People around her, she explained, were of two minds about the exodus. "Most of our people seem to be pleased that they are leaving," she said, but "others[,] fearing labor is becoming rather scarce[,] tell them frightful tales about being sold into slavery again [and] have detered [sic] a good many."[53] Probably a majority of planters combined both attitudes, even though they were contradictory. The planters' racial antipathy warred with their labor requirements. Exclusion of blacks would have solved the South's race problem but not the labor problem. In the end, planters resolved the tension in their feelings on the side of the preservation of essential labor. They chose to immobilize and subdue blacks, not send them on their way. For as a 1914 study of colonization sentiment perceptively concluded, "Every white man would be glad to have the entire black race deported—except his own laborers."[54]

Intellectual acceptance of the new system did not come easily for those whose entire lives had rested on antithetical propositions. But unable to attract immigrants or to colonize blacks without depopulating the plantations, planters had little choice but to use freedmen in their fields. In time, outright rejection of the new labor system dissipated, but in its place there often stood profound ambivalence. The confidence and buoyancy of antebellum days gave way to skepticism and resignation—more appropriate attitudes, many planters believed, for plantations without slaves. Ironically, even those few who leaped confidently from the old world to the new, welcoming free black labor, were not likely to prosper in the mire of postwar plantation agriculture.

## II

The battle for survival after the Civil War took place in a rural economy that was in a tailspin. Neither enthusiastic acceptance of the new labor system, nor unflagging energy, nor skill, nor will, nor faith, nor any other quality could guarantee victory in the planter's personal duel with poverty. Individual effort was often inadequate because the problems of postwar Southern agriculture had reached unmanageable proportions. On the heels of the war's physical devastation and the destruction of slavery, planters were confronted with liens and mortgages, declining prices and rising taxes. Threats of confiscation and subdivision proved largely imaginary, but the dangers of bankruptcy and foreclosure were potent realities. Although plantations continued to enjoy advantages in the agricultural market place, most failed to regain their antebellum prosperity. Most planters, therefore, found the mid-century revolution permanently disabling.

The planters' hardships were relative and often exaggerated by plantation folk, but privation did become a companion for many. As one young woman announced dramatically after the war, her generation had said good-by to "ease, elegance, and affluence." [55] Her prediction was accurate for many plantation families, who experienced, as one planter put it, "the dire pressure of poverty, the bitter pill of want." [56] Unlike Sherman's bummers, poverty could not always simply be endured and outlasted. As it worked its way into plantation life, planters felt bullied and victimized by forces over which they had no control. Accustomed to mastery, they felt frustrated and helpless. Enmeshed in an unyielding economic network, they felt their prized independence slip away. And in time, privation eroded the spirit and confidence of the South's old elite. Six years after Appomattox, an aristocratic South Carolinian remarked, "The war still rages, and I speak feelingly when I say that with some of us we are always having the worst of it." [57] For most, the final shot of the war only marked the beginning of a personal struggle for economic survival.

Precisely how well or how badly did planters and their estates weather the vicissitudes of the postbellum years? How persistent was the antebellum elite, how durable were the plantations, how did aristocrats and their lands fare? Unlike questions about the interior lives of planters, whose answers are necessarily impressionistic and unquantifiable, these questions lend themselves to systematic and empirical treatment. Unfortunately, certain of these have received little attention, while others remain among the most disputed concerning the postbellum South. [58]

Any consideration of the fate of planters and plantations in the postbellum South must begin with the Federal Government's refusal to undertake a program of confiscation and redistribution of land. From the beginning of the war, Northern radicals had demanded a revolution in Southern landholding. Although the government did haltingly begin to implement redistribution, it soon pulled back. By the end of the war, it was clear that the government had decided to maintain the system of large landholdings rather than replace it with a system of small yeoman farms. Planters were not forced to pay for their treason by suffering dispossession. The war ended as it had begun, with a highly unequal distribution of land in the South. [59] If planters and plantations were to disappear, it would not be as a result of a decree from Washington.

For years it was believed that economic forces had in fact accomplished what the radicals had been unable to do—that plantations had broken up into little farms, that Tara had become Tobacco Road. The census supported this notion that an agrarian revolution had occurred. According to the reports for the years 1860, 1870, and 1880, the number of Southern landholders doubled, while the average size of farms was halved. Actually, however, the census had failed, not the plantations. It had simply neglected to distinguish between landlords and tenants. Because the census marshals had recorded rented land under the renter's name, not the owner's, the impression arose that plantations had disintegrated. In 1910, however, a special census of 310 cotton counties in eleven states revealed that plantations had survived and even increased in size and had remained the most important units of Southern agricultural production.[60]

Plantations survived for a variety of reasons. While potent political forces outside the South had refused to touch the pattern of Southern landholding, hostile elements within the South were not powerful enough to accomplish the revolution on their own. Moreover, the economic system emerging in the South, while often inimical to the planters' economic well-being, actually operated in ways to preserve the plantations. The credit network of liens and blanket mortgages, for instance, made the alienation of small parcels of land difficult or impossible. The plantation's larger size, superior soil, and better credit sources meant that it continued to have the edge in competition with small farms in the uplands. And finally, plantations held together because planters worked hard to keep them together. For generations, the existence of plantations had been regarded as tied to the existence of slavery, but slavery proved to be not essential to the system.[61] Political and economic forces did impinge on the pattern of landholding in the postbellum South, but neither uprooted plantations.

The persistence of plantations did not necessarily guarantee the persistence of the old master class, however. Was the triumph of the plantation matched by a triumph of antebellum planters? Or did the transfer of land titles by judicial order, the foreclosure of mortgages, and the sale of plantations after the war leave the properties intact but dispossess their antebellum owners? What exactly was the old elite's economic fate?

Firm answers to these important questions do not yet exist, but some preliminary information is available. A recent study of five black-belt counties in Alabama reveals that only 43 percent of the elite planters who were there in 1860 remained in 1870. This is a remarkable turnover, but as the study demonstrates, the rate of planter persistence in the 1860s was only slightly less than in the 1850s. Still, we must be cautious before concluding that war, emancipation, and Reconstruction did not affect planter persistence. The study does not consider the fate of planters after 1870. While 1870 marked the effective end of Republican rule in Alabama, the economic difficulties set in motion in the 1860s did not cease with the termination of Reconstruction. The panic of 1873 worsened farming conditions, and planters found little relief for the rest of the decade. It is possible that many of those who were able to weather the early postwar years were unable or unwilling to hold on through the troubled 1870s. We must also be careful not to project the rates of persistence in Alabama's black belt to the rest of the plantation South. Central Alabama suffered far less destruction and disruption at the hands of invading armies than did most plantation areas. In the one county in Alabama's black belt that experienced major destruction, the rate of persistence of the landholding elite was only 29 percent, and this figure may be more representative of rates of planter persistence in other war-ravaged states. [62]

Neither those who left nor those who stayed nor those who bought in were likely to restore to plantations the level of afluence they had known in the antebellum South. In Marengo County, Alabama, for instance, war losses were devastating to all landowners. Between 1860 and 1870, the value of the average holding fell by 51 per cent. The losses incurred by elite landholders were relatively less severe, however, averaging about 43 per cent. Apparently, those who had much lost much, but those who had far less lost relatively even more. Again, we do not know precisely how planters fared in the 1870s, but we do know that the value of all Southern farms in 1880 was still fully 33 per cent below the level of 1860. [63]

Each type of plantation had its own peculiar burdens. None were heavier than those borne by rice. On the eve of the Civil War, the center of the rice industry was in the coastal and island areas of the Carolinas and Georgia. When rice production again reached the level of 1860, its center lay in Louisiana and Texas. Tidewater rice plantations had suffered extensive wartime destruction and deterioration, and by 1865 much of the land had been reclaimed by swamps. When Louis Manigault returned to one of his estates on the Savannah River, he declared that it had changed "from a Village to a Wilderness." The huge capital resources required for complete restoration were lacking, and the possibility of developing a tenant system did not exist because each tidewater rice plantation depended on a single, complex irrigation system. Still, modifications were made, and small-scale rice planting limped along under a task and wage-labor system. But eastern rice was no longer competitive, and on one plantation after another, rice production ceased. Typical of many was a plantation on the Altamaha River in Georgia; when the growing of rice was finally discontinued there in 1898, the land was sold to a wealthy Northerner, who used it for recreation and hunting. [64]

The sugar industry in Louisiana was also crippled by the war. Costly machinery was ruined through neglect and military destruction. Levees upon which planters depended were broken. The financial system which supported sugar was smashed. The sugar crop of 1861 was an enormous 459,000 hogsheads; that of 1865 was 15,000. Nevertheless, aided by new technologies and tools, a national tariff, and fortuitous international events, sugar gradually recovered. Like rice plantations, sugar estates experienced less decentralization than cotton plantations. Labor organization was in fact little changed, with workers continuing to live in quarters near the sugar houses but now receiving wages. Sugar regained its antebellum production levels in the 1880s, but as with cotton, the increase in production did not always mean prosperity for planters. The prominent Pugh family, for instance, managed to retain their plantations through the difficult years of Reconstruction but lost them afterward, the first in the 1880s and the last in 1910.[65]

Cotton was less hard hit than sugar or rice, but the cotton planter's search for renewed prosperity took place in similar unpropitious circumstances; he too coped with destruction, debts, and shortages of labor, credit, tools, and livestock. And in neither rice nor sugar did the end of slavery mean such a sharp break with traditional forms of plantation agriculture as occurred in cotton. By 1880, the fragmentation of the cotton plantation was almost complete. Measured either by the size of the cultivated unit or by the persistence of gang labor, fewer than 1 per cent of all farms in the cotton belt resembled antebellum plantations. Planters in the old cotton counties saw the center of cotton production shift not only westward to the virgin, alluvial soils of the lower Mississippi valley and Texas but also to small upland farms within their own states. Because banks and factors were either unable or unwilling to extend credit, crucial financial functions devolved upon country merchants. Some planters opened stores on their own plantations, becoming furnishing merchants as well as landlords for their tenants. But most planters ended the years of Reconstruction locked into staple production and entangled in an injurious credit system. Under these new conditions, cotton plantations did resume production, achieving antebellum levels in 1877. But cotton prices reached their nineteenth-century low in 1898, and cotton plantations rarely returned their antebellum profits.[66]

The long-term economic consequences of postbellum developments in the cotton South—the decrease in average size of the cultivated unit and the rise of sharecropping and the country merchant—remain somewhat cloudy. Whatever the final answers, contemporary planters found the new circumstances damaging. The changes in their income, in the value of their lands, and in the productivity of their farms, all show that they suffered. Yearly labor contracts reveal that they were continually, often desperately, juggling the terms, seeking a formula that would extract labor from freedmen and put dollars in their pockets. Their difficult, sometimes severe, economic circumstances were heightened by their memories of the past. Forced to exist on what to him seemed a "mere pittance," a Louisianan declared in 1875 that his life was an endless "struggle with rooted habits." [67] Life was distinctly crude after the war, and while some planters told tales of success and optimism, many more spoke of their hardships and discouragement.

The path of decline in the postwar rural South was winding, but it did end in real poverty for some. Failure could come abruptly. Louis Hébert, for example, a Louisiana legislator in the 1850s and a Confederate officer during the war, returned to his bayou plantation in the summer of 1865, "doing all I could by manual labor to provide food for myself, my children, and kindred then there." But before he could even begin to put his place back on its feet, the bank foreclosed his mortgage and he was "homeless." Until his death in 1901, Hébert earned his livelihood by teaching, seldom staying in one location more than a year, constantly moving from one debt-ridden Southern academy to another. [68] Similarly, creditors moved quickly after the war to foreclose on Thomas Chaplin's plantation on Saint Helena Island. Living "from hand to mouth for several years," he returned to the island in 1872, not to resume life as a planter, but to live in an "overseer's house" and for sixty dollars a month teach "a large school for negro children." He could not "stand much more thumping & tumbling about," he declared in 1886. [69]

If economic destruction was to be a planter's fate, it usually came more gradually. Strangulation was hardly less painful, however. James Gregorie of South Carolina was in desperate circumstances in 1867 and sought operating capital in the North. A New York financier, Charles Rose, responded with a loan of fifteen thousand dollars. Gregorie resumed planting, but his crop was a complete failure and he was unable to pay even the interest. He appealed for more money, and again Rose responded favorably. For six seasons Gregorie met disaster, and six times the New Yorker bailed him out. Each year, just as a rich crop of sea-island cotton was about to ripen, rain, drought, or caterpillars would destroy it, and Rose would follow bad money with good. This shrewd and successful Northern businessman had become less a creditor than a patron. He obviously enjoyed his relationship with the Southern aristocrat, extending new sums with a flourish, soothing Gregorie's anxieties, proffering naïve advice. Finally, however, in 1873, after thousands had been invested and not a penny returned, Rose informed Gregorie, through his accountant, that he would have to foreclose.[70]

Keating Simons Ball of South Carolina also spun in ever tightening circles. By 1874 his factor had cut off his credit, he was unable to find renters for his land, he had to let his taxes go unpaid, and he was personally at work in his own fields, burning stubble and hoeing. "What I am to do in the way of occupation the coming year is all dark before me," he cried out in anguish, "most Merciful Father . . . into Thy hands do I commit myself. . . ." This in a diary once jammed with details of horse races, fox hunts with the "wallet club," fancy balls, and lovely ladies.[71] Everard Green Baker of Mississippi was one of those rare souls who had begun the great "experiment" of free labor with enthusiasm. Eager to establish a "model farm," based on "scientific, systematic" principles and run with "perfect order and system," he bought a second plantation and filled the margins of his daybook and diary with the maxims of Benjamin Franklin. But he could not overcome cotton prices that were "less than the cost of production." Finally, on January 31, 1876, he made his final entry: "*Have now $41.00 & check for $300—& some little change in violin string box.*"[72]

More often, however, a planter's postwar experience was a prosaic tale of gradual decline and relative poverty. Most escaped total collapse, but few escaped hardship. And in time, pinched circumstances worked on minds and spirits. On a visit to Bolivar County, Mississippi, in 1867, a young Georgian observed that planters there were "as a general thing completely broke & worse than all, entirely destitute of anything like a spirit of enterprise." In his opinion, the "energy seems completely crushed out of them."[73] Hard times certainly eroded the confidence and good humor of the Virginian George W. Munford. At sixty-six years of age, he mauled rails, felled trees, cut ditches, and generally worked "from morn till dark," like "a nigger." But he could not save his plantation. "I am eating it up as I did my negroes & most of my other property during the war," Munford declared. He made a series of moves, each time to a smaller farm. It was hard "to bring down high notions—but they must come down." He could see no alternative but "to sell out & still reduce down, down, to a lower state, & come to the level at once of the poorer classes, face the music and live as they do." He could not shake his "dejection and gloom." Privations were difficult, but it was not knowing "whether the good old times will ever come back" that tortured him. He knew only that he was "going down hill." His only hope was that his children were "advancing in the contrary direction." [74]

But Munford's children were following the same path as their father. "I am disgusted with farming in the old beaten track," Thomas T. Munford, also a Virginia planter, declared in 1870. "I work hard all year, pay the negro's [*sic*] every cent I can get my hands on and have nothing to credit my self & farm with." Because it was impossible to make money in Virginia "at wheat, or corn, or tobacco," he bought an Alabama plantation and went into cotton production. After three successive crop failures, he sold out and returned home. [75]

Ella Clanton Thomas of Georgia left a particularly detailed and reflective chronicle of her descent from affluence. Daughter of a wealthy planter, she had brought as her dowry a plantation and thirty thousand dollars' worth of slaves. Her family largely escaped the destruction of the war, but during the next twenty-five years foreclosures became a way of life. In the 1870s she began teaching school, and in the 1880s she took in boarders. To be in debt, she said, was to "feel cramped, confined, pent up, unable to stand erect and breathe the air of freedom." She did not mind the economic loss as much as her "loss of Faith, of confidence." She had learned how "frail" she was, she said, and thought she was "fast becoming a fatalist." But it was the shame of being poor that she found most galling. "Our season of humiliation," she called it. When faced with one of their many sheriff's sales, she felt like a "woman who knew that upon a certain day . . . . she is to be beheaded." She was forced to take her eldest son out of school and put him into the fields, where he was "engaged in work which any Negro could have done as well." "*Oh! it is humiliating*," she cried. And decline was endless. "I am tired mind, body, and soul," she moaned in 1880. "Oh how at times I wish that I could be transported to some place on the seacoast where the only sound I would hear would be the ocean wave as it dashed against the shore." [76]

Unrelenting hardship caused increasing numbers of Southern planters to loosen their grips on their plantations. Despairing of ever restoring the glory and prosperity of the antebellum days, they sought to escape poverty by escaping the plantations. "I begin to conclude those who have sold their land have been rather wiser than those who bought," observed a Virginian in 1870. [77] A Louisiana man urged his brother and sister-in-law to sell their unprofitable Kentucky plantation. When they resisted, he wondered, "Are they wedded to idols?" Southerners "should all give over fancies and look at plain facts in the face," he declared. [78] A Virginian put his plantation on the market in 1873 because he foresaw no "prospects for improvement in the farming interest—or for an increase in the value of land." [79] But the market for plantations was not brisk. "I should like to sell out," a North Carolinian declared, "but there is nobody to buy." [80] "We are very anxious to sell & move but no possibility of it," echoed another planter in 1871. [81] A Mississippi woman noted that everyone seemed "dissatisfied and anxious to move." She had "California fever" herself and would go except for "the impossibility of selling property at one tenth of its value." [82]

An enormous, though still unquantified, number of plantations changed hands in the decade after the war. Banks took many, of course. And some planters had no choice but to sell out. "I must either starve or sell the land to buy some thing to live upon," one planter explained. [83] Others sold because they were dissatisfied with the life and income afforded by plantations after the war. Those who had other investments, or professions to practice, sometimes moved into towns. Probably an even greater number either wanted to sell and could not find buyers or refused to sell at such depressed prices. As Thomas T. Munford observed, "Country property seems to pay so poorly that few people care to invest." [84] With each year, therefore, more planters remained on plantations not voluntarily, but of necessity.

Almost all—those who sold out and those who held on—kept their eyes open for alternative ways of making money. James Trezevant of North Carolina said in 1869 that when property values rose he would sell his plantation and "then purchase a smaller place or rent and invest capital in some other way than planting." [85] A Virginian admitted that he was *"afraid* to lay out money" on his lands. "The profits of tillage are so very precarious &, at the best, *so low*, that money can be employed to much greater advantage in various other ways." [86] When Thomas Munford sold his plantation in 1874, he declared, "I rejoice to be free from a farm which yielded me nothing—but I want some business to occupy my time and help to make the 'pot boil.' " [87] John G. Guignard of South Carolina admitted that the tough times had caused drastic changes in his views. "I confess to you that some of my ideas are nearly revolutionized," he declared. "I am well nigh of the opinion that under some circumstances in this country a man may be poor or poorer as the no. [of] Acres of land he owns may be great or greater." Because of the new circumstances, he was "much more willing to see the proposed Steam Mill in opperation [*sic*] than I should have been. . . ." [88]

While Southern agriculture tottered on the edge of ruin after the war, Southern manufacturing recovered rapidly. [89] It appears that those planters who were resilient, adaptable, and skillful enough to diversify their investments and to find sound commercial and industrial opportunities were more likely to retain their plantations. John Houston Bills of Tennessee held onto his several plantations, and also moved heavily into stocks, government bonds, urban real estate, and railroads. [90] The McCollam sugar plantation in Louisiana recovered its prosperity, and family money also found its way into a variety of New Orleans businesses, including icehouses. [91] Sometimes postwar behavior was simply an extension of prewar practices. The Guignards of South Carolina, for instance, had always combined planting, business, and the professions, and after 1865 they remained in agriculture but also moved into brickmaking, timber-cutting, and the operation of ferries. Nonagricultural enterprises, in fact, subsidized their unprofitable plantation. [92] There was not much money in the South after the war, but what there was could most likely be found in business. [93]

That is not to say that the typical planter was a prophet or even an adherent of the New South creed, however. Certainly some, like Joseph Buckner Killebrew of Tennessee, extolled the revolutionary program of industry, yeoman agriculture, and active partnership with Yankee capitalism. [94] But few of those who stayed on the land could swallow the entire New South program. Essentially a design for an urban, industrial society, it was a call for a changed way of life. Not only did its spokesmen attack slavery, but they also lambasted planters as soft, self-indulgent snobs who were doomed to extinction in a rawer, more competitive society. The New South advocates proposed rural democracy and yeoman agriculture and launched an assault on plantations, planter hegemony, and cotton. As Sidney Lanier summarized, "The New South means small farming." [95] Planters sometimes wished to escape the plantations, but not by becoming yeoman farmers. Plantations did not pay well, but they still provided social status in the rural areas, and there was always the hope of recovery. Planters must have heard the New South message, but not many could have become whole-souled converts.

Plantations and planters survived the Civil War and Reconstruction. After 1865, land and landlords were quickly reunited with blacks and staples. But the attempt to restore antebellum patterns was hardly auspicious. The planter class suffered considerable attrition. Those planters who managed to retain their lands usually lived at significantly reduced levels. And their moods and temperaments mirrored their economic difficulties. Still, as the major landholders in an agricultural society, planters continued to wield power. Because the protection of the plantations remained a central premise, they continued to do battle with the enemies of plantation agriculture, both the old ones that had survived the war and the new ones that sprang up afterward.

### III

Although the political aspects of Reconstruction have often dominated modern perceptions of the period, politics did not fill the life of the average Southern planter. Economic survival was his first priority. Energy was funneled into his effort to salvage a living from the ruins of his plantation. In this battle to save himself, the front lines were the cotton, rice, and sugar fields. Politics remained on the periphery. In 1866, an Alabama planter reported that his neighbors remained aloof from political affairs because they had "too many private and domestic troubles to think about." [96] A year later another Alabaman said, "The subject which most concerns us here is how to manage to keep famine from the door." [97] Summing up the attitude of many, Ella Clanton Thomas declared, "With most of us the present duty—the duty of the hour—is to provide for our familys and *avoid politics*." [98]

The disengagement of planters from politics was not simply a function of their economic difficulties, however. For some, political inactivity stemmed from a profound alienation from the postbellum South. To these individuals, the North's victory and emancipation meant that nothing of value was at stake any longer in the political arena. "As I fought the Radicalism of N. England to preserve the Slave power (which I esteemed of inestimable value)," Thomas S. Watson of Virginia declared in 1868, "I am convinced that the loss of that issue by battle makes it impossible . . . to raise any other issue that could eventuate in good to us." Given the failure "to preserve the only thing that was of interest to us" and the impossibility of retrieving what was lost, Watson believed it was foolish to engage "in thwarting the plans of the North." From his perspective, Reconstruction applied "not to the *South that I loved*, but to a new & strange & terribly vicious system." Without slavery, in other words, politics had become hollow and irrelevant. All that remained for Watson was his private battle to protect "persons and property." [99]

And yet, most planters could not ignore political developments after Appomattox. To forfeit meekly their power would have been uncharacteristic of the antebellum ruling class. In addition, most planters recognized that politics impinged directly on their primary postwar objective—the reorganization and economic recovery of the plantations. Continued control of labor, land, and other resources was crucial in restoring the plantations and in maintaining a planter-dominated economic and social structure in the South. To lose control permanently was to risk complete destruction. Southern agriculture had never functioned independently of politics, and after the war, planters' workplaces remained squarely in the middle of the political struggle. Because politics and plantations were still linked, therefore, the battle to preserve plantation agriculture and planter power became a political as well as an economic affair.


Defeat had brought a revolution to the lives of Southern planters, but in the summer of 1865 they did not yet know how deeply it would cut. Planters had obviously lost slavery and national independence, but vital decisions were still to be made in Washington. How heavy a yoke would the Republicans decide to fashion? Would the sequel to war be a quick restoration or a thoroughgoing reconstruction? Planters were liable to a variety of charges, including treason, and numerous penalties, including confiscation. Could they expect sympathy or compassion from the victorious North? "Rumours innumerable of Yankee plans, the Yankee intentions toward us," Catherine Edmondston noted hurriedly in her diary a few weeks after the end of the war.[100] "What will be the fate of Virginia is beyond my ken," sighed George W. Munford. "Whether the Yankees will permit us to have any rights or property is more than I can say." [101] The soul-eroding war had ended, but apprehension and anxiety continued unabated, and planters still stared northward.

Despite the confusion surrounding Abraham Lincoln's assassination, answers to the planters' questions were not long in coming. Andrew Johnson rapidly revealed a plan of reunion that rested more on Southern conciliation and consent than upon coercion and reconstruction. Hoping to stimulate renewed loyalty among the South's traditional leaders and to build a national coalition of conservatives, the new president requested the minimum—renunciation of secession, slavery, and the Confederate debt. Instead of implementing the Confiscation Acts, under which the lands of every supporter of the Confederacy were subject to forfeiture, he halted all proceedings and issued a sweeping proclamation of amnesty and pardon, restoring most planters' political rights and land titles. Early fears that the maverick Southerner would unleash a social revolution in the South were largely dispelled. In the cause of reunion, the president promised to leave land, blacks, and political power in the hands of the old rulers.[102]

The moods and aspirations of Southern planters found expression in their responses to Johnson's program. Some simply assumed that absolute submission was the inevitable consequence of total military defeat. But considerably more urged minimal compliance as practical wisdom. Realizing the impossibility of victory on the old issues of slavery and national self-determination, yet still resolved to protect their vital interests, planters believed that acceptance of Johnson's program was a strategic necessity. Accommodation to harsh realities was not the same as servile submission. Practical conservatives rather than doctrinaire reactionaries, they sought speedy reunion in order to restore autonomy and self-determination to the South. With the reinstatement of the South's traditional rulers and the re-establishment of order and stability, they could set about rebuilding plantation society.[103] In the autumn of 1865, a wife argued with her irreconcilable husband that he must learn to live under "the new order of things." Her message was the realistic one that the sooner Southerners "can manage to be restored to civil rights, the better it will be for their interests and future prospects." Putting her finger on her husband's greatest worry, she explained that reunion would mean that white Southerners, through their state legislatures, could create "a new system" to control black labor. Without political power, she reminded him, the key to the planters' future would remain "in unfriendly hands." [104]

Advocates of rapid reintegration usually saw a clear choice between Johnson and the Radical Republicans. "If the movement of Sumner in the Senate and Thad Stevens in the House foreshadow the future of the Govt. then indeed are our darkest days yet to come," declared Howell Cobb. The Southerners' only hope, he asserted, was "the willingness and ability of President Johnson to rescue them from the fate that bigotry, hatred and passion would bring upon them." [105] Without Southern co-operation, Henry Watson, Jr., argued, Johnson would surely lose to the Radicals.[106] The ex–Confederate governor of Virginia, John Letcher, said that in his personal meeting with President Johnson, he had found him both "liberal and conciliatory," and he suggested that it was "both politic and wise to meet him in the same spirit." [107] In the opinion of these realists, considerations of power, not outdated formal principles, needed to govern action. Through minimal compliance, the South could reassert its mastery.

Others, however, saw the political situation in 1865 quite differently. For them, the emotions and issues of the war were still very much alive. They refused to accept the victory of Northern arms as final and continued to assert their allegiance to the values and institutions of the Old South. Because they were unwilling to accept as permanent any rupture in Southern continuity, they were unwilling to become participants in a political debate in which union and emancipation were taken for granted. It was useless to seek allies in the North, they reasoned, because no Northerner was willing to offer Southerners the restoration of the master-slave relationship. Old patterns could be perpetuated or restored intact only if Southerners would remain loyal to their traditions and affirm their total resistance to change. Even slavery in some form was not beyond their grasp, they thought, if Southerners would stand firm on principle and conviction.

William Henry Stiles, a Georgia planter who refused to emancipate his slaves throughout the summer of 1865, declared that he would stand his ground and "fight it out against tyranny, poverty & the misuse of power." No one would find him "singing hosannas to the Union & praising the Northern vandal as the perfection of all that is kind & noble in human nature." He swore to avoid all contact with Yankees, "those who have murdered our parents—non-combattants that never harmed them—ravished our wives, daughters & sisters —pillaged & destroyed as effectively as was ever done by Attila or Alaric—ie all our property—who have strip[ped] us of every vestage [*sic*] of freedom & reduced us to the condition of abject slaves." Unwilling to bend principle, he would never beg "for pardon when I have committed no offence." Sovereign states seceded, and he merely gave his allegiance to Georgia, "to which all allegiance is first due." [108]

Robert Toombs, observing events from Havana, denied there was significant choice between the two political factions in the North. He predicted Johnson's program would only be an opening salvo. "Poor fools! What comes next?" Sumner and his friends, Toombs predicted. The Radicals would use the Freedmen's Bureau and other Federal agencies to "regulate Labour!" Southerners would "find military rule a positive luxury in comparison to the civil regulation of labour by Congress," Toombs declared. "The true policy of the South is to stand still, do nothing, let the Yankees try their hands on Cuffee." After they failed, he explained, Southerners could rebuild according to their own blueprints. Toombs was convinced that the basic constitutional issues of the war were still unresolved. Might had nothing to do with right. But because Southerners lacked enough political power to confront the issues directly, they could only bide their time. [109]

In the autumn of 1865, former Confederates, in accordance with the restoration plans of President Andrew Johnson, met in state conventions, drew up constitutions, and held elections. New state legislatures convened and enacted legislation to meet pressing problems. Even though a significant number of planters were still too unreconstructed to join the constituencies the Johnson legislatures represented, a good deal of the early legislation was designed to facilitate the reconstruction of Southern agriculture along familiar lines. In several states, the Black Codes promised planters a disciplined, immobile, and productive labor force. Stay laws helped protect plantations from immediate foreclosure. "Confederate

Brigadiers," heavily represented in the newly elected congressional delegation, were expected to fulfill the traditional role of Southern political leaders—that of looking after the plantation interests. In addition, several states even resisted Johnson's minimum recommendations, refusing to ratify the Thirteenth Amendment, to repudiate the Confederate debt, or to admit the illegality of secession.[110]

To observers in both the North and the South, it appeared that the Confederacy was attempting to reconvene in Washington. A worried Lawrence, Massachusetts, mill owner wrote to his Southern relative expressing his consternation. "Some of the ruling class seem to abide by the issue at once & endeavor to make the best of circumstance," he admitted. But "others give only an unwilling & silent assent, while the great majority will probably never cordially recognize the U.S.G. again or be reconciled to their condition & position." [111] One angry Southern planter, who eventually found his way into the Republican party, was convinced that the South was still ruled by fire-eaters. "They lie when they declare themselves in favor of the president's policy," he declared. "They prefer him, doubtless, to the so called Radicals, but in their hearts they hate him. They cling with an undying hope to the wretched rebel cause and desire to manifest their hatred for every thing which does not immortalize that." [112]

The South's response to Johnson's plan of Reconstruction revealed that although militarily defeated, economically crippled, and politically weakened, its leaders were not prepared to ignore what they perceived as their vital interests in pursuit of reunion. Essentially unrepentant, the South adopted a public stance of acquiescence that was superficial and misleading, occasioned only by military necessity. As Michael Perman has recently demonstrated, Johnson's insistence that Southern reorganization take place with the co-operation of the region's traditional leaders meant that their wishes and aspirations were allowed to surface. Seeking renewed sectional harmony, Johnson could not present demands; he could only offer recommendations. When Southerners balked, Johnson retreated, and Southerners simply took as much easy ground as they could. New state legislatures moved swiftly to retrieve as much as possible of the traditional order and to protect themselves from any further unreasonable demands.[113]

When Congress reconvened in December, 1865, Republican legislators responded sharply to the South's Black Codes and Brigadiers. Searching for contrite and reformed ex-Confederates, they found very few, and refused to seat the Southerners. Instead, they began to shape

Reconstruction in their own way. They extended the life of the Freedmen's Bureau and passed the Civil Rights Act and the Fourteenth Amendment, each of which sent a chill down the spines of Southern planters. In 1866, Ella Clanton Thomas tersely described the congressional program as one of "extermination, confiscation, and annihilation." She could only hope that her champion, Andrew Johnson, could muster enough power to keep the Radicals from carrying out their plans. [114] "Should the Stevens, Sumner & Phil[l]ips party succeed," said another witness to the struggle between the president and Congress, "God save the South, for she will be in the jaws of wolves and tigers." [115]

In March, 1867, Southerners believed Republicans had actually taken them by the throat. When the South continued to follow Johnson's lead and rejected the Fourteenth Amendment, Congress took charge of Reconstruction altogether. It reorganized the ten obstreperous states under military rule, enfranchised blacks, and disenfranchised substantial numbers of whites, including many planters. The gentry was shocked and dismayed. Hopes that had been kindled under Johnson were extinguished. One Louisiana planter said in May that while things had not been easy under Johnson, they had been tolerable, "but now this new move to enfranchise the blacks places the whole matter once more in the cloud of doubt." [116] The congressional program jeopardized the precarious system of white control. Yankees had "disenfranchised her best citizens & enfranchised the blacks," a planter from Virginia moaned when he heard the news, and "we are destined to have negro officers of government from the highest to the lowest." [117] Everything was adrift, and the situation was more ominous than at any time since Grant had besieged Lee outside Richmond.

When a South Carolina planter heard the news in mid-March, he poured out his anger and frustration. Of "all the miserable & wretched men on Earth I am the most so," he cried. "Just look at the horrid condition our Country is in—all civil government suspended & naught but Military Rule." The military commander would be "a perfect monarch," he predicted, with "all things at his will." He could even "divide out our lands." In fact, the plantations would be "confiscated just as certain as we live." In truth, he said, "we are subjugated to the negroes completely & all of our offices will be filled by them & Sumner says he hopes to see a black man President—that damnable rascal. Brooks ought to have killed him." From the bottom of his soul he "wished the whole North & all the blacks were in hell & never to get out." [118]

Anger and fear were common spontaneous reactions, but emotion could not serve as political strategy. And a new strategy was imperative, for with the Reconstruction Act of 1867, the North's terms for reunion were law and could no longer be avoided. From his exile in Montpellier, France, George Noble Jones, owner of cotton plantations in Florida and Georgia, pondered how Southern whites would attempt to defeat the Radical program. Would it be "by refusing to register or vote and denouncing the whole thing—or by registering & defeating it after?" By not voting, he thought, they would certainly lose. He also recognized that if they voted and lost, there was the danger "that their participation in registering will be considered as an acquiescence in the constitutionality of the law." White Southerners had a difficult problem, he concluded, and he could only wish them success, for he decidedly preferred "temporary military rule to permanent equality with the Negro." [119] Like planters at home, what Jones feared most was not military domination, but civil government based on the black franchise. Also in common with the majority, however, he could not devise a strategy which would assure success. Not surprisingly, Southern planters were divided in their responses to the problem of Radical Reconstruction.

One response was simply to drop out of politics entirely. Abstention was prompted by a variety of motives. Some white Southerners, of course, had no choice, being barred from participation by Reconstruction legislation. But eligible ex-rebels were sometimes unwilling to bend principle, and refused to participate again in Yankee-dominated politics. Others were so incensed at the enfranchisement of former slaves that they divorced themselves from political affairs. "I shall never cast another vote so long as I live," vowed an angry and humiliated South Carolinian. [120] And some were simply politically adrift, appalled by the policies of the Republicans and sickened by the past record of the Democracy. A Mississippi planter who had suffered heavy damage during the war called for a pox on both their houses. It was "emphatically an age of small men," he observed, "men dwarfed in principle and intellect." He was disgusted with Republicans, and as for the old Confederate leaders, they were "political mad caps, who have destroyed our once prosperous & happy people. . . ." Who knows, he asked helplessly, "where we are drifting, where we shall make harbor?" [121]

Probably a more important consideration in the detachment of planters from politics was their sense of powerlessness. The planting counties, with their large concentration of blacks, consistently returned Republicans on election day. Since blacks voted the party of their emancipators rather than that of their former masters, the outlook was grim. Many planters decided to sit out the political struggle and wait for Northerners to come to their senses. Some had no choice, for in several black-belt counties, the Democrats did not put forward a slate of candidates, and conservative planters were left without even a continuous minority party organization they could accept. "We are certainly . . . entirely powerless," a Lowndes County, Mississippi, planter remarked in 1867, "and it is as well for us . . . to eschew politics altogether and endeavor to advance our own interests." [122] Agriculturalists in Alabama's black belt felt "that they can do nothing to help themselves politically but must wait for a change of opinion elsewhere." [123] A Virginian declared, "In matters political we have large interest but no active part. . . . we have to 'stand & wait.' " [124]. In South Carolina, almost the only native whites active in politics after 1867 were allied with the conservative wing of the Republican party. [125]

The Republican party did offer an alternative political avenue for some Southern planters. Before Congress threw its weight behind Radical Reconstruction, formal Republican organizations existed in only three Southern states, but after 1867, they sprouted everywhere. Planters could be attracted to Republicanism for any number of reasons—persistent Whiggery, consistent Unionism, hope for economic recovery and the end of lawlessness, disillusionment with the Democracy, a realization that the war made old issues irrelevant, and so on. Despite the diversity of their motives, the planters active in Republican politics usually pursued approximately the same course, seeking to control their party, moderate its apparent radicalism, and promote nationalism and economic recovery. [126]

Lewis Thompson, a formerly wealthy and politically active Whig planter from North Carolina, was representative of the minority who gravitated toward Republicanism. A friend wrote him in 1866 that "traitors North and South" were subverting reconciliation and that he believed "all truly national men from all sections of the country should unite" to prevent catastrophe. The following year Thompson came out in support of the Republican party in his state and urged citizens to renounce the "lost cause" and accept "civil and political equality among all citizens, irrespective of race or color." Recent intransigence, he argued, only made Reconstruction more severe. If it continued, the South would be largely responsible for its own subjugation. [127]

Thompson and like-minded Southerners were quickly snared in a dilemma, however. While they hoped to control Republicanism in the South, they discovered that the party was in the hands of "Northerners and negroes." Thompson was dismayed in 1867 when the Republican convention in North Carolina refused to pass resolutions condemning confiscation of plantations, opposing universal manhood suffrage, and supporting the removal of all political disabilities of white Southerners. By offering "delusive promises to the most ignorant and most unsuspecting and docile of our population," he explained, the "radicals" had carried the day. [128] A friend from Boon Hill pointed out that by the standards of the convention, neither he nor Thompson was a Republican. The friend was "completely stuned [sic] by the Idea of proping [sic] myself up with, and associating with negroes Politically, and with a party whose aims is confiscation and division of land among the negroes." To be "debased and degraded below a negro is very hard," he said, "and to join a party and Hurra for those who has put me Politically below a negro will be going it pretty strong, and as Crockett would say 'ajin natur.' . . ." [129] Increasing numbers found an association with Republicanism unnatural. Pushed out of the party by Northerners or blacks or what they perceived as radical politics, they either slipped into inactivity or drifted back into the Democratic party. [130]

The majority of Southern planters neither retreated from politics entirely nor joined the enemy's ranks. They enlisted in the motley coalition of white conservatives which struggled to defeat Republican rule in the Southern states. But whether politically active or merely fireside politicians, planters were generally agreed that the caldron of Reconstruction politics threatened to boil over with anarchy and ruin. The danger emanated from three sources, a Mississippi planter declared. Ranking the evils, he declared that the South was "accursed with (2) carpetbag, (1) Negro & (3) scalawag rule—(1) bad, (2) worse, (3) worst, & then cotton has fallen to ten cents." [131] Though not always agreeing with this particular gradation, planters generally did agree that he had, indeed, identified the devils.

Each offered its own special threat. Carpetbaggers and their Radical sponsors in the North, planters believed, despised the plantation aristocracy and were eager to destroy it through a program of free labor, confiscation, and disfranchisement. Blacks were unpredictable and potentially dangerous. They might laze about, quietly die out, or lapse into barbarism. And no one doubted that they might also be wooed by unscrupulous whites and led on a rampage against their former masters. Scalawags, whom planters increasingly characterized as native poor whites, might join with blacks and carpetbaggers to inaugurate a sweeping program of political, social, and economic democracy, completely leveling the plantation gentry and the traditional hierarchy of the South. Clearly, the planters' wartime preoccupation, almost obsession, with class and racial revolution had not died with the Confederacy.

Apparently threatened with multiple dangers, both internally and externally, planters had difficulty agreeing on a single political strategy. What, if any, political alliance to strike was difficult to decide. Since white Southerners were "saddled" with black voters, one planter reasoned in June, 1867, "we must hope to divide them and thus rule." [132] And in the period 1868–74, the Democracy, often running under the flag of the Conservative party in an effort to broaden its appeal, did follow an electoral strategy of seeking the support of black voters and dissident white Republicans. Although not without divisions in their ranks, planters made mighty efforts to see that blacks voted correctly. Donelson Caffery of Louisiana hoped to woo freedmen to his party, where they could work against Radical rule and for the "re-establishment of constitutional liberty." "I shall make speeches to the negroes at the Barbecues," he announced optimistically in 1868, and "hope they will be of service to the cause." [133] A Virginian considered running for office because his party was in desperate need of "decent gentlemen" and because he had "some strength with the darkies." Still, he feared that "the Yankees will cause the negro vote to go, in mass, for their candidate." [134] Others tried more direct means of influencing black voters. Believing that freedmen voted with "the same intelligence that a drove of cattle would," a Tennessee planter simply rounded up his laborers, gave them the right ballot, and herded them to the polls. [135]

Planters who had not yet accepted blacks as free laborers suddenly found them active as citizens, voters, and legislators. To seek after their votes was more than some could stomach. They responded to black enfranchisement as to a racial slur. Black suffrage "debased and degraded" white men and was an intolerable "humiliation," a North Carolinian asserted.[136] So long as Negroes were politically active, Ella Clanton Thomas declared in 1870, "just so long will the feeling of resentment linger in our minds." [137] Joseph Buckner Killebrew of Tennessee remembered, "I had fully made up my mind that to be governed by my former slaves was an ignominy which I should not and would not endure." [138]

More often, however, planters were less concerned with racial humiliation than they were with the consequences of black power. In 1866, John Moore predicted that black voters would "be nothing but the tools of leud and designing men, as proven in the late riot in New Orleans." [139] Stability and social order were crumbling under black rule, declared an Alabaman in September, 1867. "I am willing to do almost anything and submit to anything in preference to nigger domination," he said, "because they have neither the intelligence [n]or virtue to rule properly." [140] Even that minority of planters who expressed relatively liberal attitudes toward black suffrage usually agreed that it was an idea whose time had not come. "I say negroes are *not going to vote until we*, the *States*, give them the right, or they win it by a fight," shouted a Georgian in September, 1867. "Negroes who get able to read & write, & pay taxes of $250 real property," he explained, "may get leave to vote, bye & bye. . . ." [141] An Alabama planter agreed. "The African, in his present condition in the South, I do not consider capable of exercising the franchise discretely and prudently." Without substantial inducements to acquire learning and accumulate property, he predicted, "he will go down to his native ignorance, poverty, and barbarism." [142] Most believed blacks had already fallen to their natural level. "Our state is in a horrible condition," a South Carolina woman cried in 1871. "The negro's [sic] are making laws perfectly distruction [sic] of all property[,] order and peace." [143]

From the beginning, some conservative ex-slaveholders had sought to end their political troubles by emphasizing race and calling for a white man's party. Although it did not usually become the basic anti-Republican strategy until the mid-1870s, some Southerners in the late 1860s already thought it made eminently more sense to tighten party and color lines than to seek co-operation with blacks and dissident whites. In December, 1867, George W. Munford concluded that "the only thing that could be done was to establish a white man's party." When whites resumed control, "the Blacks will be made to know their places, or be driven from the State." [144] Six months later, William H. Heyward declared that "with a white man's civil government again," the Negroes would "be more slaves than they ever were," and white laborers would also step back into harness. [145] Radical Republicans were hammering away at class issues, and planters were frightened of a revolution from below. Racism and opposition to black suffrage would attack the threat directly, and would also erode any alliance that was in the making between poor whites and blacks. The gentry had traditionally used antagonism toward blacks as a means of manipulating poor whites, and some planters argued for continuation of the tactic after the war.

Black behavior under the Republican regimes was scrutinized by planters. No one doubted that Republican politics affected black productivity. "Their heads are full of politics," a South Carolinian declared in November, 1867, "and they have no idea of work until starvation forces them. . . ." [146] But more frightening was the thought that freed from the discipline of slavery and urged on by no-account whites, blacks were ripe for revolution. "The Rads have been trying to bring about a collession [*sic*] of the races," asserted a New Orleans man in 1868. [147] If the Republicans maintained control for much longer, a Mississippian declared, they would "ruin beyond redemption our people[,] negroes and all[,] & perhaps bring on a war of the races as predicted long ago by A. De Tocqueville." [148] Planters anxiously scanned the horizon for signs of the Radicals' success. "Many negroes have been heard to allude to St. Domingo, Jamaica, etc.," a Greensboro, Alabama, planter reported anxiously in 1867, and to say "that it is utterly impossible for the two races to live together in peace. . . ." [149] A South Carolinian claimed more concrete evidence. "Every day there is a barn burnt or a dwelling burnt or a murder committed," she said in 1871, "and there is no redress." [150] Slavery had been far more than a means of achieving white supremacy, but the restoration of race control became a minimum requirement of planters in the postbellum years.

What terrified the gentry was the specter of a fusion of "negroes and

Tories." Together, they could completely overwhelm the men of "intelligence," the "good men." If scalawags and Negroes ever took charge of the state of Georgia, C. S. Sutton announced in 1867, "repudiation—the abolition of [the] poll tax—a general division of land, & disfranchisement of Rebels will probably follow, with laws regulating the price of labor and the rent of lands—All to benefit the negro & the poor." [151] William M. Byrd of Alabama noted that a "people, white or black, to reach any exalted scale of refinement and civilization must first be taught to respect labor, learning and property." He feared that "ignorance and poverty" had gotten such a hold on Southerners that there would soon be *"a more bloody revolution."* [152] Another Alabaman agreed that they were "bound to have another revolution of *some sort."* He believed that "seven tenths of the people of the south would vote for . . . confiscation of Southern *property*. Every negro would vote for such a proposition and a vast number of the whites." And, he added, the "masses of the north would doubtless favor such a proposition." "You can form no idea how very reckless our people have become," he told his correspondent, Henry Watson, Jr. And Watson himself agreed that "no tyranny can compare with that of a mob." [153]

In time, the planters' image of the Southern white Republican became almost entirely that of a mean, opportunistic poor white. Sympathetic relationships between poor whites and planters had deteriorated with the Civil War and emancipation. The destruction of slavery had meant the destruction of the poor white's dream of slaveholding, and the rise of white sharecropping had meant that class differences in the rural South were sharpened and made dangerously visible. [154] With the stability of the antebellum social order destroyed, the gentry believed that poor whites, like blacks, had become volatile and unreliable. They feared that poor whites would respond to the Radicals' constant plea that they vote their class, not their race. Scalawags sprang from every element of Southern society, of course, but native white Republican strength was concentrated, as planters believed, in the nonplanting counties and states of the South. [155]

The potential catalyst of revolution, the element which threatened to fuse blacks and poor whites and lead them in an assault upon property and person, was the interloping Northern Republican, the carpetbagger. And carpetbaggers were everywhere, Donelson Caffery of Louisiana complained in 1868, tampering with the lower classes, preaching democracy and egalitarianism, appealing to "the sovereign freedmen & the 'white trash.' " [156] Blatant manipulation of blacks by Radicals enraged James M. Willcox of Virginia. "Congress has placed those Southern States under Negro rule and the Negroes led on by a set of wild, mean Yankees, *Carpet Baggers*, who incite them to all wicked and vicious acts, make tools of the poor deluded creatures to advance their own purposes." They shouted such nonsense as, "The black man is the equal of the white and the white the inferior race, and we of the North the only men fit to govern the Rebs. . . ." [157] In the planters' eyes, blacks, scalawags, and carpetbaggers made up a formidable coalition, one powerful enough perhaps to raise a full-blown social revolution.

The issue around which the three challenging groups were most likely to coalesce, planters believed, was the confiscation of plantations. No political topic was more consistently on planters' lips. Confiscation was an old fear, dating back to the early years of the war, when the Northern Congress passed the Confiscation Acts and Confederate propagandists argued that loss of the plantations would be the price of defeat. A year after Appomattox, on the eve of the registration of black voters in his county, William H. B. Richardson concluded, "Confiscation is inevitable in my opinion." [158] In 1867, a Mississippi man reported that the freedmen ran to the county seat "every week to know something about when the time will be they expect to have the lands & stock devied out amongst them." [159] In 1868, Henry Watson, Jr., said that the tendency in Alabama was "for a subdividing of property rather than for its aggregation." [160] With only gradual abatement, the worry persisted through the early years of the next decade, even though confiscation was last broached in Congress in March, 1867 (and then the proposal did not even reach the floor), and no black legislator ever proposed a plan of confiscation during the years of Republican government in the South. The explanation for the persistence of this fear perhaps lies in the fact that on this one matter planters clearly did "know the Negro." The black man, an Alabama gentleman observed, "wants the white man's property." [161]

Black field hands did not get their ex-masters' lands, however. Land remained in the possession of whites, if not always planters. And eventually, state by state, political power returned to conservative white Southerners. But many planters did endure for as many as ten years what they considered intolerable "Radical rule." "We are so oppressed with carpet bag & negro rule," a Mississippi planter moaned in 1872, "that we the Southern people feel we have quite gone out of existence except to work very hard for bare subsistence." [162] It is incredible, another Mississippian declared two years later, that the "North is so ignorant of the bad rule their party established in [the] South." The "outlook from here is worse than ever before," he asserted, "labor demoralized, taxes high, provisions high & this country making nothing. . . . Do not see nothing but universal Bankruptcy—of both negro and white." [163] But in the end, instead of suffering a revolution from below, white Southerners of all classes joined hands to end Republican rule. Rallying around the standard of white supremacy and applying large doses of white terrorism, they smashed the fragile Republican coalition in the South, ending the era of Reconstruction.

To what degree the restoration of home rule meant a return to power of the antebellum ruling class is not entirely clear. A quarter of a century ago, C. Vann Woodward argued brilliantly that after Reconstruction the ex-Confederate states were dominated by an elite in which new men from the middle classes had a disproportionate influence. Wartime destruction, emancipation, proscription, and economic decay had eroded the planters' political base, while the new urban middle class, with its Whiggish-industrial outlook, was in touch with the dynamic forces of the age.[164] But just how complete the rupture was, just how separated agricultural interests were from post-Reconstruction political power, has never been adequately measured.[165] That some planters were agile enough to resume political careers in the new governments is obvious. That the owners of land in a society still predominately agricultural would have considerable political leverage is likely. Nevertheless, we know that in several states in the 1880s government policies drove planters out of the Democratic party and into agricultural insurgency. Only a thorough study of the social origins and social ideas of post-Reconstruction Southern leadership can answer the question satisfactorily. What we can say with confidence is that after Reconstruction, planters faced powerful, often unprecedented, challenges from small farmers, middle-class professionals, and the new urban, industrial class. The antebellum equation of planters and political power was no longer automatically valid.

The primary political objective of Southern planters after 1865 was to make the region a safe place for plantation agriculture. They had no alternative but to accept fundamental change—the end of slavery and the failure of independence—but they also sought to maintain the continuity of the plantation. Toward that end, planters fought the challenge of the carpetbaggers, scalawags, and blacks, and struggled to reassert their control over the South's government, its resources, and especially, its labor. They won significant victories in restoring home rule and white supremacy, but they failed to re-establish unquestioned political dominance or to halt the economic deterioration of agriculture. Conservative political control did not bring an end to the mournful tone in planters' statements. Although cheered by the election of General Wade Hampton to the governorship of South Carolina, a young planter declared in 1877 that "Hampton cant do much for our *pockets.*" His gloom grew from his conviction that rice could not "be cultivated profitably for many years longer without compulsory labor, which we dont seem at all likely to have." [166] Actually, the prize sought by planters was not to be gained through Reconstruction politics at all. Slavery, the soul of the antebellum plantation, had been lost with the war.

## IV

Almost overnight, Southern planters crossed from the world of slave labor to that of compensated labor, from substantial wealth and ease to relative poverty and drudgery, from political dominance to crippled influence. Continuity in their practice of racism and rural exploitation could not mask the revolution in their lives. With emancipation, important ground was cut away forever. From the planters' perspective, the postbellum plantation was almost unrecognizable. The South, the larger context of their existence, was beginning to move in new directions, often under new leaders, with new objectives. Transformations in economic and political matters were joined by more qualitative changes, but social, cultural, and intellectual disruption was no less painful for its intangibility. In some ways, the planters' journey from slave labor to free was hardly more than a step. In a more significant sense, however, it was a leap across time.

The plantation was the gentry's home, workplace, and primary community. Slavery had largely determined its organization, its relationships, its spirit, even its architecture. The white family had dwelt in the "big house," while the slaves were clustered in the quarters, as one mistress remembered, "neither too near nor too far from the house." [167] Lines of authority were complex but eventually ran to the master and mistress, around whom revolved a busy social and economic life. Masters extended their control to the quarters through the manipulation of rations and rewards, affections and pride, but most importantly through the whip. From sunup to sundown, the bondsman's life was prescribed by the master, who fed, clothed, housed, and worked him. Each morning, slaves left for the fields, where they would work in gangs, directed by white supervisors, for the master's profit. Each evening, they returned to the quarters, where their time was largely their own until the bell sounded the beginning of another day. Integrated and unified by the master's power, tending toward self-sufficiency and therefore semiautonomy, the plantation was a complex society that welded black and white together in intimate, visceral relationships.

Emancipation altered the face, and eventually the essence, of the old plantation. As cotton planters adopted share tenancy, familiar patterns disintegrated. Under the new system, the "big house" became simply the biggest house, for freedmen deserted the quarters for their own widely scattered cabins. As black families made their own separate lives, the labor force ceased to function as a unit, direct white supervision lessened, and more individualistic patterns replaced the collective character that had typified the antebellum plantation. Despite efforts of some planters to continue to operate their plantations as integrated units rather than assembleges of small farms, the highly centralized network gave way to a loosely organized system of landlords and tenants. Some postbellum plantations were inhabited completely by strangers, for emancipation meant the rise of black mobility, white tenancy, and absentee ownership. Patterns of domination and subordination were also transformed. Planters often still fed, clothed, housed, and directed blacks, but when yearly contracts replaced bills of sale, ex-slaveholders learned to relate to their laborers as landlords, bankers, merchants, and overseers. It is not necessary to accept fully the conclusion of a Virginian who argued in 1871 that the "present condition of land holders, and of the labour of the country, is opposed to the old system entirely." [168] But the master-slave bond had been broken, and in its place stood an assortment of less compelling relationships. [169]

The transformation of the plantation was mirrored in the relationships of its inhabitants. Most important was the widespread abandonment of paternalism. Some planters had never shown much regard for the welfare of their bondsmen, of course, and these individuals often took advantage of emancipation to clear their quarters of unproductive labor. But while paternalism had never won universal acceptance, it had been the communal standard, even in the rambunctious, booming Mississippi valley. Paternalism set the gentleman off from the "cotton snob," and unnecessarily cruel masters were ostracized by decent white folks. As Eugene Genovese has argued, paternalism, with its notion that slavery imposed upon masters a burden and a duty, provided slaveholders a means of legitimizing their rule and reinforcing the slaves' dependence.[170] Planters saw slavery as a heavy and often even holy burden, an institution, one planter intoned, "rendered by *his* order, for the government of *his* creatures."[171] A Georgia father advised his son against settling where "the rush is for accumulation; the game played at is speculation . . . and there is little sympathy for the *laborers* in the race."[172] Planters were hardly opposed to private gain, but naked avarice was offset—occasionally even smothered—by competing social values.

Just as the ownership of men had often bred a peculiar sense of responsibility, so the destruction of slavery opened up new possibilities in black-white relationships. Instead of being masters and slaves, whites and blacks became employers and employees, bound together by contracts. When Northern capital penetrated the plantation country after the war, an unalloyed capitalist ethic also appeared. Antebellum planters became mere rural businessmen. Or as Ella Clanton Thomas said, she was no longer "a fashionable lady but a business woman."[173] Planting had been a source of status, but it now became a vocation. Plantations had been a way of life, but increasingly they became investments. Hundreds of labor contracts reveal that planters often sought to retain the benefits of slavery while shaving off expensive responsibilities. It was more than a slip of the pen that caused William H. B. Richardson to write in his labor contract for 1868, ". . . to be strictly as my Slaves in obeying . . . orders & instructions."[174] While demanding slave-like behavior from freedmen, planters carefully excluded from the bargain any commitment to pay doctors' bills, burial expenses, or the cost of a Sunday preacher, to provide rations for those who did not work, and so on. Even then, Thomas T. Munford concluded in 1869 that a planter could be successful by hiring Negroes "only when he wants them, & lets them go when he has nothing for them to do." [175] The desperate search for renewed prosperity put a heavy strain on unprofitable traditional relationships. Paternalism did not wear well in the Gilded Age.

Paternalism had been touted as the expression of unselfish, gracious benevolence by a white superior to a black inferior, but in practice it had depended on the fulfillment of reciprocal responsibilities. In return for fatherly treatment, blacks were expected to be good children—obedient, diligent, and even affectionate. With emancipation, black behavior violated traditional norms. Eventually, every planter encountered acts which he could only perceive as impudent, insubordinate, and disloyal. "A decently bred white man was never designated to trade with a nigger," fumed a young Alabaman in 1875; "their assumptions of familiarity are absolutely insulting." The cause of this particular explosion was one Negro's "straightforward tone." "Was there ever anything like this?" the planter muttered. [176] Ella Clanton Thomas of Georgia was revealing when she said, "Respect is a quality I demand from servants even more than obedience." [177] James Trezevant of North Carolina declared in 1869 that he wanted to sell out and go where he would "never see a d—m nigger." They "steal and kill my stock so around me that I have to sleep with one eye open." He had trained his dogs to "make noise at every thing and anything that stirs from a toad to a man and I am in the habit yet of walking around at night only instead of the whip I carried before I now carry my double barreled with a couple of buckshot. . . ." [178] Planters needed and demanded certain behavior from blacks, and when it was not forthcoming, paternalism withered.

In 1867, William H. Heyward, scion of what was once the wealthiest rice-plantation family in South Carolina, quit his plantation and moved into a Charleston hotel. "I am sometimes almost on the verge of self-destruction," he cried. "When I go to my rest at night, my wish and great desire is that I may not open my eyes another day." The simple fact was that he was "not prepared for the great change." He sympathized with his friends who continued to plant because he knew how "very trying" it was to those who "have been always accustomed to obedience to every order to be now subject to the humour of the Negro. . . ." Without the master's power to command, however, he found that not even his hotel was a refuge. He stopped eating in the main dining room because he could not stand the insolence of the black steward. He eventually gave up all his personal servants and cooked his meals in his own room because he could not stand blacks any longer and had "no desire to see them except in the field." [179]

As patriarchal omnipotence evaporated, planters were afflicted with a sense of powerlessness, or as a Mississippi woman put it, "helplessness." Blacks still stood where they always had, squarely between planters and their profits, but now planters' means of coercion seemed so limited. "I can do nothing," a Georgian cried out in frustration. "I can dismiss them or shoot them but nothing more." [180] What was lacking was that crucial middle range of coercive techniques, particularly the whip. Neither shootings nor dismissals were common, in part no doubt because they did not solve the labor problem. It is true that contracts included release clauses. One planter, for instance, contracted to pay half the crop for work but stipulated that should the Negroes "become troublesome or disobey any order . . . they are to leave the place or plantation on which they are living immediately and forfeit all claims, rights, or interest in the crop. . . ." [181] As often as not, however, dismissal was an empty threat. For example, one young manager was instructed to punish a freedman for theft, but was specifically directed not to dismiss him. The owner did not "wish to lose him from the crop," and reiterated that "his labor is now needed in the field."[182] Planters felt that they were at the mercy of their laborers, and dependence was not a good seedbed for paternalism. [183]

The reshaping of black-white relationships on the plantations was also affected by emancipation's disruption of a relatively stable laboring population. Enjoying at least temporary mobility, many blacks left old masters and never returned. "We have not one of our old hands on the plantation this year," a Mississippian reported in 1867. "They are scattered to the four winds." [184] How could a planter be held responsible for the treatment of *his* "people," when they were no longer his, or even familiar to him. And besides, now he was dealing with free blacks, not slaves, and free blacks had never met much gentleness in the South. Racial antipathy and violence were, in fact, on the rise. Characteristic was the assertion by one Virginian that audacious "nigs" needed "the application of the cudgel." [185] Railing against those "miserable nigs who steal," a South Carolinian could only "wish the rice was poison to give them their deserts." [186] Anxious whites were feverishly attempting to reassert the race and labor controls they had lost with emancipation, and they were increasingly willing to sanction any means necessary. Much was compromised in the drive for white supremacy, home rule, and personal gain.

Nevertheless, economic survival demanded that planters achieve a working relationship with freedmen. A Mississippi planter thought that a living could still be made from agriculture if the planter had "a faculty to get work out of the freedmen by management rather than coercion." [187] But many never found the key. "Tens of thousands of the best *old fashion*[ed] managers have failed in the South since the war," Thomas T. Munford declared in 1869. [188] Planters were always on the lookout for someone who thought he had discovered the secret. "In my contract," replied a successful planter to an inquiry from a distraught Alabama friend, "I furnish provisions to the hands that labour, & none other." In addition, "All lost time is charged and accounted for" and subtracted from their share of the crop. And he used the "most rigid economy" in everything. But, first and foremost, his "overseer" managed all practical operations. "I have no dealings otherwise with the hands," he declared. [189] Efficient production had once been thought to depend upon a resident planter, but now, given the changes, this planter believed he did better by keeping his distance.

The desire for distance from freedmen was not unusual. Most planters displayed an aversion to dealing directly with free blacks. "Free Negroes frets me so much," explained one man in 1871, "that I very seldom go among them." [190] The need to back away from freedmen was in part a reflection of what one scholar has recently identified as the South's evolution from a "paternalistic" to a "competitive" model of race relations. The master-slave relationship, with its enormous social distance and legally defined stations, allowed close contact, even intimacy, without threatening white status. Emancipation drastically reduced the social distance between whites and blacks, prompting whites to reject intimate contact and to seek physical separation as a buttress to their own status. [191] But planters were caught in a difficult dilemma. At the very moment they were tempted to accept whatever new plantation arrangement provided the least contact between them and their laborers, they realized that in practice physical separation would only increase the independence that they already found so troublesome in freedmen. They were torn between their social desire to maximize distance and racial separation and their economic desire to maintain supervision and agricultural efficiency. Not all planters allowed their racism to stand between them and their profits, but the repugnance they felt for free blacks often did impinge on the satisfaction of immediate economic needs.[192]

Despite the magnitude of the pressures acting against paternalism, however, emancipation did not always mark the end of the planters' feelings of genuine concern for their laborers. Old standards of responsibility and integrity had some staying power. The aristocratic tradition did not die with the old regime or even with the old aristocrats. Postwar plantations still linked the two races on the land, the one dominant and the other subordinate. Some Southerners still valued quiet living, family honor, and magnanimous, gentle treatment of one's inferiors. And in time, certain changes provided paternalism with more nourishment. Transient labor decreased as freedmen were immobilized by shares and liens, and deferential behavior among blacks rose in tandem with their powerlessness.

Planters who re-established some degree of prosperity were probably most likely to maintain paternal relations with their laborers. Wealthy John Houston Bills of Tennessee, for instance, continued many of the small traditions of the slave regime, such as having blacks marry in his home and treating them to a wedding dinner.[193] But prosperity was no prerequisite to continued concern. An Alabama woman, who for years owed "so many debts" that she was "almost crazy about them," found that when she sold the freedmen's cotton in 1876, "it did not pay one rent, [and] the negroes did not get anything, poor creatures[;] it is hard on them, as well as us." Despite the fact that every one of her own children was out of school, "trying hard to make money," she gave each black tenant five dollars, "and it seems so little that it is no comfort for me to think about it." [194] In 1875, Dolly Burge, who faced a plantation "all run down [,] no stock[,] no hands & nothing," cosigned a note for one of her former bondsmen. Three weeks later he ran off without paying. "I cannot meet it & dont know what to do." [195]

But postwar paternalism was often a very pale imitation. Northern-born Henry Watson, Jr., having spent thirty-three years in Alabama and four years abroad during the war, decided after his discouraging visit to his plantation in the autumn of 1865 to move to Massachusetts. He kept his plantation, however, and made annual visits. In 1876, he wrote from Alabama about how all the servants had rushed up to see him when he arrived, to "be noticed," to talk of old times, and to express their "imaginary wants." They always seemed to be getting into "some scrape," he said indulgently, "and want me to get them out of it." He was pleased with how well they were doing —working, buying useful items, keeping clean. Everything was splendid, in fact, "abundance prevails everywhere." [196] But for all Watson's solicitous behavior, he had really betrayed the paternal ideal. He had moved to the North, visited Alabama but once a year, and maintained no direct, continuous involvement in the lives of his workers. He was play-acting, reaping the psychic rewards of paternalism without really fulfilling his own obligations. Like so many Southern conservatives in the postwar period, he had subordinated aristocratic ideals to save himself.

Slavery had been a kind of log jam behind which forces of social and cultural change had stacked up, and with emancipation, the South moved toward the mainstream of American development. Torrents of change, sometimes inconsequential except to the beholder, poured into planters' lives—often with the effect of salt on fresh wounds. One woman was angry that blacks had begun using two names. It was "no unusual thing to read of an Andrew Jackson or George Washington having been convicted of larceny," she declared. [197] Others were unable to accept the changes the war had worked on friends and relatives. "I never see cousin Tom," a Mississippi woman sighed, "but I mourn the change in him from the genial, social, charming companion he used to be to the careworn man." [198] A Georgian was upset by the "habitual profanity" of her husband, caused by his "loss of property." [199] A Charlestonian lamented the change in attitude of aristocratic youth toward education. "All say 'whats the use of Latin & Greek or Mathematics—let me go into business.' Business, of course," he snorted, "meaning the making of money." [200] "What has become of the gentlemen of the country, the men of the 'old Regime'?" echoed a plantation mistress. "Do you observe how money is worshipped now? More than ever before the men of high character —of sterling worth and integrity—without wealth, have no influence." [201] Many a plantation dweller agreed with the Virginian who declared that emancipation would surely mean the disappearance of "our old fashioned and true *lady & gentleman*." [202]

The fate of one antebellum institution can perhaps stand as a symbol for the social and cultural change that penetrated the planters' world. Tournaments—medieval pageants—had been a striking and unique Southern manifestation of the prewar romantic mood. Gaudy knights and demure ladies had gathered on sunny afternoons, and bugles sounded and sabers flashed as Brian de Bois-Guilbert, Ivanhoe, Bernardo del Carpio, and others matched swordsmanship and riding skills. Not every plantation dweller was immersed in Sir Walter Scott, but many were. Lucy Judkins Durr of Alabama said that she was raised on "Scott & Carlyle." "With Scott it was 'some must work while others play,' " she remembered, while "with Carlyle it was 'some must work while others think.' " [203] Catherine Edmonston of North Carolina, in a rare quiet moment during the war, reflected on her favorite literature, tales of "Lords and Ladies in olden times." She loved the "glow of romance thrown by these old Chevaliers upon their age, the Knightly Courtesy, the mixture of the impossible, the incomprehensible, with the daily life. . . ." Southern fighting men, she said, had adopted as their own "the law of Knightly honour and chivalry." [204]

Defeat did not eliminate the tournament from Southern life. Outside Asheville, North Carolina, in November, 1865, Ivanhoe crowned Maggie McDowell "Queen of Love and Beauty." A year later, crowds in the Cape Fear region agreed that their tournament was the grandest they had ever seen. [205] But postwar tournaments were not the same as those of earlier days. After Ella Clanton Thomas attended one near her Georgia plantation in 1868, she complained that the grand prize, a bridle, was too common, too utilitarian, for a chivalric event. "This is an eminently practical age," she lamented. She had even overheard "several young men say that if the judges would make up a prize of money they would ride for it." [206] In 1870, James Wilson White learned that a "grand Tournament" was scheduled near his home in Fort Mill, South Carolina. "I may attend," he said, "but will not participate, for men of my age . . . don't care about such things, especially when they revelled in the reality—for a space of four long years." [207] When another observer heard that knights had recently jousted in his neighborhood, he chided, "I think the entire batch had better drop the 'lance' and 'take up the shovel and the hoe.' . . ." And finally, to complete the revolution, in 1871 in North Carolina, black Ivanhoes took the field in their own privately sponsored event. [208] Defeat, social revolution, and Gilded Age materialism seriously challenged the romantic aristocratic mentality. Tournaments did not die, but like so much of the postbellum South, they retained little more than the form, while much of the original substance drained away.

Turn-of-the-century Southerners, looking back over Southern history since the war, often were struck by the drastic alteration of the social landscape. George Cary Eggleston, who had loved the "soft, dreamy, deliciously quiet life" of the old order, thought it had been entirely shattered.[209] Thomas Nelson Page, the man primarily responsible for the rise of the plantation myth after the war, agreed that a society of courage, hospitality, magnanimity, affection, and honor had disappeared with the defeat.[210] Philip Alexander Bruce thought "the new South . . . already directly the opposite of the old." In the place of the society of planters stood the society of the courthouse, peopled with professionals. He found it remarkable how completely the planter class had "vanished and how wholly the country is given over to the former lower ranks."[211] John Spencer Bassett in 1896 was also struck by the "disappearance of the planter type."[212] Years later, William Alexander Percy of Mississippi, speaking of the post-Reconstruction generation, said, "There was no embattled aristocracy, for the descendents of the old-timers were already a rather seedy remnant, and there was no wealth. White folks and colored folks—that's what we were—and some of us were nice and some weren't."[213]

Late-nineteenth-century opinion about change in the South is not very reliable, for both romantic reactionaries and progressive New South types joined in mythmaking. Those who loved the Old South were often unable to find a single significant remnant from the past, while those who were eager to transform the South often mistook their own optimistic rhetoric for reality. We know now that the South was still distinctive, that much had survived and that much that looked new actually had roots in the antebellum years. But emancipation had caused a basic transformation, and survivals were often empty shells. Thus when Southerners spoke of the plantation and the cultural changes that had enveloped it, their perception was more right than wrong.

Their opinion was given dramatic confirmation by one Southerner who was able to view the scene from a unique perspective. In 1888, George Scarborough Barnsley returned to his native Georgia after an absence of more than twenty years. He had left his father's plantation in 1867 to reconstruct his life in Latin America. He established himself as a planter and a doctor in Brazil, but not totally satisfied with his new home after two decades, he returned to Georgia. A Southern Rip Van Winkle, he saw the postwar South with fresh vision and he was appalled.

Part of his shock stemmed from the fact that he had become a "Brazilian." After the vastness of Latin America, he felt "cramped in the U.S." Everything looked tiny, dry, and desolate. But the South had also changed. The old "civilization" of the plantation had crumbled and in its place stood something "mean and ugly." He remembered freedom and independence, yet now his "every act was spied upon." He could not even "fish on Sundays!" Southern hospitality had given way to stinginess. "Blue-blazes—I had been living where negroes gave away copper coins, and food or rest was never denied, but kindly and hospitably given by the poorest of the poor." Institutions which had once been honored in the South and were still honored in Brazil were treated shabbily. Gentility, it seemed, had no part in the postwar South. The court, for instance, "was crowded, the floor filthy with tobacco spittle, men in shirt sleeves, bad accomodations, talking, etc." When his own case came before the bench, instead of arguing the facts, the prosecuting lawyer "commenced abusing me and my family for being as he said aristocrats. . . ." The impression grew that he had "gotten into a country where people were prejudiced, narrow-minded, and selfish." And that was not the impression he had of the country he had left two decades earlier. After six years in Georgia, he left once again for South America. "I was glad to get back to Brazil," he recalled, "where I could do as I pleased," with "perfect freedom to think as it suited me." There, at least, one never saw "disagreeable, roudy scrambling in the street or stores." He lived out his life in this more congenial climate, dying in 1916 in Rio de Janeiro.[214]

Change had not been totally alien to the Old South, but that conservative society had hobbled modern ideas. Appomattox was an explosion in the minds of the gentry. Sometimes large-scale violence changes nothing, but in this case it seemed to change everything. "I am almost tempted to doubt my self sometimes and ask if this is really I, to doubt my own identity," declared Octavia Otey.[215] Her concern about identity was not a mere dramatic flourish, for the summer of 1865 had been the South's moment of fundamental historical disjuncture. Masters without slaves, thrust into an alien, unpredictable world, planters felt a loss of historical continuity, a loss of sameness and wholeness. Jefferson Davis called it a "break in time." "What an emptiness it all is," a North Carolina woman sighed.[216] And to a Georgia planter, "All that we were seemed to be passing away." [217]

Revolutions confront individuals with difficult ideological problems. "In this world, nothing is fixed and stationary," Octavia Otey concluded two years after Appomattox; "all things are changing constantly, and *I know but too well.*" [218] In his recent discussion of revolutionary change, Robert Jay Lifton identifies three basic individual stances toward rapid movement in history. He labels the three patterns of response transformation, restoration, and accommodation. Transformation is future-oriented, involving a negative vision of the past and a willingness to remake existence into something fundamentally new. Restoration is past-oriented, involving an urge to return to tradition and flee from an inauthentic future. Both contain seeds of totalism, readiness for an all-or-nothing plunge. Accommodation, however, entails willingness to compromise, an acceptance of a blend of past, present, and future. Its focus is on immediate circumstances, the goal being to carve out a place in the new environment, while at the same time to maintain integrity. Of the three, accommodation is most difficult to sustain, Lifton explains, for it does not provide a complete, clear ideology which orders all things and makes all decisions lucid.[219]

These are universal psychological patterns, and Southerners, naturally, found their way into every category. Joseph Buckner Killebrew of Tennessee was a transformationist; he celebrated emancipation, welcomed the New South, and optimistically looked forward to factories, small farms, and prosperity.[220] Octavia Otey of Alabama was a restorationist, wretched in the postwar South. "How strange life seems to me now," she declared. "I feel as if I were floating on a strong current, through strange countries, whose every appearance was new to me." Her thoughts, she said, were *"ever* turn[ed] *backward."* [221] Ella Clanton Thomas of Georgia was an accommodationist; she tried to maintain standards but at the same time succeed in the new world. "It is not 'the moldering past' . . . to which my thoughts refer," she said, "but the never forgotten present." [222]

The majority of Southern planters were similar to Ella Clanton Thomas, struggling desperately to accommodate themselves to new realities but also unwilling, and often unable, to turn their backs entirely on the plantation past. In one way, they were ill prepared for the crisis, for their social insularity and personal arrogance had not nourished in them vibrant and healthy adaptive mechanisms. But more important, planters had traditionally acted in what they had perceived as the best interest of the plantation system. Even after emancipation, when their commitment to agriculture waned, preservation of the plantation usually remained the central priority in their lives. The plantation gave them a standard by which they could evaluate the rush of change.

The planters' readjustments proved that men and women are capable of surprisingly rapid shifts in ideas and ideologies, even when these are related to the central issues of their existence. After the defeat, planters had little choice but to find a place for themselves in the accepted intellectual framework of the day, just as they had little choice but to reconstruct plantations without slaves. Slavery, that seemingly indispensable first premise, was relegated fairly soon to a past that was seen as ended once and for all. Planters did not have the luxury of pining for an irretrievable institution. In place of the labor and race controls of slavery, Southerners developed sharecropping and liens, segregation and militant white supremacy. Whites regained control, and the bottom rail remained on the bottom. But the concepts of black inferiority and white supremacy were paltry replacements for the mature proslavery ideology. Slavery had provided planters with a total, complex world view, while the scope of its post-emancipation substitute seemed seriously foreshortened and incomplete.

Planters could become at home in this New South only by ceasing to be the people they had been. Insofar as they retained their antebellum identities, they could not feel at ease. And for all their practical and intellectual adjustments, planters could not eradicate entirely their antebellum selves. Most adjusted merely enough to make their way, rarely enough to make real peace. Plantations were reorganized, but prosperity was elusive. Fundamental ideas gave way, but old habits and feelings lived on. Planters did not recognize the new order as superior to the old. Individuals may have made a successful transition, but the antebellum planter class did not. With emancipation, the slaveholders' basis for unity disappeared, and with that, much of their pride, *élan*, and confidence. Planters never again regained an identity as sharply drawn, as universally accepted, and as completely satisfying as that of master. Plantations survived, but plantation life was transformed. "The houses, indeed, are still there, little changed, it may be, on the outside," George Bagby declared, in words planters would have understood, "but the light, the life, the charm are gone forever. 'The soul is fled.' " [223]

# Notes

## Manuscript Collections

| | |
|---|---|
| ADAH | Alabama State Department of Archives and History, Montgomery |
| Duke | Duke University Library, Durham, North Carolina |
| Emory | Emory University Library, Atlanta, Georgia |
| GaHS | Georgia Historical Society, Savannah |
| LSU | Louisiana State Department of Archives and History, Louisiana State University, Baton Rouge |
| NCAH | North Carolina State Department of Archives and History, Raleigh |
| SCHS | South Carolina Historical Society, Charleston |
| SCL | South Caroliniana Library, University of South Carolina, Columbia |
| SHC | Southern Historical Collection, University of North Carolina, Chapel Hill |
| TSLA | Tennessee State Library and Archives, Nashville |
| Tulane | Tulane University Library, New Orleans, Louisiana |
| UGa | University of Georgia Library, Athens |
| UVa | University of Virginia Library, Charlottesville |

## Journals

| | |
|---|---|
| AgH | *Agricultural History* |
| AHR | *American Historical Review* |

| Annals | *Annals of the American Academy of Political and Social Science* |
|--------|----------------------------------------------------------------|
| CWH | *Civil War History* |
| JEH | *Journal of Economic History* |
| JMH | *Journal of Mississippi History* |
| JNH | *Journal of Negro History* |
| JSH | *Journal of Southern History* |
| LH | *Labor History* |
| LaH | *Louisiana History* |
| LaHQ | *Louisiana Historical Quarterly* |
| MVHR | *Mississippi Valley Historical Review* |
| PSQ | *Political Science Quarterly* |
| SAQ | *South Atlantic Quarterly* |
| SwHQ | *Southwestern Historical Quarterly* |
| VaMHB | *Virginia Magazine of History and Biography* |
| WMQ | *William and Mary Quarterly* |

## CHAPTER ONE: THE PLANTERS' REVOLUTION

[1]John Berkley Grimball Diary, Dec. 19, 1860, SHC.

[2]Robert Toombs to the People of Georgia, Dec. 23, 1860, in Ulrich Bonnell Phillips, ed., *The Correspondence of Robert Toombs, Alexander H. Stephens, and Howell Cobb*, vol. 2, 525.

[3]Kenneth Clark to Lewis Thompson, Nov. 26, 1860, Lewis Thompson Papers, SHC.

[4]Daniel Perrin Bestor to Thomas Jefferson Bestor, Jan. 11, 1861, in Arthur E. Bestor, Jr., "Letters from a Southern Opponent of Sectionalism, September, 1860, to June, 1861," *JSH*, 12 (Feb., 1946), 117.

[5]James M. Willcox to Susannah Willcox, April 14, 1861, James M. Willcox Letters and Papers, Duke.

[6] John Hartwell Cocke to Charles C. Cocke, Oct. 11, 1860, John Hartwell Cocke Papers, UVa.

[7]John Houston Bills Diary, June 8, 1861, John Houston Bills Papers, SHC.

[8]C. D. Whittle to L. N. Whittle, Feb. 2, 1861, Lewis Neale Whittle Papers, SHC.

[9]D. P. Bestor to T. J. Bestor, Jan. 28, 1861, in Bestor, "Letters," 116.

[10]John Houston Bills Diary, Jan. 8, 1861, John Houston Bills Papers, SHC.

[11]Andrew McCollam, Jr., to Andrew McCollam, Nov. 23, 1860, Andrew McCollam Papers, SHC.

[12]Alfred Huger to [illegible], Oct. 4, 1856, Alfred Huger Papers, Duke.

[13]J. Carlyle Sitterson, "The William J. Minor Plantations: A Study in Ante-Bellum Absentee Ownership," *JSH*, 9 (Feb., 1943), 61.

[14]Quoted in Lillian A. Pereyra, *James Lusk Alcorn: Persistent Whig*, 43.

¹⁵Henry Selby Clark to his wife, Jan. 12, 1861, Henry Selby Clark Letters, SHC.

¹⁶Alexander Stephens to J. Henley Smith, July 10, 1860, in Phillips, ed., *Correspondence of Toombs, Stephens, and Cobb*, vol. 2, 487.

¹⁷John Houston Bills Diary, Nov. 28, 1860, John Houston Bills Papers, SHC.

¹⁸Kenneth Clark to Lewis Thompson, Nov. 26, 1860, Lewis Thompson Papers, SHC.

¹⁹William Kirkland to Octavia Otey, Nov. 18, 1860, Wyche and Otey Family Papers, SHC.

²⁰John Houston Bills Diary, Nov. 29, 1860, John Houston Bills Papers, SHC.

²¹Mrs. Jane Brown to Mrs. J. L. Bailey, Dec. 29, 1860, John Lancaster Bailey Papers, SHC.

²²Mary Ann Whittle to Lewis Neale Whittle, Dec. 1, 1860, Lewis Neale Whittle Papers, SHC.

²³Alexander Stephens to J. Henley Smith, July 10, 1860; Stephens to [unknown], Nov. 25, 1860; and Stephens to J. Henley Smith, Dec. 31, 1860, in Phillips, ed., *Correspondence of Toombs, Stephens, and Cobb*, vol. 2, 487, 504, 526–27.

²⁴D. P. Bestor to T. J. Bestor, Jan. 11, 1861, in Bestor, "Letters," 115.

²⁵William Henry King, "Colonel James Moore King, A Southern Gentleman, 1792–1877" (1932), William Henry King Memoirs, SHC.

²⁶Alfred Huger to Evan Edwards, Aug. 26, 1858, Alfred Huger Papers, Duke.

²⁷Alfred Huger to [illegible], Oct. 4, 1856, Alfred Huger Papers, Duke.

²⁸Alfred Huger to Evan Edwards, Aug. 26, 1858, Alfred Huger Papers, Duke.

²⁹Carl N. Degler, *The Other South: Southern Dissenters in the Nineteenth Century*, 116.

³⁰Alfred Huger to [illegible], Oct. 4, 1856, Alfred Huger Papers, Duke.

³¹Alfred Huger to James L. Petigru, Oct. 8, 1861, Alfred Huger Papers, Duke.

³²Andrew McCollam to Ellen McCollam, Jan. 27, 1861, Andrew McCollam Papers, SHC.

³³John Houston Bills Diary, Jan. 8, 1861, John Houston Bills Papers, SHC.

³⁴William Henry King, "Colonel James Moore King," William Henry King Memoirs, SHC.

³⁵C. D. Whittle to L. N. Whittle, June 13, 1861, Lewis Neale Whittle Papers, SHC.

³⁶James M. Willcox to Susannah Willcox, April 14, 1861, James M. Willcox Letters and Papers, Duke.

³⁷John Houston Bills Diary, April 15, 1861, John Houston Bills Papers, SHC.

³⁸John Mering, "Persistent Whiggery in the Confederate South: A Reconsideration," *SAQ*, 69 (1970), 124–43; Degler, *The Other South*, 158–63.

³⁹Final judgment on William Barney's thesis must be reserved. His subject is actually lower- and middle-level politicians, and his analysis of them tells us a great deal about the way parties were developing in 1860. But it remains to be seen whether or not rank-and-file Whigs and Democrats duplicated the social characteristics of the party leaders. William L. Barney, *The Road to Secession: A New Perspective on the Old South*, 135; William L. Barney, *The Secessionist Impulse: Alabama and Mississippi in 1860*, passim.

⁴⁰For a full discussion of Southern Unionism, see Degler, *The Other South*, chs. 3–5. Taking a position contrary to mine, Degler argues that Unionism persisted throughout the war in a significant portion of the planter class. For my discussion of

planter Unionism in the war years, see pp. 55–58.

[41]Mrs. Catherine Ann Edmondston Diaries, Dec. 22, 1860, NCAH.

[42]John Bones to Robert Hughes, March 29, 1861, Hughes Family Papers, SHC.

[43]Quoted in Donald E. Reynolds, *Editors Make War: Southern Newspapers in the Secession Crisis*, 196.

[44]Edmund Ruffin to John Perkins, March 22, 1861, John Perkins Papers, SHC.

[45]John Perkins to Dr. Delong and others, Sept. 28, 1861, John Perkins Papers, SHC.

[46]Mrs. Catherine Ann Edmondston Diaries, Feb. 13, 1861, NCAH.

[47]William Kirkland to Octavia Otey, May 22, 1861, Wyche and Otey Family Papers, SHC.

[48]Alfred Huger to William Ravenel, June 24, 1865, William Ravenel Paper, SHC.

[49]John Hartwell Cocke to E. C. DeLavan, July 1, 1862, John Hartwell Cocke Papers, UVa.

[50]David Gavin Diary, Dec. 6, 1860, SHC. Occasionally a planter would opt for consistency. Henry Watson, Jr., a Massachusetts-born planter who had settled in Alabama, opposed secession during the crisis. However, once it had occurred, he said, "But a separation having taken place by our inherent *right of revolution*, not of secession, and it seeming to be the *will of the people*, that we should be independent, I hold that we are right in maintaining our independence. . . ." Henry Watson, Jr., to J. A. Wemyss, Aug. 6, 1861, Henry Watson, Jr., Papers, Duke.

[51]Andrew McCollam to Ellen McCollam, May 9, 1861, Andrew McCollam Papers, SHC.

[52]Ella Gertrude (Clanton) Thomas Journal, May 27, 1861, Duke.

[53]Alfred Huger to W. B. Pringle, March 14, 1862, Alfred Huger Papers, Duke.

[54]D. P. Bestor to T. J. Bestor, Feb. 25, 1861, in Bestor, "Letters," 118.

[55]Everard Green Baker Diary, April 24, 1861, SHC.

[56]D. P. Bestor to T. J. Bestor, Jan. 11, 1861, in Bestor, "Letters," 115.

[57]Alexander Stephens to [unknown], Nov. 25, 1860, in Phillips, ed., *Correspondence of Toombs, Stephens, and Cobb*, vol. 2, 504.

[58]That the American Revolution had actually divided Southern society, caused widespread destruction, and been a threat to the continuance of slavery was either unknown or ignored. History did have something to teach planters in 1861, but they were not very receptive students. See Benjamin Quarles, "Lord Dunmore as Liberator," WMQ, 15 (Oct., 1958), 494–507.

[59]Alfred Huger to William Porcher Miles, Jan. 23, 1858, Alfred Huger Papers, Duke.

[60]Alfred Huger to W. B. Pringle, March 14, 1862, Alfred Huger Papers, Duke.

[61]The pivotal exposition is John Higham, *From Boundlessness to Consolidation: The Transformation of American Culture, 1848–1860*. But also important are Rowland T. Berthoff, *An Unsettled People: Social Order and Disorder in American History*; William W. Freehling, "The Editorial Revolution, Virginia, and the Coming of the Civil War: A Review Essay," *CWH*, 16 (March, 1970), 64–72; and David Donald, "The Proslavery Argument Reconsidered," *JSH*, 37 (Feb., 1971), 3–18.

[62]David Brion Davis, *The Slave Power Conspiracy and the Paranoid Style, passim*.

[63]George C. Rogers, Jr., *The History of Georgetown County, South Carolina*, 386.

[64]Mary Ann Whittle to Lewis N. Whittle, Oct. 29, 1860, Lewis Neale Whittle Papers, SHC.

[65]C. D. Whittle to L. N. Whittle, Nov. 7, 1860, Lewis Neale Whittle Papers, SHC.

[66]Jack P. Maddex, Jr., *The Virginia Conservatives, 1867–1879: A Study in Reconstruction Politics*, 23.

[67]Frederick Law Olmsted, *A Journey in the Seaboard Slave States*, 491.

[68]Alfred Huger to Dr. Benjamin Huger, Sept. 16, 1853, Alfred Huger Papers, Duke.

[69]George Hairston to Bettie Hairston, Oct. 10, 1861, Hairston and Wilson Family Papers, SHC.

[70]Tobias Gibson to Mrs. Young, April 6, 1862, Gibson and Humphreys Family Papers, SHC.

[71]Alfred Huger to Mr. Wickham, June 1, 1858, Alfred Huger Papers, Duke.

[72]David Gavin Diary, June 12, 1860, SHC.

[73]Ella Gertrude (Clanton) Thomas Journal, March 31, 1861, Duke.

[74]Howell Cobb to the People of Georgia, Dec. 6, 1860, in Phillips, ed., *Correspondence of Toombs, Stephens, and Cobb*, vol. 2, 506.

[75]Alfred Huger to Robert Gourdin, Aug. 23, 1859, Alfred Huger Papers, Duke.

[76]David Gavin Diary, April 22, 1858, and June 22, 1861, SHC.

[77]W. P. Craighill to Benjamin Allston, May 27, 1860, Robert Francis Withers Allston Papers, SCHS.

[78]Alfred Huger to Robert Gourdin, Aug. 23, 1859, Alfred Huger Papers, Duke.

[79]David Gavin Diary, Dec. 6, 1860, and July 1, 1861, SHC.

[80]Alexander Stephens to J. Henley Smith, Jan. 20, 1860, and Sept. 16, 1860, in Phillips, ed., *Correspondence of Toombs, Stephens, and Cobb*, vol. 2, 457, 498.

[81]David Gavin Diary, June 12, 1860, SHC.

[82]Alfred Huger to W. B. Pringle, March 14, 1862, Alfred Huger Papers, Duke.

[83]Ella Gertrude (Clanton) Thomas Journal, 1861, Duke.

[84]Randall Lee Gibson to Cora Bell Gibson [wartime], Gibson and Humphreys Family Papers, SHC.

[85]Iredele Jones to Cadwallader Jones, Jr., Jan. 20, 1863, Cadwallader Jones, Jr., Papers, SHC.

[86]Maddex, *The Virginia Conservatives*, 23. For a path-breaking analysis of the conservative reaction in Georgia, see Michael P. Johnson, "Secession and Conservatism in the Lower South: The Social and Ideological Bases of Secession in Georgia, 1860–1861" (Ph.D. dissertation, Stanford University, 1973), chs. 6–8.

[87]Jesse T. Carpenter, *The South as a Conscious Minority, 1789–1861: A Study in Political Thought*, 260.

[88]David Gavin Diary, July 21, 1861, SHC.

[89]Louis Hartz, *The Liberal Tradition in America: An Interpretation of American Political Thought since the Revolution*, 145.

[90]Lester B. Baltimore, "Southern Nationalists and Southern Nationalism, 1850–1870" (Ph.D. dissertation, University of Missouri, 1968), 26–32.

[91]C. D. Whittle to L. N. Whittle, Oct. 30, 1860, Lewis Neale Whittle Papers, SHC.

[92]Henry Watson, Jr., to M. L. Filley, March 17, 1861, Henry Watson, Jr., Papers, Duke.

[93]Eric Foner, "The Causes of the American Civil War: Recent Interpretations and New Directions," *CWH*, 20 (Sept., 1974), 210. In explaining the absence of overt class hostility in the antebellum South, Roger W. Shugg says simply, "Race prejudice . . . filled the void of class hatred." *Origins of Class Struggle in Louisiana: A Social History of White Farmers and Laborers during Slavery and After, 1840–1875*, 30.

[94]Quoted in Carpenter, *The South as a Conscious Minority*, 5.

[95]Mrs. Catherine Ann Edmondston Diaries, Nov. 25, 1860, and Feb. 10, 1861, NCAH.

[96]Mrs. Catherine Ann Edmondston Diaries, Feb. 18, 1861, NCAH.

[97]See, for example, William Clark to Lewis Thompson, Dec. 22, 1860, Lewis Thompson Papers, SHC; Alfred Iverson to David C. Barrow, Aug. 23, 1860, Colonel David Crenshaw Barrow Papers, UGa; and Cary Charles Cocke to John Hartwell Cocke, Jan. 10, 1861, John Hartwell Cocke Papers, UVa. For an important discussion of this theme, see Freehling, "The Editorial Revolution, Virginia, and the Coming of the Civil War," 68–71.

[98]W. P. Craighill to Benjamin Allston, May 27, 1860, Robert Francis Withers Allston Papers, SCHS.

[99]Iveson Brookes to Sarah Brookes, Feb. 25, 1836, Iveson L. Brookes Letters and Papers, Duke.

[100]Biography accompanying Iveson L. Brookes Letters and Papers, Duke.

[101]Susan L'Engle to Edward M. L'Engle, April 15, 1861, Edward McCrady L'Engle Papers, SHC.

[102]Charles Smallwood Diary, May 3, 1861, SHC.

[103]Edward Fontaine Diary, April 14, 1861, quoted in John K. Bettersworth, ed., *Mississippi in the Confederacy: As They Saw It*, 55.

[104]Mrs. Catherine Ann Edmondston Diaries, April 15, 1861, NCAH.

[105]Mrs. Catherine Ann Edmondston Diaries, May 2, 1861, NCAH.

[106]William Kirkland to Octavia Otey, April 30, 1861, Wyche and Otey Family Papers, SHC.

[107]Samuel David Sanders to Mary Sanders, Nov. 27, 1861, Samuel David Sanders Letters, Emory.

[108]Annie I. Jones to Cadwallader Jones, April, 1861, Cadwallader Jones, Jr., Papers, SHC.

[109]Everard Green Baker Diary, April 24, 1861, SHC.

[110]John S. Dobbins to William Dobbins, April 28, 1861, John S. Dobbins Papers, Emory.

[111]Charles Smallwood Diary, May 1, 1861, SHC.

[112]Henry Watson, Jr., to Dr. John H. Parrish, July 15, 1861, and July 30, 1861, Henry Watson, Jr., Papers, Duke.

[113]Henry S. Clark to his wife, Feb. 5, 1861, Henry Selby Clark Letters, SHC.

[114]Quoted in Reynolds, *Editors Make War*, 201.

[115]Edward Fontaine Diary, quoted in Bettersworth, ed., *Mississippi in the Confederacy*, 58.

[116]William Wallace White Diaries, April, 1861, SHC.

[117]Duncan [illegible] to Andrew McCollam, Oct. 9, 1861, Andrew McCollam Papers, SHC.

[118]John Houston Bills Diary, April 15, 1861, John Houston Bills Papers, SHC.

[119]Henry Watson, Jr., to Allen C. Jones, April 22, 1861, Henry Watson, Jr., Papers, Duke.

[120]Henry Watson, Jr., to Dr. John H. Parrish, Aug. 9, 1861, Henry Watson, Jr., Papers, Duke.

[121]Tobias Gibson to Mrs. Young, April 6, 1862, Gibson and Humphreys Family Papers, SHC.

[122]Alfred Huger to Mr. Vanderhorst, Dec. 1, 1861, Alfred Huger Papers, Duke.

[123]William Howard Russell, *My Diary North and South*, vol. 1, 141–43.

[124]Benjamin Ballard to Lewis Thompson, Sept. 17, 1862, Lewis Thompson Papers, SHC.

[125]Edmund Ruffin to John Perkins, Aug. 16, 1862, John Perkins Papers, SHC.

[126]Benjamin Ballard to Lewis Thompson, Sept. 17, 1862, Lewis Thompson Papers, SHC.

[127]Henry L. Graves to "Aunt Libby," Oct. 28, 1862, Graves Family Papers, SHC.

[128]David Gavin Diary, Oct. 19, 1861, SHC.

[129]Rev. C. C. Jones to Charles C. Jones, Jr., March 24, 1862, in Robert Manson Myers, ed., *The Children of Pride: A True Story of Georgia and the Civil War*, 866.

[130]Alfred Huger to R. Bunch, Oct. 20, 1857, Alfred Huger Papers, Duke.

[131]Rowland Berthoff has recently suggested the name "War for Social Security." *An Unsettled People*, 296.

[132]Randall Lee Gibson to Tobias Gibson, Feb. 20, 1861, Gibson and Humphreys Family Papers, SHC.

## CHAPTER TWO: PLANTATIONS UNDER SIEGE

[1]James M. Willcox to Susannah Willcox, June 10, 1863, James M. Willcox Letters and Papers, Duke.

[2]Philip Alexander Bruce, "Social and Economic Revolution in the Southern States," *Contemporary Review*, 78 (July, 1900), 61.

[3]Charles Smallwood Diary, Feb. 2, 1862, SCH.

[4]Ella Gertrude (Clanton) Thomas Journal, Dec. 3, 1861, Duke.

[5]Mrs. Catherine Ann Edmondston Diaries, June 1, 1862, NCAH.

[6]Caroline E. Merrick, *Old Times in Dixie Land: A Southern Matron's Memories*, 47.

[7]Miss Mary E. Robarts to Mrs. Mary Jones, Dec. 30, 1862, in Robert Manson Myers, ed., *The Children of Pride: A True Story of Georgia and the Civil War*, 1006.

[8]Alexander McBee to Vardry A. McBee, May 5, 1864, and May 25, 1864, McBee Family Papers, SHC.

[9]William A. Hardy to Lewis Thompson, June 3, 1861, Lewis Thompson Papers, SHC.

[10]Robertson Blacklock and Co. to James Sparkman, Dec. 3, 1861, Sparkman Family Papers, SHC.

[11]Quoted in Albert D. Kirwan, ed., *The Confederacy*, 54. Historians have engaged in extensive discussions concerning the food supply in the antebellum South. For a recent, persuasive argument, see Robert E. Gallman, "Self-Sufficiency in the Cotton Economy of the Antebellum South," *AgH*, 44 (Jan., 1970), 5–23.

[12]Quoted in Paul W. Gates, *Agriculture and the Civil War*, 16.

[13]John Kirkland to Octavia Otey, April 29, 1861, Wyche and Otey Family Papers, SHC.

[14]Charles P. Roland, *Louisiana Sugar Plantations during the American Civil War*, 42.

[15]J. A. Wemyss to Henry Watson, Jr., Jan. 28, 1862, Henry Watson, Jr., Papers, Duke.

[16]William A. Hardy to L. Thompson, June 3, 1861, Lewis Thompson Papers, SHC.

[17]H. E. Sterkx, *Partners in Rebellion: Alabama Women in the Civil War*, 131.

[18]Quoted in Kirwan, ed., *The Confederacy*, 61.

[19]Dolly Burge Diary, May 5, 1862, Burge-Gray Papers, Emory.

[20]J. A. Wemyss to Henry Watson, Jr., Jan. 28, 1862, Henry Watson, Jr., Papers, Duke.

[21]Daniel Perrin Bestor to Thomas Jefferson Bestor, Jan. 7, 1860, in Arthur E. Bestor, Jr., "Letters from a Southern Opponent of Sectionalism, September, 1860, to June 1861," *JSH*, 12 (Feb., 1946), 115.

[22]Rev. C. C. Jones to Charles C. Jones, Jr., March 14, 1862, in Myers, ed., *Children of Pride*, 859.

[23]Gates, *Agriculture and the Civil War*, 370–73; T. Conn Bryan, *Confederate Georgia*, 118–21. Tobacco figures are not available for the war years.

[24]Quoted in John K. Bettersworth, ed., *Mississippi in the Confederacy: As They Saw It*, 215–16.

[25]David C. Barrow to "Georgia," April 12, 1863, Colonel David Crenshaw Barrow Papers, UGa.

[26]Quoted in Sterkx, *Partners in Rebellion*, 43.

[27]Bettersworth, ed., *Mississippi in the Confederacy*, 224.

[28]Robert Toombs to George Hill and others, June 11, 1862, in Ulrich Bonnell Phillips, ed., *The Correspondence of Robert Toombs, Alexander H. Stephens, and Howell Cobb*, vol. 2, 613.

[29]Rev. C. C. Jones to Charles C. Jones, Jr., April 21, 1862, in Myers, ed., *Children of Pride*, 882.

[30]E. Merton Coulter, "The Movement for Agricultural Reorganization in the Cotton South during the Civil War." *AgH*, 1 (Jan., 1927), 6–7.

[31]This discussion of James Lusk Alcorn is based on the United States Census Bureau's 1860 Census, Schedules No. 1 (Free), No. 2 (Slave), and No. 4 (Agriculture) for Coahoma County, Mississippi, on microfilm in the University of North Carolina Library; James Lusk Alcorn Papers, SHC; P. L. Rainwater, ed., "Letters of James Lusk Alcorn," *JSH*, 5 (May, 1939), 196–209; and Lillian A. Pereyra, *James Lusk Alcorn: Persistent Whig*.

[32]Quoted in Roland, *Louisiana Sugar Plantations*, 110.

[33]Quoted in James W. Silver, ed., *Mississippi in the Confederacy: As Seen in Retrospect*, 273.

[34]Quoted in Bettersworth, ed., *Mississippi in the Confederacy*, 218.

[35]Isaac Shoemaker Diary, April 15, 1864, Duke.

[36]Dolly Burge Diary, June 3, 1862, Burge-Gray Papers, Emory.

[37]Bettie Brownrigg to Mrs. J. L. Bailey, Oct. 16, 1861, John Lancaster Bailey Papers, SHC.

[38]Charles Smallwood Diary, April 2, 1862, and Feb. 20, 1863, SHC.

[39]Alexander McBee to Vardry A. McBee, Aug. 26, 1863, McBee Family Papers, SHC.

[40]Richard Ivanhoe Cocke to Charles Ellis, April 15, 1864, Munford-Ellis Family Papers, Duke.

[41]Jonathan M. Wiener, "Planter Persistence and Social Change: Alabama, 1850–1870" (paper presented at the annual meeting of the Organization of American Historians, Boston, April, 1975).

[42]C. D. Whittle to L. N. Whittle, July 24, 1860, Lewis Neale Whittle Papers, SHC. A Mississippi gentleman said, "A Man would do better to have a good Negro driver, than to have an overseer, & not oversee him, for they are as a class a worthless set of vagabonds, to treat them as Gentlemen turns their heads completely." Everard Green Baker Diary, July 1, 1858, SHC. A recent study argues that a majority of planters did use black drivers to manage the field operations of their plantations, but the study seriously underestimates the number of white overseers in the antebellum South. Robert William Fogel and Stanley L. Engerman, *Time on the Cross: The Economics of American Negro Slavery*, 200–201, 210–12.

[43]Thomas Thompson to "Pat," March 7, 1864, Lewis Thompson Papers, SHC.

[44]Mrs. E. W. Stiles to William Stiles, Oct. 10, 1862, Mackay and Stiles Family Papers, SHC.

[45]William McKinley to David C. Barrow, Nov. 1, 1861, Colonel David Crenshaw Barrow Papers, UGa.

[46]"An Old Man" to Lewis Neale Whittle, July 25, 1863, Lewis Neale Whittle Papers, SHC.

[47]Quoted in Bettersworth, ed., *Mississippi in the Confederacy*, 77.

[48]Quoted in Bryan, *Confederate Georgia*, 123.

[49]Mrs. Mary Jones to Charles C. Jones, Jr., May 19, 1863, May 29, 1863, and Sept. 24, 1863, in Myers, ed., *Children of Pride*, 1062, 1066, 1104; Anne Firor Scott, *The Southern Lady: From Pedestal to Politics, 1830–1930*, 34–36. Some women, such as Sallie Radford Munford of Virginia, bridled at having to play the "woman's part." "I do long sometimes to be a man that I too might fight for so glorious a cause," she said in June, 1863. She complained about "how hard it was to wait, and that *patiently*, until others shall strike the decisive blow." Quoted in Douglas Southall Freeman, *The South to Posterity: An Introduction to the Writing of Confederate History*, 108.

[50]A. H. Boykin to his wife, May 7, 1861, Boykin Family Papers, SHC.

[51]Mrs. Catherine Ann Edmondston Diaries, Feb. 12, 1862, NCAH.

[52]Though most women entered their new duties enthusiastically, not all succeeded. One wife begged her husband to come back home. The plantation was going to pot, she said, and she was "tired of playing the heroine." Mrs. A. H. Boykin to her husband, July 4, 1862, Boykin Family Papers, SHC. The literature on women in the Confederacy is large and growing. The most recent discussion is Bell Irvin Wiley, *Confederate Women*.

[53]George Hairston to Bettie Hairston, Oct. 10, 1861, Hairston and Wilson Family Papers, SHC. Women were also apparently allowed to nurse the wounded while they talked. Henry Graves described the women in Richmond: "Young and beautiful ladies sitting on couches of the wounded soldiers talking to them, fanning, feeding & cheering them. Who would not fight for such women?" Henry L. Graves to Iverson L. Graves, June 6, 1862, Graves Family Papers, SHC.

[54]Dolly Burge Diary, Dec. 31, 1861, Burge-Gray Papers, Emory.

[55]Henry Effingham Lawrence to Frances Lawrence, Dec. 10, 1862, Brashear Family Papers, SHC.

[56]Octavia Otey Diary, Sept. 10, 1864, Wyche and Otey Family Papers, SHC.

[57]Charles Smallwood Diary, April 7, 1864, SHC.

[58]Memorandum, 1864, Heyward and Ferguson Family Papers, SHC.

[59]Account slip, Feb., 1864, Gregorie and Elliott Family Papers, SHC.

[60]S. M. Hunt to "Jennie," Oct. 15, 1861, Hughes Family Papers, SHC.

[61]Sally Sparkman to Mrs. J. L. Bailey, Jan. 29, 1862, John Lancaster Bailey Papers, SHC.

[62]Dolly Burge Diary, June 3, 1862, Burge-Gray Papers, Emory.

[63]William Cooper Diaries, Jan. 9, 1865, SHC. Some planters were on the creditor side with respect to this problem and were angry about having to accept Confederate money in payment for debts. "This law benefits the debtors but is ruin to men who loaned money," David Gavin complained. David Gavin Diary, Oct. 29, 1863, SHC. John Houston Bills fumed that the currency was almost worthless but that he had to accept it "because the pressure of public opinion demands it." John Houston Bills Diary, March 20, 1862, John Houston Bills Papers, SHC.

[64]Robert Toombs to Linton Stephens, Dec. 1, 1862, in Phillips, ed., *Correspondence of Toombs, Stephens, and Cobb*, vol. 2, 609.

[65]James H. Nichols to William Porcher Miles, Oct. 21, 1861, William Porcher Miles Papers, SHC.

[66]D. L. Rivers to John Perkins, April 9, 1863, John Perkins Papers, SHC.

[67]S. M. Hunt to "Jennie," Oct. 15, 1861, Hughes Family Papers, SHC.

[68]James H. Nicholas to William Porcher Miles, Oct. 21, 1861, William Porcher Miles Papers, SHC.

[69]Frank E. Vandiver, *Their Tattered Flags*, 95.

[70]Lemuel P. Conner to "Fanny," March 30, 1863, Lemuel Parker Conner Family Papers, LSU.

[71]Robert Toombs to W. M. Burwell, Aug. 29, 1863, in Phillips, ed., *Correspondence of Toombs, Stephens, and Cobb*, vol. 2, 627.

[72]Ella Gertrude (Clanton) Thomas Journal, Oct. 22, 1864, Duke.

[73]William King Diary, July, 1864, William King Papers, SHC.

[74]This discussion of Catherine Edmondston is based on Mrs. Catherine Ann Edmondston Diaries, NCAH.

[75]Charles Ellis to Powhatan Ellis, March 8, 1865, Munford-Ellis Family Papers, Duke.

[76]Robert Toombs to Linton Stephens, Dec. 1, 1862, in Phillips, ed., *Correspondence of Toombs, Stephens, and Cobb*, vol. 2, 609.

[77]Frank W. Klingberg, *The Southern Claims Commission*, 160.

[78]*Ibid.*, 103–105.

[79]Walter McGehee Lowrey, "The Political Career of James Madison Wells," *LaHQ*, 31 (Oct., 1948), 995–1009.

[80]Quoted in Herbert H. Lang, "J. F. H. Claiborne at 'Laurel Wood' Plantation, 1853–1870," *JMH*, 18 (Jan., 1956), 11–12.

[81]Stephen E. Ambrose, "Yeoman Discontent in the Confederacy," *CWH*, 8 (Sept., 1962), 259–68; Georgia Lee Tatum, *Disloyalty in the Confederacy, passim*.

[82]George M. Fredrickson, *The Black Image in the White Mind: The Debate on Afro-American Character and Destiny, 1817–1914*, 61–68, 93–94.

[83]Alfred Huger to W. T. Seale, Aug. 8, 1854, Alfred Huger Papers, Duke. The

Alabama fire-eater William L. Yancey expressed the same thought more completely before a Northern audience in 1860. "Your fathers and my fathers built this government on two ideas: the first is that the white race is the citizen, and the master race, and the white man is the equal of every other white man. The second idea is that the Negro is the inferior race." Quoted in Fredrickson, *The Black Image*, 61.

[84]James Wilson White to Sam White, Nov. 29, 1864, James Wilson White Papers, SHC.

[85]Joseph Hubbard Saunders to Laura A. Saunders, July 25, 1862, Joseph Hubbard Saunders Papers, SHC.

[86]Cadwallader Jones, Jr., to Fanny I. Erwin, Jan. 11, 1862, Cadwallader Jones, Jr., Papers, SHC.

[87]Charles C. Jones, Jr., to Rev. C. C. Jones, Feb. 21, 1862, in Myers, ed., *Children of Pride*, 850.

[88]Mrs. Catherine Ann Edmondston Diaries, June 27, 1861, NCAH.

[89]John Dobbins to Joseph Dobbins, May 31, 1863, John S. Dobbins Papers, Emory.

[90]Dolly Burge Diary, Dec. 31, 1865, Burge-Gray Papers, Emory.

[91]Ella Gertrude (Clanton) Thomas Journal, April 17, 1862, Duke.

[92]Vardry McBee to Vardry A. McBee, April 14, 1859, McBee Family Papers, SHC.

[93]Quoted in Dolly Burge Diary, Feb. 14, 1862, Burge-Gray Papers, Emory.

[94]Mrs. Catherine Ann Edmondston Diaries, March 20, 1862, and May 28, 1861, NCAH.

[95]J. A. Wemyss to Henry Watson, Jr., Jan. 28, 1862, Henry Watson, Jr., Papers, Duke.

[96]Mrs. Catherine Ann Edmondston Diaries, May 10, 1862, NCAH.

[97]Rev. C. C. Jones to Charles C. Jones, Jr., March 3, 1862, in Myers, ed., *Children of Pride*, 855.

[98]Dolly Burge Diary, Nov. 22, 1864, Burge-Gray Papers, Emory.

[99]William King Diary, July 11, 1864, William King Papers, SHC.

[100]Quoted in Gates, *Agriculture and the Civil War*, 34.

[101]Isaac Applewhite to Governor Pettus, July 15, 1862, in Bettersworth, ed., *Mississippi in the Confederacy*, 227.

[102]Quoted in E. Merton Coulter, "Movement for Agricultural Reorganization in the Cotton South during the Civil War," 7.

[103]Ambrose, "Yeoman Discontent in the Confederacy," 266.

[104]Quoted in Horace Montgomery, *Johnny Cobb: Confederate Aristocrat*, 53.

[105]S. M. Hunt to Jennie [illegible], Oct. 15, 1861, Hughes Family Papers, SHC.

[106]Dolly Burge Diary, May 1, 1862, Burge-Gray Papers, Emory.

[107]Mrs. Catherine Ann Edmondston Diaries, Dec., 1861, NCAH.

[108]Diary of Thomas Watson, June 19, 1864, Watson Papers, UVa.

[109]L. W. Hopkins to James Gregorie, Oct. 11, 1863, Gregorie and Elliott Family Papers, SHC.

[110]C. Chesnut to Mrs. Manning, Nov. 8, 1863, Williams-Chesnut-Manning Papers, SCL.

[111]Elisha Laurey to John Dobbins, April 3, 1864, John S. Dobbins Papers, Emory.

[112]Mrs. Catherine Ann Edmondston Diaries, Aug. 26, 1862, NCAH; Sallie Dillard to Mrs. J. L. Bailey, March 26, 1863, John Lancaster Bailey Papers, SHC.

[113]Alfred Huger to W. T. Seale, Aug. 8, 1854, Alfred Huger Papers, Duke.

[114]Quoted in Kirwan, ed., *The Confederacy*, 264–65.

[115]Mrs. Catherine Ann Edmondston Diaries, June 10, 1863, May 10, 1862, and Feb. 13, 1862, NCAH; Ella Gertrude (Clanton) Thomas Journal, Jan. 1, 1862, Duke.

[116]Randall Lee Gibson to Cora Bell Gibson [wartime], Gibson and Humphreys Family Papers, SHC.

[117]The tendency toward interpreting the conflict in terms of class antagonism was seen in a grim proposal made in August, 1862, by Edmund Ruffin. Ruffin's son's plantation on the James River had been destroyed by Northern soldiers, and he suggested a strategy of "vengeance." The South, he said, should capture some Northern cities—Chicago, Philadelphia, and Cincinnati, for example—and hold them for ransom; if the Federal Government refused to pay, Southerners should turn them over to the oppressed Northern classes, who would certainly plunder them and burn them to the ground. Edmund Ruffin to John Perkins, Aug. 22, 1862, John Perkins Papers, SHC. It is quite likely that Unionists among the planters minimized the cultural differences between the North and South. William King of Cobb County, Georgia, a planter with strong pro-Union sentiments, found the officers of the invading army men of "education, polish and laudable sentiments." He claimed that he did not meet "a single individual whose deportment and language has not been gentlemanly." The officers told him, he said, that "we are one people, the same language, habits and religion, and ought to be one people." He was saddened only by one trait: "the bitter hatred the Northern men seem to feel towards the poor Negro." William King Diary, July 3, 1864, and July 27, 1864, William King Papers, SHC.

[118]Henry Watson, Jr., to Dr. John H. Parrish, April 9, 1864, Henry Watson, Jr., Papers, Duke.

[119]*Congressional Globe*, 38 Cong., 1 Sess., 1185–90. Wendell Phillips demanded that the "intellectual, social, aristocratic South" be "annihilated." Quoted in James M. McPherson, *The Struggle for Equality: Abolitionists and the Negro in the Civil War and Reconstruction*, 221–22.

[120]Rev. C. C. Jones to Chas. C. Jones, Jr., May 9, 1861, in Myers, ed., *Children of Pride*, 676.

[121]Henry Watson, Jr., to [illegible], Jan. 24, 1861, Henry Watson, Jr., Papers, Duke.

[122]Rev. C. C. Jones to Charles C. Jones, Jr., Nov. 15, 1860, in Myers, ed., *Children of Pride*, 628.

[123]Mrs. Catherine Ann Edmondston Diaries, April 10, 1863, NCAH.

[124]William King Diary, July 18, 1864, William King Papers, SHC.

[125]Ella Gertrude (Clanton) Thomas Journal, Jan. 3, 1865, and Feb. 12, 1865, Duke.

[126]Bell Irvin Wiley, *The Plain People of the Confederacy*, 62–65. The planters' fears of upheaval proved unfounded, but they were not totally irrational, for the last stages of an unsuccessful war provide the most likely circumstances for a revolutionary thrust from below. See Chalmers Johnson, *Revolutionary Change*, 91–104.

[127]Henry Watson, Jr., to Dr. John H. Parrish, April 9, 1864, Henry Watson, Jr., Papers, Duke.

[128]Mrs. Catherine Ann Edmondston Diaries, Sept. 28, 1862, NCAH.

## CHAPTER THREE: A LOSS OF MASTERY

[1]Daniel R. Hundley, *Social Relations in Our Southern States*, 49, *passim*.

[2]Frederick Law Olmsted, *The Cotton Kingdom*, *passim*.

[3]One perpetuator of the myth of the planter as a disinterested, ineffectual manager was George Bagby. In his description of the "Virginia gentleman," he said that "the whole of the character is fully told only when you come to open his 'secretary.' There you will find his bonds, accounts, receipts, and even his will, jabbed into pigeon-holes or lying about loose in the midst of a museum of powder-horns, shot-gourds, turkey-yelpers, flints, screws, pop-corn, old horseshoes and watermelon seed." George W. Bagby, *The Old Virginia Gentleman and Other Sketches*, 57. Several historians have recently attempted to replace one myth with another. Rejecting the notion that planters were primitive businessmen, they argue that planters actually anticipated the Frederick W. Taylor school of scientific management. See R. Keith Aufhauser, "Slavery and Scientific Management," *JEH*, 33 (Dec., 1973), 811–24; and Robert William Fogel and Stanley L. Engerman, *Time on the Cross: The Economics of American Negro Slavery*, 200–206.

[4]Alfred Huger to John Preston, Dec. 11, 1856, Alfred Huger Papers, Duke.

[5]Charles C. Jones, Jr., to Rev. C. C. Jones, July 25, 1862; Rev. C. C. Jones to Charles C. Jones, Jr., July 10, 1862, in Robert Manson Myers, ed., *The Children of Pride: A True Story of Georgia and the Civil War*, 940, 929.

[6]George M. Fredrickson, *The Black Image in the White Mind: The Debate on Afro-American Character and Destiny, 1817–1914*, 43–70.

[7]Mrs. Catherine Ann Edmondston Diaries, June 27, 1863, and March 26, 1862, NCAH.

[8]Henry Watson, Jr., to Sarah Carrington, Jan. 28, 1861, Henry Watson, Jr., Papers, Duke.

[9]Mrs. Mary Jones to Charles C. Jones, Jr., May 28, 1863, in Myers, ed., *Children of Pride*, 1063.

[10]Alfred Huger to J. Harleston Read, Nov. 9, 1854, Alfred Huger Papers, Duke.

[11]H. L. Green to his sister, Oct. 29, 1854, Crabtree Jones Papers, NCAH.

[12]Clipping from Sarah J. B. Cain's scrapbook, signed "North Carolina planter," Oct. 12, 1857, John Lancaster Bailey Papers, SHC. While in New York in 1859, a Louisianan wrote to his wife, "I have seen more misery since I have been in this city than I have since I have ben in the union[;] it is awful." He had also seen a great many "expensive things," he said, but he thought that if the money had been spent on "the poore of this City it would have been a greate deal better." Robert A. Newell to Sarah Newell, June 1, 1859, Robert A. Newell Papers, LSU.

[13]Mrs. Catherine Ann Edmondston Diaries, June 1, 1862, NCAH.

[14]David Gavin Diary, Dec. 17, 1859, SHC.

[15]C. D. Whittle to L. N. Whittle, Oct. 30, 1860, Lewis Neale Whittle Papers, SHC.

[16]William Cooper Diaries, April, 1862, SHC.

[17]Henry A. Middleton to Harriott Middleton, Nov. 5, 1862, Langdon Cheves Collection, SCHS.

[18]S. M. Hunt to "Jennie," Oct. 15, 1861, Hughes Family Papers, SHC.

[19]William Kirkland to Octavia Otey, May 22, 1861, Wyche and Otey Family Papers, SHC.

[20]Fanny I. Erwin to Cadwallader Jones, Jr., Jan. 17, 1863, Cadwallader Jones, Jr., Papers, SHC.

[21]John Houston Bills Diary, Dec. 13, 1862, John Houston Bills Papers, SHC.

[22]Charles C. Jones, Jr., to Rev. C. C. Jones, Sept. 27, 1862; Rev. C. C. Jones to Charles C. Jones, Jr., Sept. 30, 1862, in Myers, ed., *Children of Pride*, 967, 969. Because planters believed that emancipation was Lincoln's aim from the beginning, some responded to the proclamation calmly, thinking it a mere formality. See, for example, Ella Gertrude (Clanton) Thomas Journal, Oct. 7, 1862, Duke.

[23]Diary of Thomas Watson, July 4, 1862, Watson Papers, UVa.

[24]Hugh Torrance to Mrs. T. M. Reid, Feb. 16, 1863, George F. Davidson Papers, Duke.

[25]Mrs. Catherine Ann Edmondston Diaries, March 23, 1863, NCAH.

[26]Louis Manigault Diary, Sept., 1862, in Albert V. House, ed., "Deterioration of a Georgia Rice Plantation during Four Years of Civil War," *JSH*, 9 (Feb., 1943), 106.

[27]An appeal to the governor, May 2, 1862, James M. Chestnut, Jr., Letters and Papers, Duke. Even if the Yankees and the Southern nonslaveholders could not convince the slaves to pick up the torch and knife, the planters feared, they could tempt them into running away. C. C. Jones pointed out that runaways destroyed slavery just as effectively as barn burners. And, besides, they might "pilot an enemy into your *bedchamber!*" Rev. C. C. Jones to Charles C. Jones, Jr., July 10, 1862, in Myers, ed., *Children of Pride*, 929.

[28]Charles P. Roland, *Louisiana Sugar Plantations during the American Civil War*, 3; Harold D. Woodman, *King Cotton and His Retainers: Financing and Marketing the Cotton Crop of the South, 1800–1925*, 209, 245.

[29]William King Diary, Sept. 3, 1864, William King Papers, SHC.

[30]Hugh Torrance to Mrs. T. M. Reid, Feb. 16, 1863, George F. Davidson Papers, Duke.

[31]M. McIllhenny to "Ned," June 8, 1863, Weeks Family Papers, Tulane.

[32]Langdon Cheves II to William T. Haskell, March 5, 1862, Langdon Cheves Collection, SCHS. Eugene Genovese brilliantly analyzes the process by which slaves took what masters perceived as privileges and reinterpreted them as rights, which they demanded. Eugene D. Genovese, *Roll, Jordan, Roll: The World the Slaves Made*, *passim*.

[33]J. A. Wemyss to Henry Watson, Jr., Jan. 28, 1862, Henry Watson, Jr., Papers, Duke.

[34]Quoted in John K. Bettersworth, ed., *Mississippi in the Confederacy: As They Saw It*, 224.

[35]James Allen to his wife, Jan., 1864, James Allen and Charles B. Allen Papers, SHC.

[36]John Houston Bills Diary, Oct. 8, 1861, John Houston Bills Papers, SHC.

[37]Quoted in Harrison A. Trexler, "The Opposition of Planters to the Employment of Slaves as Laborers by the Confederacy," *MVHR*, 27 (1940), 213.

[38]*Ibid.*, 217.

[39]Quoted in T. Conn Bryan, *Confederate Georgia*, 132.

[40]Report of William M. Shannon, 1864, Miscellaneous Manuscripts, SCHS.

[41]James H. Brewer, *The Confederate Negro: Virginia's Craftsmen and Military Laborers, 1861–1865*, 152–53.

[42]Susan Dabney Smedes, *Memorials of a Southern Planter*, 196–97.

[43]James B. Heyward to Maria Heyward, Dec. 25, 1864, Heyward and Ferguson Family Papers, SHC.

[44]John Edwin Fripp Diary, 1864 or 1865, John Edwin Fripp Papers, SHC.

[45]Mrs. Catherine Ann Edmondston Diaries, Feb. 12, 1862, March 31, 1862, May 10, 1862, and Sept. 9, 1862, NCAH.

[46]James Lusk Alcorn to Amelia Alcorn, Dec. 18, 1862, James Lusk Alcorn Papers, SHC.

[47]M. M. Green to Mary Jones, Dec. 7, 1863, Crabtree Jones Papers, NCAH.

[48]A. J. Fremantle, *Three Months in the Southern States: April–June 1863*, 45. After Port Royal fell and it appeared that Federal troops would drive up the Savannah River, the Manigaults, simply as a precautionary measure, removed ten slaves from their plantation, "selecting such as we deemed most likely would cause trouble." Charles and Louis Manigault Records, June 12, 1862, GaHS.

[49]Quoted in Bryan, *Confederate Georgia*, 125.

[50]Quoted in H. E. Sterkx, *Partners in Rebellion: Alabama Women in the Civil War*, 132.

[51]Alfred Huger to Thomas Bee Huger, Sept. 15, 1854, Alfred Huger Papers, Duke. Agreeing with Huger's sentiment, another South Carolinian argued that a master should never "desert his negroes." In fact, she declared, "where negroes are deserting to the enemy, their master left them first." Mrs. Manning to John Manning, June 17, 1861, Williams-Chesnut-Manning Papers, SCL.

[52]N. W. E. Long to his wife, June 17, 1862, and Feb. 18, 1863, N. W. E. Long Confederate Soldier's Letters, Emory.

[53]William King Diary, Sept. 6, 1864, William King Papers, SHC.

[54]"Max" to "Buss," Sept. 19, 1862, Williams-Chesnut-Manning Papers, SCL.

[55]Rev. C. C. Jones to Mrs. Eliza G. Robarts, July 5, 1862, in Myers, ed., *Children of Pride*, 925.

[56]Louis Manigault Diary, June 12, 1862, in House, ed., "Deterioration of a Georgia Rice Plantation," 102.

[57]Mrs. Catherine Ann Edmondston Diaries, Sept. 9, 1862, NCAH.

[58]Petition to the Federal Military Command, Georgetown District, March 6, 1865, Sparkman Family Papers, SHC.

[59]Rev. C. C. Jones to Mrs. Eliza G. Robarts, July 5, 1862, in Myers, ed., *Children of Pride*, 925.

[60]Mrs. Mary Jones to Charles C. Jones, Jr., May 28, 1863, in Myers, ed., *Children of Pride*, 958.

[61]Quoted in James W. Silver, ed., *Mississippi in the Confederacy: As Seen in Retrospect*, 286.

[62]Quoted in P. L. Rainwater, ed., "Letters of James Lusk Alcorn," *JSH*, 5 (May, 1939), 207.

[63]Ella Gertrude (Clanton) Thomas Journal, July 21, 1861, Duke.

[64]Henry Graves to a cousin, Oct. 10, 1864, Graves Family Papers, SHC.

[65]A. F. Rightor to Andrew McCollam, Aug. 10, 1864, Andrew McCollam Papers, SHC.

[66]Ella Gertrude (Clanton) Thomas Journal, Dec. 31, 1863, June 28, 1864, July 12, 1864, and March 29, 1865, Duke.

[67]David Gavin Diary, July 8, 1863, SHC.

[68]William Cooper Diaries, April, 1865, SHC.

[69]Fremantle, *Three Months in the Southern States*, 19–22.

[70]Octavia Otey Diary, Oct. 3, 1864, Wyche and Otey Family Papers, SHC.

[71]Quoted in J. Carlyle Sitterson, "The Transition from Slave to Free Economy on the William J. Minor Plantations," *AgH*, 17 (Oct., 1943), 219.

[72]Ella Gertrude (Clanton) Thomas Journal, Dec. 26, 1864, and March 29, 1865, Duke.

[73]Louis Bringier to "Stella," Dec. 31, 1864, Louis Amedee Bringier Papers, LSU.

[74]C. D. Whittle to L. N. Whittle, July 24, 1860, and Sept. 29, 1860, Lewis Neale Whittle Papers, SHC.

[75]Robert Newell to Sarah Newell, Jan. 24, 1863, Robert A. Newell Papers, LSU.

[76]Henry L. Graves to Iverson Graves, Feb. 29, 1864, Graves Family Papers, SHC.

[77]Quoted in Bryan, *Confederate Georgia*, 125.

[78]John L'Engle to Edward L'Engle, March 11, 1863, Edward McCrady L'Engle Papers, SHC.

[79]Rev. John Jones to Mrs. Mary Jones, Dec. 7, 1863, in Myers, ed., *Children of Pride*, 1121.

[80]Ella Gertrude (Clanton) Thomas Journal, May 29, 1865, Duke.

[81]Quoted in Bell Irvin Wiley, *The Plain People of the Confederacy*, 83.

[82]C. Chesnut to Mrs. Manning, Nov. 8, 1863, Williams-Chesnut-Manning Papers, SCL.

[83]Ella Gertrude (Clanton) Thomas Journal, Jan. 2, 1858, and May 23, 1864, Duke.

[84]Dolly Burge Diary, Nov. 8, 1864, Burge-Gray Papers, Emory.

[85]Quoted in Frank W. Klingberg, *The Southern Claims Commission*, 108.

[86]Robert Brent Toplin, "The Specter of Crisis: Slaveholder Reactions to Abolitionism in the United States and Brazil," *CWH*, 18 (June, 1972), 132; Robert Brent Toplin, *The Abolition of Slavery in Brazil*, 225–46.

[87]The following discussion of Bills is based entirely on material from the twenty-seven volumes of the John Houston Bills Diary, John Houston Bills Papers, SHC.

[88]For a provocative discussion of this topic, see Chalmers Johnson, *Revolutionary Change*, 35–110.

[89]Arguing what he calls the principle of conservation of cognitive structure, Anthony Wallace reaches persuasive conclusions about what happens to thought systems when social systems become disrupted. His argument helps explain why the minds of individual planters did not automatically reflect social reality. First, Wallace argues, individuals will not abandon their particular world view, even when faced with direct evidence of its current inutility, without having had an opportunity to construct a new viewpoint. Second, their confrontation with contradictory evidence will arouse anxiety-denial responses. And third, the abandonment of an old ideology is easier when convincing substitutes are made available. Anthony F. Wallace, *Culture and Personality*, *passim*.

[90]William King Diary, July 24, 1864, William King Papers, SHC.

[91]Rev. John Jones to Mrs. Mary S. Mallard, July 1, 1864, in Myers, ed., *Children of Pride*, 1189.

[92]Ella Gertrude (Clanton) Thomas Journal, September 17, 1864, Duke.

⁹³Louis Manigault Diary, June 12, 1862, in House, "Deterioration of a Georgia Rice Plantation," 102.

⁹⁴A. H. Boykin to his wife, Dec. 4, 1861, Boykin Family Papers, SHC.

⁹⁵James W. Silver, *Confederate Morale and Church Propaganda, passim.*

⁹⁶Dolly Burge Diary, Nov. 8, 1864, Burge-Gray Papers, Emory.

⁹⁷For a fuller discussion, see Sudie Duncan Sides, "Women and Slaves: An Interpretation Based on the Writings of Southern Women" (Ph.D. dissertation, University of North Carolina, 1969), *passim;* and Anne Firor Scott, *The Southern Lady: From Pedestal to Politics, 1830–1930,* 46–52.

⁹⁸Ella Gertrude (Clanton) Thomas Journal, Jan. 3, 1865, Duke. In the most famous of Southern Civil War diaries, Mary Boykin Chesnut said, "Under slavery, we live surrounded by prostitutes. . . ." Ben Ames Williams, ed., *A Diary from Dixie by Mary Boykin Chesnut,* 21.

⁹⁹Dolly Burge Diary, Nov. 8, 1864, Burge-Gray Papers, Emory.

¹⁰⁰Kenneth M. Stampp, *The Southern Road to Appomattox,* 18.

¹⁰¹Clement Eaton, *The Mind of the Old South,* 24–41; Martin Boyd Coyner, Jr., "John Hartwell Cocke of Bremo: Agriculture and Slavery in the Ante-Bellum South" (Ph.D. dissertation, University of Virginia, 1961), *passim.*

¹⁰²The discussion of John Hartwell Cocke in this and the following paragraph is based on his "Journal or Commonplace Book, 1863–1864," John Hartwell Cocke Papers, UVa.

¹⁰³Henry L. Graves to "Aunt Sibbie," Sept. 4, 1861, Graves Family Papers, SHC.

¹⁰⁴Mrs. Catherine Ann Edmondston Diaries, May 2, 1862, NCAH.

¹⁰⁵Frederick G. Skinner to Charles Ellis, Sept. 8, 1865, Munford-Ellis Family Papers, Duke.

¹⁰⁶Quoted in Robert F. Durden, *The Gray and the Black: The Confederate Debate on Emancipation,* 233–34.

¹⁰⁷*Ibid.,* 7, 234.

¹⁰⁸Quoted in Charles H. Wesley, "The Employment of Negroes as Soldiers in the Confederate Army," *JNH,* 4 (July, 1919), 246. At about the same moment, General Robert E. Lee arrived at the same conclusion. In January, 1865, he said that the South "must decide whether slavery shall be extinguished by our enemies and the slaves used against us, or use them ourselves at the risk of the effects which may be produced upon our social institutions." *Ibid.,* 249.

¹⁰⁹Durden, *The Gray and the Black,* 70.

¹¹⁰*Ibid.,* 232, 114.

¹¹¹Quoted in Nathaniel W. Stephenson, "The Question of Arming the Slaves," *AHR,* 18 (Jan., 1913), 300. Also see John Brawner Robbins, "Confederate Nationalism: Politics and Government in the Confederate South, 1861–1865" (Ph.D. dissertation, Rice University, 1964), 119–21; and John E. Fisher, "Statesman of the Lost Cause: R. M. T. Hunter and the Sectional Controversy, 1847–1887" (Ph.D. dissertation, University of Virginia, 1968), 237–39.

¹¹²Lawrence J. Friedman, *The White Savage: Racial Fantasies in the Postbellum South,* 15–16.

¹¹³Quoted in Durden, *The Gray and the Black,* 142.

¹¹⁴Charles Ellis to Powhatan Ellis, Jan. 8, 1865, Munford-Ellis Family Papers, Duke.

¹¹⁵Crenshaw Hall to "Laura," March 12, 1865, Bolling Hall Papers, ADAH.

[116]Mrs. Catherine Ann Edmondston Diaries, Dec. 30, 1864, NCAH. Also see the Ella Gertrude (Clanton) Thomas Journal, Nov. 11, 1864, Duke.

[117]Quoted in Friedman, *White Savage*, 14. Interestingly, a large number of planters did not comment at all on the slave-arming idea. It is possible that working planters dismissed the idea so thoroughly as to pay it little notice, but more likely, they simply lacked accurate information about the new program. Illustrative of the muddled communications in the last chaotic days of the Confederacy was the statement of Thomas Barrow on March 29, 1865, that "Congress has only passed a bill to put negroes in as teamsters and engineers, not as soldiers." Thomas Barrow to "Poole," March 29, 1865, Colonel David Crenshaw Barrow Papers, UGa.

[118]Thomas B. Alexander and Richard E. Beringer, *The Anatomy of the Confederate Congress: A Study of the Influences of Member Characteristics on Legislative Voting Behavior, 1861–1865, passim.*

[119]*Ibid.*, 256–57.

[120]William H. Stiles to his wife, July 25, 1865, MacKay and Stiles Family Papers, SHC.

[121]Mrs. Catherine Ann Edmondston Diaries, May 8, 1865, NCAH.

[122]Ella Gertrude (Clanton) Thomas Journal, May 8, 1865, and Oct. 9, 1865, Duke; Mary Elizabeth Massey, "The Making of a Feminist," *JSH*, 39 (Feb., 1973), 10.

[123]Joseph Buckner Killebrew Autobiography, I, 191, SHC.

[124]Diary of Thomas Watson, June 10, 1864, Watson Papers, UVa.

[125]"Notes on Brazil during the years of 1867 to 1880," George Scarborough Barnsley Papers, SHC.

[126]Quoted in Stampp, *The Southern Road to Appomattox*, 21.

[127]*Ibid.*, 20–21.

[128]Wiley T. Burge to Dolly Burge, June 1, 1865, Burge-Gray Papers, Emory.

[129]John Parrish to Henry Watson, Jr., June 19, 1865, and July 30, 1865, Henry Watson, Jr., Papers, Duke.

[130]Quoted in Bettersworth, ed., *Mississippi in the Confederacy*, 354.

[131]Most helpful to me in understanding ideologies and how they change have been Wallace, *Culture and Personality*; Karl Mannheim, *Ideology and Utopia* (New York: Harcourt, Brace and Co., 1936); and Thomas Kuhn, *The Structure of Scientific Revolutions*, Second ed. (Chicago: University of Chicago Press, 1970). For the impact of disasters upon belief systems, I found particularly helpful Martha Wolfenstein, *Disaster: A Psychological Essay*; and Robert Jay Lifton, *History and Human Survival: Essays on the Young and Old, Survivors and the Dead, Peace and War, and on Contemporary Psychohistory.*

## CHAPTER FOUR: BRICKS WITHOUT STRAW

[1]Willie Lee Rose, *Rehearsal for Reconstruction: The Port Royal Experiment, passim.*

[2]Magnolia Plantation Journals, Aug. 11, 1862, Nov. 1, 1862, Tulane; J. Carlyle Sitterson, "Magnolia Plantation, 1852–1862: A Decade of a Louisiana Sugar Estate," *MVHR*, 25 (Sept., 1938), 206.

[3]Quoted in Barnes Fletcher Lathrop, "The Pugh Plantations, 1860–1865: A Study of Life in Lower Louisiana" (Ph.D. dissertation, University of Texas, 1945), 177.

[4]William F. Messner, "Black Violence and White Response: Louisiana, 1862," *JSH*, 41 (Feb., 1975), 19–27.

[5]Lathrop, "The Pugh Plantations," 200.

[6]Quoted in Charles P. Roland, *Louisiana Sugar Plantations during the American Civil War*, 57.

[7]Quoted in Frank W. Klingberg, *The Southern Claims Commission*, 204.

[8]Thomas McGruder to "My dear friends," Dec. 28, 1863, Thomas Affleck Papers, LSU.

[9]Joe Gray Taylor, "Slavery in Louisiana during the Civil War," *LaH*, 8 (Winter, 1967), 27–33.

[10]Ellen McCollam to Andrew McCollam, Jr., March 26, 1863, Andrew McCollam Papers, SHC.

[11]Quoted in J. Carlyle Sitterson, "The Transition from Slave to Free Economy on the William J. Minor Plantations," *AgH*, 17 (Oct., 1943), 217–18.

[12]For a full description of the new labor program and how it fit within the broad war and Reconstruction strategy of the Federal Government, see two excellent studies: Louis S. Gerteis, *From Contraband to Freedman: Federal Policy toward Southern Blacks, 1861–1865*, 65–115; and James Peyton McCrary, "Moderation in a Revolutionary World: Lincoln and the Failure of Reconstruction in Louisiana" (Ph.D. dissertation, Princeton University, 1972), *passim*.

[13]J. Thomas May, "Continuity and Change in the Labor Program of the Union Army and the Freedmen's Bureau," *CWH*, 17 (Sept., 1971), 245–51.

[14]Thomas Gale to his wife, July 17, 1863, Gale and Polk Family Papers, SHC.

[15]Bell Irvin Wiley, "Vicissitudes of Early Reconstruction Farming in the Lower Mississippi Valley," *JSH*, 3 (Nov., 1937), 444.

[16]But for statements supporting the notion that the desires of the army and of the planters converged in the new labor program, see May, "Continuity and Change," 254, and Messner, "Black Violence and White Response," 36.

[17]McCrary, "Moderation in a Revolutionary World," 130; Taylor, "Slavery in Louisiana," 29.

[18]Quoted in James M. McPherson, *The Struggle for Equality: Abolitionists and the Negro in the Civil War and Reconstruction*, 290.

[19]James Lusk Alcorn to Amelia Alcorn, March 22, 1864, James Lusk Alcorn Papers, SHC.

[20]Quoted in Lathrop, "The Pugh Plantations," 300–303.

[21]Quoted in Wiley, "Vicissitudes of Early Reconstruction Farming," 444–50.

[22]McCrary, "Moderation in a Revolutionary World," 130.

[23]Quoted in Sitterson, "The Transition from Slave to Free Economy," 220.

[24]Quoted in Lathrop, "The Pugh Plantations," 343.

[25]Still helpful is Roger W. Shugg, *Origins of Class Struggle in Louisiana: A Social History of White Farmers and Laborers During Slavery and After, 1840–1875*, 134–55, 196–205, although for the war years it is now superseded by McCrary, "Moderation in a Revolutionary World."

[26]Quoted in Wiley, "Vicissitudes of Early Reconstruction Farming," 442.

[27]Isaac Shoemaker Diary, Feb., 1864, Duke. His principles went beyond words. He

voluntarily agreed to pay the Confederate owner of the plantation he managed a rent of four dollars an acre because he had "a particular objection to taking a place & farming it without consent of & compensation to the owner." Isaac Shoemaker Diary, March 4, 1864, Duke.

²⁸*Ibid.*, March 20, 1864, April 2, 1864, April 24, 1864, April 28, 1864, and May 4, 1864.

²⁹Quoted in McCrary, "Moderation in a Revolutionary World," 129. Herbert Gutman brilliantly analyzes the meaning for the working class of the transition from a preindustrial to an industrial society. While the shift from slave to free labor was different, it still shares some of the same characteristics. Herbert G. Gutman, "Work, Culture, and Society in Industrializing America, 1815–1919," *AHR*, 78 (June, 1973), 531–88.

³⁰Roland, *Louisiana Sugar Plantations*, 75–77; Taylor, "Slavery in Louisiana," 27–33.

³¹Quoted in Sitterson, "The Transition from Slave to Free Economy," 219; Shugg, *Origins of Class Struggle in Louisiana*, 191–92.

³²Quoted in Sitterson, "The Transition from Slave to Free Economy," 220–21.
³³*Ibid.*, 221.

³⁴Whitelaw Reid, *After the War: A Tour of the Southern States, 1865–1866*, 34.

³⁵William R. Taylor, *Cavalier and Yankee: The Old South and American National Character*, 316–18; Edmund Ruffin to John Perkins, Aug. 22, 1862, John Perkins Papers, SHC.

³⁶George Scarborough Barnsley, "Notes on Brazil during the years of 1867 to 1880," George Scarborough Barnsley Papers, SHC.

³⁷Julia Louisa (Hentz) Keyes Manuscript, SHC.

³⁸Mrs. Elizabeth B. Waddell to Mrs. J. L. Bailey, Jan. 29, 1866, John Lancaster Bailey Papers, SHC.

³⁹William Heyward to John Jenkins, July 22, 1865, John Jenkins Papers, SCL.

⁴⁰Lawrence F. Hill, "The Confederate Exodus to Latin America," *SwHQ*, 39 (Oct., 1935), 122.

⁴¹Andrew F. Rolle, *The Lost Cause: The Confederate Exodus to Mexico*, 140.

⁴²"Loula" [Grimes] to "Poss" [Grimes], May 22, 1865, Graves Family Papers, SHC.

⁴³George W. Munford to Mrs. E. T. Munford, May 9, 1865, Munford-Ellis Family Papers, Duke.

⁴⁴Thomas McGruder to "My dear friends," Dec. 28, 1863, Thomas Affleck Papers, LSU.

⁴⁵Rolle, *The Lost Cause*, 8.

⁴⁶Robert Toombs to Alexander Stephens, Dec. 15, 1865, in Ulrich Bonnell Phillips, ed., *The Correspondence of Robert Toombs, Alexander H. Stephens, and Howell Cobb*, vol. 2, 673.

⁴⁷William H. B. Richardson to James B. Richardson, July 24, 1866, James Burchell Richardson Letters and Papers, Duke.

⁴⁸J. D. Porter to Charles Nathan, Oct. 14, 1867, J. D. Porter Letters, SHC.

⁴⁹Quoted in Hill, "The Confederate Exodus to Latin America," 110–11.

⁵⁰G. S. Crafts to William Porcher Miles, April 13, 1867, William Porcher Miles Papers, SHC.

⁵¹F. W. Johnstone to James Sparkman, Feb. 7, 1869, Sparkman Family Papers, SHC.

52Lucy Judkins Durr, "Brazilian Recollections," Judkins-Durr Papers, ADAH.

53Henry Graves to his brother, Sept. 2, 1867, Graves Family Papers, SHC.

54Robert E. Shalhope, "Race, Class, Slavery, and the Antebellum Southern Mind," JSH, 37 (Nov., 1971), 566. One prospective citizen of Mexico thought the "despotism of one man is better than the despotism of a sectional majority." Jeremiah Morton to John Hartwell Cocke, Feb. 22, 1866, John Hartwell Cocke Papers, UVa.

55George Scarborough Barnsley, "Notes on Brazil during the years of 1867 to 1880," George Scarborough Barnsley Papers, SHC.

56See Julia Keyes's descriptions of the young Southern cavaliers in Brazil, in Julia Louisa (Hentz) Keyes Manuscript, SHC.

57 Lucy Judkins Durr, "Brazilian Recollections," Judkins-Durr Papers, ADAH.

58George Scarborough Barnsley, "Notes on Brazil during the years of 1867 to 1880," George Scarborough Barnsley Papers, SHC.

59Henry M. Price to Lafayette McLaws, April 20, 1866, Lafayette McLaws Papers, SHC.

60Shalhope, "Race, Class, Slavery, and the Antebellum Southern Mind," 572–73. One other obvious difference between Brazil and Mexico—geography—did seem to affect the emigrants' decision to go to one or the other. Mexico's proximity meant that it attracted more Southerners who were simply looking for a place to run to rather than for a new, permanent homeland. Flight to Mexico was often a temporary strategy—retreat to a vantage point from which to watch developments in the South. Southern political figures, consequently, including several governors and former governors, flocked to Mexico. Brazil, on the other hand, seemed to demand a more serious commitment to permanent exile, for it certainly did not provide a convenient window from which to view the homeland.

61Not every planter adopted this image of Mexicans, however. A Texas planter, who desperately wanted to get away from "free negroes . . . and low whites," refused to go to Mexico unless he could "people it with Scotch and English," because he knew those "greasers." Thomas Affleck Diary, Sept., 1863, and Thomas Affleck to his wife, Feb. 24, 1866, Thomas Affleck Papers, LSU.

62For an excellent analysis of changing white attitudes toward free blacks in the antebellum South, see Ira Berlin, Slaves without Masters: The Free Negro in the Antebellum South.

63Quoted in Hill, "The Confederate Exodus to Latin America," 180.

64J. D. Porter to Charles Nathan, Oct. 14, 1867, J. D. Porter Letters, SHC.

65C. G. Gunter to W. A. Gunter, Dec. 21, 1865, Gunter and Poellnitz Papers, SHC.

66C. G. Gunter to W. A. Gunter, Aug. 23, 1866, Gunter and Poellnitz Papers, SHC.

67Harris Gunter to W. A. Gunter, Aug. 24, 1866, Gunter and Poellnitz Papers, SHC.

68C. G. Gunter to W. A. Gunter, Sept. 25, 1866, Gunter and Poellnitz Papers, SHC.

69C. G. Gunter to W. A. Gunter, Dec. 23, 1866, Gunter and Poellnitz Papers, SHC.

70Nearly half a century later, emigré George Barnsley remembered that Charles Gunter had been a respected planter who treated his slaves well, "but certainly they had to get a move on themselves." George Scarborough Barnsley, "Original of Reply to a

Circular for information of the Ex-Confederate emigrants, April, 1915," George Scarborough Barnsley Papers, SHC.

[71]Harris Gunter to W. A. Gunter, Nov. 6, 1866, Gunter and Poellnitz Papers, SHC.

[72]The discussion of Andrew McCollam's journey to Brazil which begins in this paragraph is based upon the diary he kept from May, 1866, through Sept., 1866. Andrew McCollam Papers, SHC.

[73]McCollam's sense of superiority and his assumption of a relatively highly developed Protestant ethic were common among Americans who visited Brazil. See Carl N. Degler, *Neither Black nor White: Slavery and Race Relations in Brazil and the United States,* 246–48.

[74]As Carl Degler has explained, descriptions of Brazilian race relations by Americans are suspect because visitors from the United States did not recognize mulattoes as a separate caste. They could not "see" brown, only black and white. *Ibid.,* 196.

[75]Robert Brent Toplin, *The Abolition of Slavery in Brazil,* 14–19.

[76]Douglas Audenried Grier, "Confederate Emigration to Brazil, 1865–1870" (Ph.D. dissertation, University of Michigan, 1968), 88–90.

[77]Blanche Henry Clark Weaver, "Confederate Emigration to Brazil," *JSH,* 27 (Feb., 1961), 47–50.

[78]Diary of Andrew McCollam's Cuban Trip, February-March, 1867, Andrew McCollam Papers, SHC.

[79]Robert Toombs to Alexander Stephens, Dec. 15, 1865, in Phillips, ed., *Correspondence of Toombs, Stephens, and Cobb,* vol. 2, 675.

[80]Whitelaw Reid, *After the War,* 194–98.

[81]George Scarborough Barnsley, "Notes on Brazil during the years of 1867 to 1880," George Scarborough Barnsley Papers, SHC.

[82]Rev. John Jones to Mrs. Mary Jones, Aug. 21, 1865, in Robert Manson Myers, ed., *The Children of Pride: A True Story of Georgia and the Civil War,* 1293.

[83]John Dobbins to Elisha Laurey, Jan. 29, 1866, John S. Dobbins Papers, Emory.

[84]R. R. Porter to Col. Barrow, Oct. 8, 1865, Colonel David Crenshaw Barrow Papers, UGa.

[85]George Scarborough Barnsley, "Reflections on Brazilian Emigration, 1865–1880," George Scarborough Barnsley Papers, SHC.

[86]Mrs. Caroline S. Jones to Mrs. Mary Jones, April 30, 1865, in Myers, ed., *Children of Pride,* 1268.

[87]Octavia Otey Diary, Dec. 25, 1865, Wyche and Otey Family Papers, SHC.

[88]Mrs. Elizabeth B. Waddell to J. L. Bailey, Jan. 29, 1866, John Lancaster Bailey Papers, SHC. For an excellent introduction to the psychology of planters at the moment of emancipation, see Willie Lee Rose, "Masters without Slaves" (paper presented at the annual meeting of the American Historical Association, New York, December, 1966).

[89]Lillian A. Pereyra, *James Lusk Alcorn: Persistent Whig,* 69–73.

[90]Henry Watson, Jr., to John H. Parrish, April 9, 1864, Henry Watson, Jr., Papers, Duke.

[91]Henry Watson, Jr., to John H. Parrish, Aug. 7, 1865; Henry Watson, Jr., to William P. Webb, Oct. 2, 1865, Henry Watson, Jr., Papers, Duke.

[92]Henry Watson, Jr., to [illegible], Jan. 2, 1866; Henry Watson, Jr., to Sereno Watson, Dec. 10, 1865, Henry Watson, Jr., Papers, Duke.

[93]Howell Cobb to William Stiles, Sept. 10, 1865, Mackay and Stiles Family Papers, SHC.

[94]For the impressions of Northern newspapermen, see J. T. Trowbridge, *The South: A Tour of Its Battle Fields and Ruined Cities*; and John R. Dennett, *The South As It Is: 1865–1866*.

[95]William Henry Stiles to his wife, July 1, 1865, Mackay and Stiles Family Papers, SHC.

[96]Jeremiah Morton to John Perkins, June 6, 1866, John Perkins Papers, SHC.

[97]Quoted in Wendell Holmes Stephenson, "A Quarter-Century of a Mississippi Plantation: Eli J. Capell of 'Pleasant Hill,' " *MVHR*, 23 (Dec., 1936), 372.

[98]For examples from Alabama, see John B. Myers, "Black Human Capital: The Freedmen and the Reconstruction of Labor in Alabama, 1860–1880" (Ph.D. dissertation, Florida State University, 1974), 94, 117.

[99]Thomas Watson to Mrs. V. H. Robertson, Dec. 31, 1867, Watson Papers, UVa.

[100]William H. Heyward to James B. Heyward, April 17, 1866, Heyward and Ferguson Family Papers, SHC.

[101]Robert L. Brandfon, *Cotton Kingdom of the New South: A History of the Yazoo Mississippi Delta from Reconstruction to the Twentieth Century*, 136–37; William H. Heyward to James B. Heyward, April 17, 1866, Heyward and Ferguson Family Papers, SHC.

[102]A. Main to Andrew McCollam, Jr., Feb. 27, 1866, Andrew McCollam Papers, SHC.

[103]Henry Watson, Jr., to J. A. Wemyss, Jan. 26, 1866, Henry Watson, Jr., Papers, Duke.

[104]F. B. Conner to L. P. Conner, Sept. 9, 1866, Nov. 3, 1866, and Feb. 3, 1867, Lemuel Parker Conner Family Papers, LSU.

[105]R. Izard Middleton to Henry A. Middleton, May 29, 1871, Langdon Cheves Collection, SCHS.

[106]John Dobbins to Elisha Laurey, Jan. 29, 1866, John S. Dobbins Papers, Emory.

[107]Kenneth Clark to Lewis Thompson, Aug. 27, 1865, Lewis Thompson Papers, SHC.

[108]Henry Graves to his sister, Jan. 22, 1866, Graves Family Papers, SHC.

[109]Thomas Munford to his mother, Nov. 13, 1865, Munford-Ellis Family Papers, Duke.

[110]Alexander McBee to Vardry A. McBee, March 10, 1867, McBee Family Papers, SHC.

[111]John Berkley Grimball Diary, Nov. 18, 1865, SHC.

[112]Louis D. DeSaussure to A. H. Boykin, Sept. 13, 1865, Sept. 29, 1865, and Dec. 4, 1865, Boykin Family Papers, SHC.

[113]James Varner to Lewis Thompson, July 12, 1866, Lewis Thompson Papers, SHC.

[114]N. N. Ballard to Lewis Thompson, Sept. 2, 1865, Lewis Thompson Papers, SHC.

[115]George W. Munford to Charles Ellis, Jan. 9, 1866, Munford-Ellis Family Papers, Duke.

[116]G. E. Manigault to James B. Heyward, May 22, 1865, Heyward and Ferguson Family Papers, SHC.

[117]Everard Green Baker Diary, May 31, 1865, and Sept. 26, 1865, SHC.

[118]J. A. Wemyss to Henry Watson, Jr., July 14, 1865, Henry Watson, Jr., Papers, Duke.

[119]Charles M. Wallace to Joyce Wallace, Oct. 12, 1865, John Clopton Papers, Duke.

[120]May, "Continuity and Change," 245–54.

[121]For a contrary view of planters' perceptions, see the recent study by William McFeely, who argues, consistent with his thesis that the Freedmen's Bureau actually functioned as a planters' bureau, that planters viewed contracts as promising and progressive business arrangements. Far from being new, he declares, contracts marked the restoration of something old and valuable. The Bureau had rescued planters from their difficulty—they no longer had to feel impotent. William S. McFeely, *Yankee Stepfather: General O. O. Howard and the Freedmen*, 152–53. Some planters did breathe a sigh of relief when they signed their labor contracts. At last, Catherine Edmondston said on January 1, 1866, we have "begun to taste some of the immunities of free negroism." Mrs. Catherine Ann Edmondston Diaries, Jan. 1, 1866, NCAH. But most planters continued to feel powerless and to experience doubt about the new labor system long after the first year of freedom.

[122]Myers, "Black Human Capital," 83–84.

[123]F. B. Conner to L. P. Conner, Feb. 3, 1867, Lemuel Parker Conner Family Papers, LSU.

[124]Thomas Affleck to his wife, March 3, 1866, Thomas Affleck Papers, LSU.

[125]Samuel Andrew Agnew Diary, July 20, 1865, SHC.

[126]Robert Toombs to Alexander Stephens, Dec. 15, 1865, in Phillips, ed., *Correspondence of Toombs, Stephens, and Cobb*, vol. 2, 675.

[127]Frederick G. Skinner to Charles Ellis, Sept. 18, 1865, Munford-Ellis Family Papers, Duke.

[128]E. Taliaferro to L. N. Whittle, June 10, 1865, Lewis Neale Whittle Papers, SHC.

[129]Theodore Brantner Wilson, *The Black Codes of the South, passim.*

[130]Joseph Buckner Killebrew Autobiography, I, 213, SHC.

[131]Cary Charles Cocke to R. D. Powell, Aug., 1867, John Hartwell Cocke Papers, UVa.

[132]Samuel Andrew Agnew Diary, Nov. 27, 1865, SHC. Early contracts often required freedmen "to work on this place as heretofore and to perform all other work that may be required of us." Labor contract, July 29, 1865, John H. Randolph Papers, LSU.

[133]R. Izard Middleton to Henry A. Middleton, Oct. 30, 1866, Langdon Cheves Collection, SCHS.

[134]In the rapidly growing literature on the black response to emancipation, I found most helpful Leon F. Litwack, "Free at Last," in *Anonymous Americans: Explorations in Nineteenth-Century Social History*, edited by Tamara K. Hareven, 131–71; Joël Williamson, *After Slavery: The Negro in South Carolina during Reconstruction, 1861–1877*; and Peter Kolchin, *First Freedom: The Responses of Alabama's Blacks to Emancipation and Reconstruction.*

[135]Mrs. Mary Jones to Mrs. Mary S. Mallard, Nov. 17, 1865, in Myers, ed., *Children of Pride*, 1308. Refusing to rent proved not to be a temporary reaction. As late as 1880, impressive new research demonstrates, renting to blacks for a fixed fee

accounted for only 3.4 per cent of all land in the cotton South. Roger L. Ransom and Richard Sutch, "The Ex-Slave in the Post-Bellum South: A Study of the Economic Impact of Racism in a Market Environment," *JEH*, 33 (March, 1973), 137.

[136]William McBurney to T. B. Ferguson, Feb. 1, 1866, Heyward and Ferguson Family Papers, SHC.

[137]Quoted in Trowbridge, *The South*, 391. Many hundreds of labor contracts are extant for 1865, 1866, and 1867, and they mirror the confusion of Southern agriculture and the ambiguous status of black labor.

[138]Henry Watson, Jr., to Walter S. Pitkin, Dec. 22, 1865, Henry Watson, Jr., Papers, Duke.

[139]Octavia Otey Diary, Jan. 29, 1867, Wyche and Otey Family Papers, SHC.

[140]Joseph H. Saunders to his cousin, Aug. 26, 1866, Joseph Hubbard Saunders Papers, SHC.

[141]James Baker to his sister, Jan. 12, 1866, Joseph Hubbard Saunders Papers, SHC.

[142]A. C. Jones to Cadwallader Jones, July 29, 1866, Cadwallader Jones, Jr., Papers, SHC.

[143]Rev. John Jones to Mrs. Mary Jones, Aug. 21, 1865, in Myers, ed., *Children of Pride*, 1291.

[144]Eugene D. Genovese, *The World the Slaveholders Made: Two Essays in Interpretation*, 121–22.

[145]R. Izard Middleton to Henry A. Middleton, Sept. 5, 1866, Langdon Cheves Collection, SCHS.

[146]Quoted in Williamson, *After Slavery*, 98.

[147]John B. Cocke to John Hartwell Cocke, June 6, 1865, John Hartwell Cocke Papers, UVa.

[148]Quoted in Thomas Wagstaff, "Call Your Old Master—'Master': Southern Political Leaders and Negro Labor during Presidential Reconstruction," *LH*, 10 (Summer, 1969), 33–34. An early historian of this subject concluded that "the planter was far more completely emancipated from the bonds of slavery than was the Negro." Charlton Watson Tebeau, "The Planter in the Lower South, 1865–1880" (Ph.D. dissertation, University of Iowa, 1933), 11. An excellent recent dissertation with white emancipation as its central theme is Robert Arthur Gilmour, "The Other Emancipation: Studies in the Society and Economy of Alabama Whites during Reconstruction" (Ph.D. dissertation, The Johns Hopkins University, 1972).

[149]W. H. Stiles to his wife, Sept. 22, 1865, Mackay and Stiles Family Papers, SHC.

[150]Mrs. Catherine Ann Edmondston Diaries, May 13, 1865, June 26, 1865, and July 2, 1865, NCAH. She thought there was no end to the freedman's foolishness. "Thinks he ought to have Land because his forefathers cleared it and he has worked it, cant beleive [sic] 'Mr. Governor' i.e.—the Government—is going to give him his bare freedom with nothing to maintain it, & many other Agrarian notions. . . ." (Oct. 1, 1865.)

[151]Mrs. Mary Jones to Charles C. Jones, Jr., May 28, 1866, in Myers, ed., *Children of Pride*, 1341. Doubtless, Mary Jones had been deeply hurt by the behavior of blacks on her plantations, and she responded by closing off her affection. But it is also possible that she was unconsciously using the episode as a means of emancipating herself from her self-imposed and increasingly difficult burden. "They have relieved me of the constant

desire and effort to do something to promote their comfort," she said. Paternalism was a heavy load for sensitive souls, especially for those who had so few resources with which to respond. *Ibid.*, 1341.

[152]Dolly Burge Diary, May 29, 1865, Burge-Gray Papers, Emory.

[153]S. Porcher Gaillard Plantation Book, Nov. 15, 1866, SCL.

[154]William Cooper Diaries, May 19, 1865, SHC.

[155]J. D. Collins to John A. Cobb, July 31, 1865, in Phillips, ed., *Correspondence of Toombs, Stephens, and Cobb*, vol. 2, 666.

[156]Andrew McCollam to Andrew J. and Edmond McCollam, July 7, 1866, Andrew McCollam Papers, SHC.

[157]Charles C. Jones, Jr., to Mrs. Mary Jones, Feb. 24, 1866, in Myers, ed., *Children of Pride*, 1321.

[158]A. Graves to Henry Graves, May 19, 1867, Graves Family Papers, SHC.

[159]The McCollam plantation in Louisiana, for example, prospered, despite Andrew McCollam's persistent wanderings in search of a new plantation country. One son wrote his peripatetic father in 1867 that the freedmen were working well and that the crops looked splendid. His only problem, he said tolerantly, was "an unusual number of conjugal jars, and consequent separations of bed and board." Edmond McCollam to Andrew McCollam, March 9, 1867, Andrew McCollam Papers, SHC.

[160]William H. Graham to Henry Graves, Dec. 12, 1866, Graves Family Papers, SHC.

[161]John Floyd King to Lin Caperton, Nov. 15, 1866, Thomas Butler King Papers, SHC.

[162]Tebeau, "The Planter in the Lower South," 61.

[163]Quoted in E. Merton Coulter, "The Movement for Agricultural Reorganization in the Cotton South during the Civil War," *AgH*, 1 (Jan., 1927), 11.

[164]*Southern Cultivator*, Jan.–Feb., 1863, 14, in *ibid.*, 12.

[165]Jennie Newton to George Barnsley, July 31, 1865, George Scarborough Barnsley Papers, SHC.

[166]Mrs. Eva B. Jones to Mrs. Mary Jones, June 27, 1865, in Myers, ed., *Children of Pride*, 1275.

[167]George W. Munford to Charles Ellis, Jan. 9, 1866, Munford-Ellis Family Papers, Duke.

[168]Samuel Andrew Agnew Diary, Jan. 3, 1866, and Jan. 9, 1866, SHC.

[169]Fanny I. Erwin to Cadwallader Jones, Jr., June 6, 1866, Cadwallader Jones, Jr., Papers, SHC.

[170]Frances Aglionby to her sister, May 22, 1865, Frances (Walker) Yates Aglionby Papers, Duke.

[171]Mrs. Caroline Thornton to Charles Ellis, Feb. 20, 1866, Munford-Ellis Family Papers, Duke.

[172]A. Graves to Henry Graves, May 19, 1867, Graves Family Papers, SHC.

[173]Godfrey Barnsley to George Barnsley, May 11, 1870, George Scarborough Barnsley Papers, SHC. But of course not all planters were willing to get their hands dirty. The South Carolina aristocrat William Heyward said in June, 1866, "If the reality ever comes on me that I must labor, I am sure I cannot do it. I must then lie down and die." Quoted in Williamson, *After Slavery*, 116.

[174]J. A. Wemyss to Henry Watson, Jr., Dec. 28, 1866, Henry Watson, Jr., Papers, Duke.

[175]George W. Munford to William Munford, June 10, 1866, Munford-Ellis Family Papers, Duke.

[176]John G. Guignard III to James S. Guignard III, March 27, 1867, in Arney R. Childs, ed., *Planters and Business Men: The Guignard Family of South Carolina, 1795–1930,* 210.

[177]Quoted in Ulrich Bonnell Phillips, "Plantations with Slave Labor and Free," *AHR,* 30 (July, 1925), 748. Writing to his sister about his young nephews, a Virginian said in 1859, "When Shelton & Rol get to be men it will be better for them to have land & negroes than money. Young men squander money, and learn badness, often; when they would not do so, if their property was land and slaves." Thomas S. Watson to F. C. Watson, March 4, 1859, Watson Papers, UVa.

[178] Randall Lee Gibson to Louisiana Gibson, Feb. 13, 1867, Gibson and Humphreys Family Papers, SHC.

[179]James M. Willcox to Susannah Willcox, Nov. 2, 1865, James M. Willcox Letters and Papers, Duke.

[180]Henry Watson, Jr., to James A. Wemyss, Sept. 5, 1865, Henry Watson, Jr., Papers, Duke.

[181]Thomas T. Munford to George W. Munford, 1869, Munford-Ellis Family Papers, Duke.

[182]John Berkley Grimball Diary, Dec. 6, 1865, Feb. 4, 1866, and Oct. 24, 1868, SHC.

[183]John G. Guignard III to James S. Guignard III, Sept. 4, 1868, in Childs, ed., *Planters and Business Men,* 90. When parents expressed concern about the future of their daughters, they were likely to indicate their fear that they were not growing into proper ladies. One mother was desperately trying to gather money "so as to send Ellen to school somewhere, she is going rapidly to seed, without culture, grace or refinement." Mrs. E. C. Rives to Susannah Willcox, June 7, 1866, James M. Willcox Letters and Papers, Duke.

[184]John Floyd King to Lin Caperton, July 31, 1865, Thomas Butler King Papers, SHC.

[185]Thomas Barrow to D. C. Barrow, June 27, 1867, Colonel David Crenshaw Barrow Papers, UGa.

[186]Quoted in Sitterson, "The Transition from Slave to Free Economy," 223–24.

[187]Henry Graves to his aunt, Nov. 19, 1862; Henry Graves to his sister, Jan. 2, 1866, Graves Family Papers, SHC.

[188]George W. Munford to "Fanny," July 23, 1870, Munford-Ellis Family Papers, Duke. For an excellent example of a family clinging to agriculture but finding business an increasingly vital part of their affairs, see the account of the Guignard family of South Carolina in Childs, ed., *Planters and Business Men,* 81–98.

[189]James Baker to his sister, Jan. 12, 1866, Joseph Hubbard Saunders Papers, SHC.

[190]F. B. Conner to L. P. Conner, Aug. 21, 1866, Lemuel Parker Conner Family Papers, LSU.

[191]Henry Watson, Jr., to Hon. J. Dixon, Dec. 20, 1867, Henry Watson, Jr., Papers, Duke.

[192]John Dobbins to Elisha Laurey, Jan. 29, 1866, John S. Dobbins Papers, Emory.

[193]John Edwin Fripp Diary, probably 1867, John Edwin Fripp Papers, SHC.

[194]John Floyd King to Lin Caperton, Sept. 8, 1866, Thomas Butler King Papers, SHC.

[195]John Houston Bills Diary, June 15, 1867, John Houston Bills Papers, SHC.

[196]Thomas S. Watson to Mrs. V. H. Robertson, June 21, 1867, Watson Papers, UVa.

[197]William Heyward to James Gregorie, Jan. 12, 1868, Gregorie and Elliott Family Papers, SHC.

[198]Thomas Ellis to George Wythe Munford, Sept. 25, 1867, Munford-Ellis Family Papers, Duke.

[199]John Floyd King to Lin Caperton, Jan. 31, 1867, Thomas Butler King Papers, SHC.

[200]Thomas Affleck to Henry Lafone, May 7, 1866, Thomas Affleck Papers, LSU.

[201]Thomas A. Collman to John Dobbins, Nov. 28, 1867, John S. Dobbins Papers, Emory.

[202]Thomas S. Watson to Mrs. V. H. Robertson, June 21, 1867, Watson Papers, UVa.

[203]*Southern Cultivator*, June, 1868, 207, in Bell Irvin Wiley, "Salient Changes in Southern Agriculture since the Civil War," *AgH*, 13 (April, 1939), 65. Charles C. Jones, Jr., advised his mother to sell out in 1867 because "Negroes and Negro labor are so entirely unreliable that a sum certain is far better than a speculative interest in the results of labor." Charles C. Jones, Jr., to Mrs. Mary Jones, Oct. 30, 1867, in Myers, ed., *Children of Pride*, 1403.

[204]J.M. Washburn to Andrew McCollam, May 27, 1866, Andrew McCollam Papers, SHC.

[205]William McBurney to T. B. Ferguson, Feb. 14, 1866, Heyward and Ferguson Family Papers, SHC.

[206]Howell Cobb to J. H. Wilson, June 14, 1865, in Richard N. Current, ed., *Reconstruction [1865–1877]*, 38–40.

[207]Howell Cobb to his wife, Dec., 1866, in Phillips, ed., *Correspondence of Toombs, Stephens, and Cobb*, vol. 2, 684.

[208]William H. Heyward to James B. Heyward, April 17, 1866, Heyward and Ferguson Family Papers, SHC.

[209]C. D. Whittle to "My Beloved Boy," Dec. 29, 1867, Lewis Neale Whittle Papers, SHC.

# CHAPTER FIVE: "THE SOUL IS FLED"

[1]Charles R. Anderson, ed., *Sidney Lanier: Poems and Letters*, 100.

[2]Everard Green Baker Diary, May 31, 1865, SHC.

[3]Charles C. Jones, Jr., to Mrs. Mary Jones, May 28, 1866, in Robert Manson Myers, ed., *The Children of Pride: A True Story of Georgia and the Civil War*, 1338.

[4]W. A. James to Andrew McCollam, May 19, 1868, Andrew McCollam Papers, SHC.

[5]Quoted in Paul M. Gaston, *The New South Creed: A Study in Southern Mythmaking*, 22.

[6]Quoted in John C. Calhoun II, "Life and Labor in the New South," in *The Transformation of American Society, 1870–1890*, edited by John A. Garraty, 27.

[7]Ann Hairston to Bettie Hairston, Jan. 22, 1870, Hairston and Wilson Family Papers, SHC.

[8]John Moore to Jos. R. Snyder, Oct. 11, 1866, Kean and Prescott Family Papers, SHC.

[9]B. W. Merritt to William Merritt, Feb. 22, 1866, William H. E. Merritt Papers, Duke.

[10]James Baker to his sister, Jan. 12, 1866, Joseph Hubbard Saunders Papers, SHC.

[11]Jennie Newton to George Barnsley, July 31, 1865, George Scarborough Barnsley Papers, SHC.

[12]R. Izard Middleton to Henry A. Middleton, Oct. 6, 1868, Langdon Cheves Collection, SCHS.

[13]A. C. Jones to Cadwallader Jones, Jr., July 29, 1866, Cadwallader Jones, Jr., Papers, SHC.

[14]W. A. James to John McCollam, Feb. 21, 1868, Andrew McCollam Papers, SHC.

[15]Henry Watson, Jr., to Walter S. Pitkin, Dec. 22, 1865, Henry Watson, Jr., Papers, Duke.

[16]Kimbrough Jones to "Cousin William," June 27, 1867, Crabtree Jones Papers, NCAH.

[17]C. G. Farmer to John Dobbins, July 1, 1867, John S. Dobbins Papers, Emory.

[18]W. J. Britton to L. Thompson, July 31, 1867, Lewis Thompson Papers, SHC.

[19]Mrs. W. H. Stiles to her children, Aug. 20, 1865, MacKay and Stiles Family Papers, SHC.

[20]William Heyward to James Gregorie, June 4, 1868, Gregorie and Elliott Family Papers, SHC.

[21]John C. Calhoun, *A Disquisition on Government and Selections from the Discourse*, edited by C. Gordon Post, 42.

[22]Quoted in Chester McArthur Destler, "David Dickson's 'System of Farming' and the Agricultural Revolution in the Deep South, 1850–1885," *AgH*, 31 (July, 1957), 33.

[23]Charles Nordhoff, *The Cotton States in the Spring and Summer of 1875*, 56.

[24]Certainly this motive was at work eight years later when John C. Calhoun II, an Arkansas planter and grandson of the South Carolinian, testified before Congress on labor relations in the South. "Friendly and harmonious" was his description of relations between planters and their black laborers. "The planter feels an interest in the welfare of his laborers," he explained, "and the latter in turn look to him for advice and assistance." At the same time, however, he asked for "the total elimination from Federal politics of the so-called negro question." All the South needed, he declared, was "just to be left alone." Calhoun, "Life and Labor in the New South," 30.

[25]F. B. Conner to Lemuel P. Conner, Nov. 30, 1866, Lemuel Parker Conner Family Papers, LSU.

[26]Keating S. Ball Plantation Day Book, 1870, John Ball and Keating Simons Ball Books, SHC.

[27]R. Izard Middleton to Henry A. Middleton, Dec. 12, 1870, and March 20, 1877, Langdon Cheves Collection, SCHS.

[28]George W. Munford to Thomas T. Munford, Dec. 4, 1870, Munford-Ellis Family Papers, Duke.

[29]Davis Whittle to L. N. Whittle, Dec. 26, 1879, Lewis Neale Whittle Papers, SHC.

[30]Quoted in W. McKee Evans, Ballots and Fence Rails: Reconstruction on the Lower Cape Fear, 208.

[31]Joseph Buckner Killebrew Autobiography, I, 340, SHC.

[32]Bruce Clayton, The Savage Ideal: Intolerance and Intellectual Leadership in the South, 1890–1914, 140.

[33]Quoted in Eugene D. Genovese, The Political Economy of Slavery: Studies in the Economy and Society of the Slave South, 231.

[34]Quoted in Donald J. Millet, "Some Aspects of Agricultural Retardation in Southwest Louisiana, 1865–1900," LaH, 11 (Winter, 1970), 41.

[35]B. W. Merritt to William Merritt, Jan. 3, 1866, William H. E. Merritt Papers, Duke.

[36]Henry McCollam to Andrew McCollam, Nov. 16, 1869, Andrew McCollam Papers, SHC.

[37]Quoted in Rowland T. Berthoff, "Southern Attitudes toward Immigration, 1865–1914," JSH, 17 (Aug., 1951), 331. Also see Bert James Loewenberg, "Efforts of the South to Encourage Immigration, 1865–1900," SAQ, 33 (Oct., 1934), 363–85. Henry Watson, Jr., attempted to establish the Alabama Cotton Planters' Association in 1866 because "of the great deficiency and difficulty of procuring laborers . . . and of the inefficiency of the labor of Freedmen and its uncertainty when obtained. . . ." "An Act to incorporate the ACPA," 1866, Henry Watson, Jr., Papers, Duke.

[38]Godfrey Barnsley to Lucian Barnsley, Sept. 16, 1869, George Scarborough Barnsley Papers, SHC.

[39]R. Izard Middleton to Henry A. Middleton, Aug. 28, 1871, Langdon Cheves Collection, SCHS.

[40]William M. Lawton to editors of the New York Journal of Commerce, July 17, 1869; William M. Lawton to Robert Mure, July 19, 1869; William M. Lawton to James R. Sparkman, Aug. 2, 1869, Sparkman Family Papers, SHC.

[41]John Floyd King to Lin Caperton, Jan. 18, 1866, and Feb. 19, 1866, Thomas Butler King Papers, SHC.

[42]R. E. Conner to L. P. Conner, July 1, 1879, Lemuel Parker Conner Family Papers, LSU.

[43]Alfred Holt Stone, "The Italian Cotton Grower: The Negro's Problem," SAQ, 4 (Jan., 1905), 42–47.

[44]Walter L. Fleming, "Immigration to the Southern States," PSQ, 20 (1905), 278–81.

[45]The most comprehensive study focused on the colonization impulse is P. J. Staudenraus, The African Colonization Movement, 1816–1865. But several broader studies are also important: Winthrop D. Jordan, White over Black: American Attitudes toward the Negro, 1550–1812, 542–69; Ira Berlin, Slaves without Masters: The Free Negro in the Antebellum South, passim; and George M. Fredrickson, The Black Image in the White Mind: The Debate on Afro-American Character and Destiny, 1817–1914, 25–26, 149, 166.

[46]Quoted in Joel Williamson, After Slavery: The Negro in South Carolina during Reconstruction, 1861–1877, 252.

⁴⁷See, for example, C. S. Sutton to John Dobbins, July 14, 1866, John S. Dobbins Papers, Emory.

⁴⁸Quoted in Williamson, *After Slavery*, 78.

⁴⁹Philip Alexander Bruce, *The Plantation Negro as a Freedman*, 79.

⁵⁰Henry Shelton Sanford, "American Interests in Africa," *The Forum*, 9 (1889), 428.

⁵¹Randall Lee Gibson to Henry Sanford, July 3, 1890, Henry Shelton Sanford Papers, TSLA.

⁵²John T. Morgan, "The Future of the Negro," *North American Review*, 139 (July, 1884), 83.

⁵³Ann Hairston to Bettie Hairston, Jan. 22, 1870, Hairston and Wilson Family Papers, SHC.

⁵⁴Walter L. Fleming, "Deportation and Colonization: An Attempted Solution of the Race Problem," in *Studies in Southern History and Politics Inscribed to William Archibald Dunning*, 30.

⁵⁵Jennie Newton to George Barnsley, July 31, 1865, George Scarborough Barnsley Papers, SHC.

⁵⁶W. H. B. Richardson to James B. Richardson, Aug. 8, 1868, James Burchell Richardson Letters and Papers, Duke.

⁵⁷William Heyward to James Gregorie, Sept. 7, 1871, Gregorie and Elliott Family Papers, SHC.

⁵⁸As recently as 1971, Gerald N. Grob could observe that there had been virtually no demographic studies of the South during Reconstruction that utilized the manuscript census data for 1860–1880. "Reconstruction: An American Morality Play," in *American History: Retrospect and Prospect*, edited by George Athan Billias and Gerald N. Grob, 229. In the past five years, however, historians and economists, using the manuscript census and much else besides, have initiated sophisticated analyses of the social and economic systems of the postbellum South. We now have several dissertations, a large number of articles (most of them appearing in the *Journal of Economic History* and *Agricultural History*), and a book—Stephen J. DeCanio, *Agriculture in the Postbellum South: The Economics of Production and Supply*. In addition, two important books are promised, one by Roger Ransom and Richard Sutch and the other by Robert Higgs.

⁵⁹Louis S. Gerteis, *From Contraband to Freedman: Federal Policy toward Southern Blacks, 1861–1865, passim*; Herman Belz, "The New Orthodoxy in Reconstruction Historiography," *Reviews in American History*, 1 (March, 1973), 106–13.

⁶⁰C. Vann Woodward, *Origins of the New South, 1877–1913*, 178–79; Paul S. Taylor, "Plantation Agriculture in the United States: Seventeenth to Twentieth Centuries," *Land Economics*, 30 (May, 1954), 142; Sheldon VanAucken, "A Century of the Southern Plantation," *VaMHB*, 58 (July, 1958), 362; Barnes F. Lathrop, "History of the Census Returns," *SwHQ*, 51 (April, 1948), 293–312.

⁶¹Roger Wallace Shugg, "Survival of the Plantation System in Louisiana," *JSH*, 3 (Aug., 1937), 323–25; Ulrich Bonnell Phillips, "The Decadence of the Plantation System," *Annals*, 35 (Jan., 1910), 37.

⁶²Jonathan M. Wiener, "Planter Persistence and Social Change: Alabama, 1850–1870" (paper presented at the annual meeting of the Organization of American Historians, Boston, April, 1975).

⁶³Jonathan M. Wiener, "Planter-Merchant Conflict in Reconstruction Alabama,"

*Past and Present*, 68 (Aug., 1975), 73–80; Eugene M. Lerner, "Southern Output and Agricultural Income, 1860–1880," in *The Economic Impact of the American Civil War*, edited by Ralph Andreano, 90–103.

[64]Charlton Watson Tebeau, "The Planter in the Lower South, 1865–1880" (Ph.D. dissertation, University of Iowa, 1933), 11–16, 111–13; "Visit to 'Gowrie' and 'East Hermitage' Plantations, Savannah River, 22 March, 1867," Charles and Louis Manigault Records, GHS; W. McKee Evans, *Ballots and Fence Rails: Reconstruction on the Lower Cape Fear*, *passim*; William Allister Noble, "Sequent Occupance of Hopeton-Altama, 1816–1956" (M. A. thesis, University of Georgia, 1956), 98.

[65]Tebeau, "The Planter in the Lower South," 17–20, 113–19; J. Carlyle Sitterson, *Sugar Country: The Cane Sugar Industry in the South, 1753–1950*; *passim*, Joe Gray Taylor, *Louisiana Reconstructed: 1863–1877*, 315–406; Barnes Fletcher Lathrop, "The Pugh Plantations, 1860–1865: A Study of Life in Lower Louisiana" (Ph.D. dissertation, University of Texas, 1945), 428–44.

[66]The best introduction to the economics of the postbellum cotton South is Harold D. Woodman, *King Cotton and His Retainers: Financing and Marketing the Cotton Crop of the South, 1800–1925*, 249–95. In the recent flood of literature on the topic, I found particularly helpful three articles by Roger L. Ransom and Richard Sutch: "Debt Peonage in the Cotton South after the Civil War," *JEH*, 32 (Sept., 1972), 641–69; "The Ex-Slave in the Post-Bellum South: A Study of the Economic Impact of Racism in a Market Environment," *JEH*, 33 (March, 1973), 131–48; "The 'Lock-In' Mechanism and Overproduction of Cotton in the Postbellum South," *AgH*, 49 (April, 1975), 405–25. For an excellent economic study of a unique plantation area, see Robert L. Brandfon, *Cotton Kingdom of the New South: A History of the Yazoo Mississippi Delta from Reconstruction to the Twentieth Century*.

[67]A. Tureaud to Stella Bringier, Oct. 25, 1875, Louis Amedee Bringier Papers, LSU.

[68]Louis Hébert Autobiography, SHC.

[69]Thomas Chaplin Journal, SCHS.

[70]This summary is based on a series of exchanges between James Gregorie and Charles Rose between 1867 and 1873, concluding with W. R. Wheelock to James Gregorie, Dec. 22, 1873, Gregorie and Elliott Family Papers, SHC. For a remarkably similar relationship, see that of Rose with another South Carolina planter, John Jenkins. Their correspondence also ends with a notice of foreclosure: C. G. Memminger to John Jenkins, April 19, 1881, John Jenkins Papers, SCL.

[71]This account is based on Keating Simons Ball's Diary from March 5, 1849 to Dec. 31, 1874, John Ball and Keating Simons Ball Books, SHC.

[72]This account is based on the Everard Green Baker Diary from Feb. 13, 1849, to Jan. 31, 1876, SHC.

[73]Pope Barrow to David C. Barrow, April 24, 1867, Colonel David Crenshaw Barrow Papers, UGa.

[74]George W. Munford to Thomas T. Munford, Aug. 21, 1869, and July 2, 1870; George W. Munford to Fanny Munford, July 23, 1870; George W. Munford to his wife, Dec. 27, 1870; George W. Munford to Charles Talbott, Feb. 10, 1871, Munford-Ellis Family Papers, Duke.

[75]Thomas T. Munford to George Munford, Nov. 14, 1870, and Dec. 20, 1874, Munford-Ellis Family Papers, Duke.

[76]This account is based on the remarkable Ella Gertrude (Clanton) Thomas Journal for the years 1855 to 1880, Duke. For another aspect of her life, see Mary Elizabeth Massey, "The Making of a Feminist," *JSH*, 39 (Feb., 1973), 3–22.

[77]Ann Hairston to Bettie Hairston, Jan. 22, 1870, Hairston and Wilson Family Papers, SHC.

[78]Randall Lee Gibson to Louisiana Gibson, Feb. 13, 1867, Gibson and Humphreys Family Papers, SHC.

[79]James B. Urquhart to Burges Urquhart, April 10, 1873, Lewis Thompson Papers, SHC.

[80]James Trezevant to J. W. White, March 25, 1869, James Wilson White Papers, SHC.

[81]Davis Whittle to L. N. Whittle, June 18, 1871, Lewis Neale Whittle Papers, SHC.

[82]Elizabeth Brownrigg Waddell to Mrs. J. L. Bailey, Jan. 28, 1871, John Lancaster Bailey Papers, SHC. Of course, not every planter who experienced economic difficulties wanted to sell his land. James L. Hubard of Virginia claimed in 1873 that he had been "twisted and turned, and half scalped by the savage times," but he concluded, "We will have to keep our lands and do nothing rash—they'll be worth something in the future." James L. Hubard to Philip A. Hubard, Feb. 5, 1873, Hubard Family Papers, UVa.

[83]D. C. Clark to Thomas Thompson, Feb. 4, 1870, Lewis Thompson Papers, SHC.

[84]Thomas T. Munford to George W. Munford, 1869, Munford-Ellis Family Papers, Duke.

[85]James Trezevant to J. W. White, March 25, 1869, James Wilson White Papers, SHC.

[86]Thomas S. Watson to Mrs. V. H. Robertson, March 27, 1868, Watson Papers, UVa.

[87]Thomas T. Munford to George W. Munford, Dec. 20, 1874, Munford-Ellis Family Papers, Duke.

[88]John Gabriel Guignard III to James Sanders Guignard III, July 24, 1869, in Arney R. Childs, ed., *Planters and Business Men: The Guignard Family of South Carolina, 1795–1930*, 190.

[89]Lerner, "Southern Output and Agricultural Income, 1860–1880," 90–103.

[90]John Houston Bills Diary, Aug. 3, 1870, John Houston Bills Papers, SHC.

[91]See the postwar letters in the Andrew McCollam Papers, SHC, and J. Carlyle Sitterson, "The McCollams: A Planter Family of the Old and New South," *JSH*, 6 (Aug., 1940), 347–67.

[92]See the postwar letters of the Guignard family in Childs, ed., *Planters and Business Men*.

[93]In his study of the postwar careers of more than six hundred Confederate officials, William Hesseltine found that the largest increases came in the fields of banking, railroads, and industry. Unfortunately, the way he selected his group limits its usefulness for the study of planters. William Best Hesseltine, *Confederate Leaders in the New South*, 16–21, 95–96.

[94]Joseph Buckner Killebrew Autobiography, SHC. For a full discussion of this unusual Southerner, see Samuel Boyd Smith, "Joseph Buckner Killebrew and the New South Movement in Tennessee" (Ph.D. dissertation, Vanderbilt University, 1962).

[95]The best study of New South ideology is Gaston, *The New South Creed*. Bruce

Clayton traces the intellectual wing of the New South movement into the twentieth century in *The Savage Ideal*. The starting point for any investigation of the relationship of planters to the New South is, of course, Woodward, *Origins of the New South*.

[96]Henry Watson, Jr., to Hon. Jas. Dixon, Dec. 20, 1866, Henry Watson, Jr., Papers, Duke.

[97]W. W. James to John McCollam, Feb. 21, 1868, Andrew McCollam Papers, SHC.

[98]Ella Gertrude (Clanton) Thomas Journal, Oct., 1868, Duke. In 1873, a Georgian reported that he had recently been appointed to several local offices, but he noted in his diary, "Prefer to drop all offices unless they pay." June 3, 1873, James Daniel Frederick Diary, UGa.

[99]Thomas S. Watson to Mrs. V. H. Robertson, Oct. 15, 1868, Watson Papers, UVa.

[100]Mrs. Catherine Ann Edmondston Diaries, May 7, 1865, NCAH.

[101]George Munford to Mrs. E. T. Munford, April 21, 1865, Munford-Ellis Family Papers, Duke.

[102]Michael Perman, *Reunion without Compromise: The South and Reconstruction, 1865–1868*, 68–81.

[103]*Ibid.*, 82–95.

[104]Mrs. W. H. Stiles to her husband, Oct. 18, 1865, Mackay and Stiles Family Papers, SHC.

[105]Howell Cobb to his wife, Dec. 7, 1865, in Ulrich Bonnell Phillips, ed., *The Correspondence of Robert Toombs, Alexander H. Stephens, and Howell Cobb*, vol. 2, 672.

[106]Henry Watson, Jr., to John Parrish, Aug. 7, 1865, Henry Watson, Jr., Papers, Duke.

[107]John Letcher to George W. Munford, Aug. 2, 1865, Munford-Ellis Family Papers, Duke.

[108]William H. Stiles to his wife, July 1, 1865, Mackay and Stiles Family Papers, SHC.

[109]Robert Toombs to Alexander H. Stephens, Dec. 15, 1865, in Phillips, ed., *Correspondence of Toombs, Stephens, and Cobb*, vol. 2, 673–75.

[110]Eric L. McKitrick, *Andrew Johnson and Reconstruction*, 186–213; Perman, *Reunion without Compromise*, 77–95.

[111]W. A. Durant to Henry R. Slack, Aug. 1, 1866, Slack Family Papers, SHC.

[112]B. F. Moore to Lewis Thompson, Sept. 3, 1866, Lewis Thompson Papers, SHC.

[113]Perman, *Reunion without Compromise*, 110–81.

[114]Ella Gertrude (Clanton) Thomas Journal, Oct. 9, 1866, Duke.

[115]Jeremiah Morton to John Perkins, June 6, 1866, John Perkins Papers, SHC.

[116]John Floyd King to Lin Caperton, May 19, 1867, Thomas Butler King Papers SHC.

[117]George W. Munford to William Munford, July 28, 1867, Munford-Ellis Family Papers, Duke.

[118]William H. B. Richardson to James B. Richardson, March 21, 1867, James Burchell Richardson Letters and Papers, Duke.

[119]George Noble Jones to his son, June 20, 1867, George Noble Jones Papers, Duke.

[120]William H. B. Richardson to James B. Richardson, March 21, 1867, James Burchell Richardson Letters and Papers, Duke.

[121]W. J. Ritton to Lewis Thompson, Aug. 10, 1867, Lewis Thompson Papers, SHC.

[122]George Hairston to Bettie Hairston, March 11, 1867, Hairston and Wilson Family Papers, SHC.

[123]Henry Watson, Jr., to W. R. [illegible], Aug. 28, 1868, Henry Watson, Jr., Papers, Duke.

[124]Cary Charles Cocke to R. D. Powell, Aug., 1867, John Hartwell Cocke Papers, UVa.

[125]Williamson, *After Slavery*, 353.

[126]The literature on postwar white Southern Republicanism is growing rapidly. For a thorough review of historical viewpoints, as well as an interesting perspective, see Carl N. Degler, *The Other South: Southern Dissenters in the Nineteenth Century*, 191–229.

[127]R. J. Powell to Lewis Thompson, June 29, 1866; "To the People of North Carolina," 1867, is signed by Thompson, Lewis Thompson Papers, SHC.

[128]"To the People of North Carolina," 1867, Lewis Thompson Papers, SHC.

[129]W. A. Smith to Lewis Thompson, April 16, 1867, Lewis Thompson Papers, SHC.

[130]A few planters moved into the Republican party and stayed, satisfied with its policy and their position within it. James Lusk Alcorn of Mississippi urged the gentry to heed the example of the English nobles who had bent to the winds of democratic reform in 1832 and had thus retained their place as the "natural leaders of the people." In his own life, Alcorn proved that those who bent the most (and perhaps those who owned plantations in the uniquely rich Yazoo delta) were the ones most likely to remain upright. Not only did he become governor in 1870 and maintain his plantations' prosperity, but he was able, in the old tradition, to hand a plantation to each of his sons. Lillian A. Pereyra, *James Lusk Alcorn: Persistent Whig*, 99, 105, 186.

[131]J. T. W. Hairston to Bettie Hairston, Oct. 11, 1874, Hairston and Wilson Family Papers, SHC.

[132]George Noble Jones to his son, June 20, 1867, George Noble Jones Papers, Duke.

[133]Donelson Caffery to "My Dearest," Aug. 23, 1868, Caffery Family Papers, SHC.

[134]Thomas S. Watson to Mrs. V. H. Robertson, June 20, 1867, Watson Papers, UVa.

[135]Joseph Buckner Killebrew Autobiography, I, 233, SHC.

[136]W. A. Smith to Lewis Thompson, April 16, 1867, Lewis Thompson Papers, SHC.

[137]Ella Gertrude (Clanton) Thomas Journal, Sept. 6, 1870, Duke.

[138]Joseph Buckner Killebrew Autobiography, I, 233, SHC. Conservative Northerners often sent their commiserations and advice on the matter of black suffrage. One Massachusetts industrialist suggested that Southerners be philosophical. After all, the South had the Negro and the North the Irish. "The practice of the doctrine of political equality requires faith & smothering of pride when the most highly educated, purest & best men walk up to the ballot with an Irishman who is stepped [*sic*] in tobacco & bad liquor, easily swayed by strong passions, by unprincipled demagogues & crafty intolerable spiritual advisers," he admitted, "and yet thus far it has worked well." He knew it seemed like a "rash experiment," but this was "the country where its people dare experiment with men as well as with wood, iron or water." Warren Durant to Henry R. Slack, Feb. 7, 1867, Slack Family Papers, SHC. A Philadelphian's mood was more in line with the feelings of the planters. "Financially you'll improve," he observed. "But

socially what a future! What a dreadful mistake it was to give the negro the franchise!"
Dr. J. Marion Sims to James Sparkman, Dec. 27, 1868, Sparkman Family Papers,
SHC.

139John Moore to Jos. R. Snyder, Oct. 11, 1866, Kean and Prescott Family Papers,
SHC.

140A. Brunner to H. W. J., Aug. 24, 1867, Henry Watson, Jr., Papers, Duke.

141William McKinley to Kate McKinley Taylor, Sept. 16, 1867, Colonel David
Crenshaw Barrow Papers, UGa.

142William M. Byrd, "Written in 1868 on the condition of the Country," William
M. Byrd Papers, SHC.

143Sallie Boykin to her son, Jan. 12, 1871, Boykin Family Papers, SHC.

144George W. Munford to Thomas J. Munford, Dec. 15, 1867, Munford-Ellis
Family Papers, Duke.

145William Heyward to James Gregorie, June 4, 1868, Gregorie and Elliott Family
Papers, SHC.

146R. Izard Middleton to Henry A. Middleton, Nov. 13, 1867, Langdon Cheves
Collection, SCHC. Thomas Watson of Virginia complained that his young servants
had "grown beyond all endurance!" "They all look forward, the boys, to being members
of Congress," he explained, and "the girls to being wives (or mistresses! Thad Stevens
kept one) of the members of Congress." Thomas S. Watson to Mrs. V. H. Robertson,
Sept. 9, 1868, Watson Papers, UVa.

147Godfrey Barnsley to George Barnsley, Sept. 14, 1868, George Scarborough
Barnsley Papers, SHC.

148W. J. Britton to Lewis Thompson, July 31, 1867, Lewis Thompson Papers, SHC.

149John Parrish to Henry Watson, Jr., June 20, 1867, Henry Watson, Jr., Papers,
Duke.

150Sallie Boykin to her son, Jan. 12, 1871, Boykin Family Papers, SHC.

151C. S. Sutton to John Dobbins, June 1, 1867, John S. Dobbins Papers, Emory.

152William M. Byrd, "Written in 1868 on the condition of the Country," William
M. Byrd Papers, SHC.

153John Parrish to Henry Watson, Jr., Aug. 6, 1867; Henry Watson, Jr., to W. R.
[illegible], Aug. 28, 1868, Henry Watson, Jr., Papers, Duke.

154Roger W. Shugg, *Origins of Class Struggle in Louisiana: A Social History of
White Farmers and Laborers during Slavery and After, 1840–1875*, 29–31; Robert
Arthur Gilmour, "The Other Emancipation: Studies in the Society and Economy of
Alabama Whites during Reconstruction" (Ph.D. dissertation, The Johns Hopkins
University, 1972), 258.

155Allen W. Trelease, "Who Were the Scalawags?" *JSH*, 29 (Nov., 1963), 445–68.

156Donelson Caffery to "My Dearest," Aug. 23, 1868, Caffery Family Papers, SHC.

157James M. Willcox to Susannah Willcox, July 20, 1868, James M. Willcox Letters
and Papers, Duke.

158William H. B. Richardson to James Burchell Richardson, July 24, 1866, James
Burchell Richardson Letters and Papers, Duke.

159C. G. Farmer to John Dobbins, July 1, 1867, John S. Dobbins Papers, Emory. A
few days earlier, a Virginian had declared that Benjamin Wade wanted "to inaugurate a
system of confiscation & military plunder of the South. That old Devil has lately spoken
in Kansas in favor, not only of *universal* suffrage (white & *black women* you see!) but

saying expressly *that property is too unequally distributed!*" Thomas S. Watson to Mrs. V.H. Robertson, June 20, 1867, Watson Papers, UVa.

[160]Henry Watson, Jr., to W. R. [illegible], Aug. 28, 1868, Henry Watson, Jr., Papers, Duke.

[161]A. Brunner to H. W. J., Aug. 24, 1867, Henry Watson, Jr., Papers, Duke.

[162]Everard Green Baker Diary, July 5, 1872, SHC.

[163]J. T. W. Hairston to Bettie Hairston, Sept. 22, 1874, Hairston and Wilson Family Papers, SHC.

[164]Woodward, *Origins of the New South, passim.*

[165]Dewey Grantham argues that in some states farmers got substantial favorable legislation under Redeemer rule, and that this fact indicates that agricultural elements were stronger in Bourbonism than we usually think. Dewey W. Grantham, Jr., "The Southern Bourbons Revisited," *SAQ*, 60 (1961), 289–90. For a recent survey of historical interpretations of the Bourbon regimes, see George Brown Tindall, *The Persistent Tradition in New South Politics*, 1–23.

[166]R. Izard Middleton to Mrs. Henry A. Middleton, April 20, 1877, Langdon Cheves Collection, SCHS.

[167]Lucy Judkins Durr, "Brazilian Recollections," Judkins-Durr Papers, ADAH.

[168]Charles C. Cocke to John B. Cocke, Aug. 2, 1871, John Hartwell Cocke Papers, UVa.

[169]E. Merton Coulter, "A Century of a Georgia Plantation," *MVHR*, 16 (Dec., 1929), 343–46; VanAucken, "A Century of the Southern Plantation," 356–87; Woodman, *King Cotton and His Retainers*, 258–312. Rice and sugar plantations, mainly because of capital requirements, did reorganize around their antebellum patterns, with wage labor replacing slavery. These units, however, made up only a small fraction of Southern plantations. Ulrich Bonnell Phillips, "Plantations with Slave Labor and Free," *AHR*, 30 (July, 1925), 749–50.

[170]Eugene D. Genovese, *Roll, Jordan, Roll: The World the Slaves Made, passim.*

[171]Alfred Huger to J. Harleston Read, Nov. 9, 1854, Alfred Huger Papers, Duke.

[172]Charles C. Jones to Charles C. Jones, Jr., June 7, 1859, in Myers, ed., *Children of Pride*, 487.

[173]Ella Gertrude (Clanton) Thomas Journal, Jan. 2, 1871, Duke.

[174]"Contract between W. B. Richardson & Freedmen," Jan. 1, 1868, James Burchell Richardson Letters and Papers, Duke.

[175]Thomas T. Munford to George W. Munford, 1869, Munford-Ellis Family Papers, Duke. When he inherited his father's estate in 1868, Thomas Thompson asked the old family financial adviser for some guidelines. "The main point is to have the money invested helping to get an income which itself will again be invested," the retainer replied. P. H. Winston to Thomas Thompson, Feb. 4, 1868, Lewis Thompson Papers, SHC.

[176]B. Bragg, Jr., to John Bragg, Dec. 27, 1875, John Bragg Papers, SHC.

[177]Ella Gertrude (Clanton) Thomas Journal, April 10, 1871, Duke.

[178]James Trezevant to J. W. White, March 25, 1869, James Wilson White Papers, SHC.

[179]William Heyward to James Gregorie, June 4, 1868, Gregorie and Elliott Family Papers, SHC.

[180]Ella Gertrude (Clanton) Thomas Journal, June 1, 1869, Duke.

[181]Quoted in Coulter, "A Century of a Georgia Plantation," 343–46. In 1867, George W. Munford explained his technique of handling labor. "When a hand becomes intolerable from impudence or idleness," he said, "I discharge him, pay him off & get a new one in his place. . . ." George W. Munford to Thomas T. Munford, Aug. 3, 1867, Munford-Ellis Family Papers, Duke.

[182]John Cobb to Pope Barrow, April 17, 1866, Colonel David Crenshaw Barrow Papers, UGa.

[183]It was not only the gentry who remained on plantations that suffered pangs from the loss of the power to command. Young Wade Manning found employment in a bank in Columbia, South Carolina, where clerks were used "just as hard and as unceasingly as ordinary 'working animals.' " It was galling, he said, to be "every man's servant & nothing but a mere machine." Wade Manning to Ellen, June 28, 1870, Williams-Chesnut-Manning Papers, SCL.

[184]Carrie Kincaid to Mrs. Elizabeth Anderson, Aug. 20, 1867, Kincaid-Anderson Family Papers, SCL.

[185]Davis Whittle to L. N. Whittle, Dec. 26, 1879, Lewis Neale Whittle Papers, SHC.

[186]Ellen Allston to Ben Allston, Nov. 21, 1874, Robert Francis Withers Allston Papers, SCHS.

[187]George Hairston to Bettie Hairston, March 11, 1867, Hairston and Wilson Family Papers, SHC.

[188]Thomas T. Munford to George W. Munford, 1869, Munford-Ellis Family Papers, Duke.

[189]J. B. Bethea to John Bragg, Jan. 4, 1875, John Bragg Papers, SHC.

[190]Daniel McNeill to William McLaurin, Feb. 27, 1871, William H. McLaurin Papers, SHC.

[191]Pierre L. van den Berghe, *Race and Racism: A Comparative Perspective,* 25–37. C. Vann Woodward uses van den Berghe's thesis in his intriguing essay "The Strange Career of a Historical Controversy," in Woodward, *American Counterpoint: Slavery and Racism in the North-South Dialogue,* 243–46.

[192]Peter Kolchin, *First Freedom: The Responses of Alabama's Blacks to Emancipation and Reconstruction,* 47–48. For the argument that it is best to view the planter as "income maximizer," see Joseph Reid, "Sharecropping as an Understandable Market Response: The Post-Bellum South," *JEH,* 33 (March, 1973), 114.

[193]John Houston Bills Diary, May 23, 1870, John Houston Bills Papers, SHC.

[194]Octavia Otey Diary, Jan. 24, 1871, and Feb. 4, 1876, Wyche and Otey Family Papers, SHC.

[195]Dolly Burge Diary, Dec. 12, 1875, and Jan. 1, 1876, Burge-Gray Papers, Emory.

[196]Henry Watson, Jr., to his mother, Jan. 30, 1876, Henry Watson, Jr., Papers, Duke.

[197]Ella Gertrude (Clanton) Thomas Journal, May 7, 1869, Duke.

[198]Elizabeth Brownrigg Waddell to Mrs. J. L. Bailey, Jan. 28, 1871, John Lancaster Bailey Papers, SHC.

[199]Ella Gertrude (Clanton) Thomas Journal, Jan. 9, 1870, Duke.

[200]G. S. Crafts to William Porcher Miles, Sept. 14, 1878, William Porcher Miles Papers, SHC.

[201]Fanny Conner to Lemuel Conner, March 10, 1869, Lemuel Parker Conner Family Papers, LSU.

[202]Thomas S. Watson to Mrs. V. H. Robertson, Feb. 10, 1868, Watson Papers, UVa.

[203]Lucy Judkins Durr, "Brazilian Recollections," Judkins-Durr Papers, ADAH.

[204]Mrs. Catherine Ann Edmondston Diaries, Aug. 26, 1862, and July 8, 1863, NCAH.

[205]News clipping, Nov. 28, 1865, John Lancaster Bailey Papers, SHC; Evans, *Ballots and Fence Rails*, 212. Sometimes, in fact, tournaments sprouted where they had never appeared before. Citizens of New Iberia Parish, Louisiana, for example, held their first tournament in 1877. "Formal Program" and news clipping, Aug. 11, 1877, Weeks Family Papers, Tulane.

[206]Ella Gertrude (Clanton) Thomas Journal, Dec. 3, 1868, Duke.

[207]J. W. White to "Emma," Sept. 29, 1870, James Wilson White Papers, SHC.
[208]Quoted in Evans, *Ballots and Fence Rails*, 212.

[209]George Cary Eggleston, "The Old Regime in the Old Dominion," *Atlantic Monthly*, 36 (Nov., 1875), 603–6.

[210]Thomas Nelson Page, "The Old Planters'," *The Century Magazine*, 78 (May, 1909), 3–21. For the image of the plantation in literature, see Francis Pendleton Gaines, *The Southern Plantation*.

[211]Philip Alexander Bruce, "Social and Economic Revolution in the Southern States," *Contemporary Review*, 78 (July, 1900), 58–73.

[212]Quoted in Clayton, *The Savage Ideal*, 22.

[213]William Alexander Percy, *Lanterns on the Levee: Recollections of a Planter's Son*, 120.

[214]George Scarborough Barnsley, "Original of Reply to a Circular for information of the Ex-Confederate emigrants, April, 1915," George Scarborough Barnsley Papers, SHC.

[215]Octavia Otey Diary, Dec. 29, 1867, Wyche and Otey Family Papers, SHC.
[216]Mrs. Catherine Ann Edmondston Diaries, Oct. 1, 1865, NCAH.

[217]Rev. John Jones to Mrs. Mary Jones, July 28, 1865, in Myers, ed., *Children of Pride*, 1281.

[218]Octavia Otey Diary, April 2, 1867, Wyche and Otey Family Papers, SHC.

[219]Robert Jay Lifton, *History and Human Survival: Essays on the Young and Old, Survivors and the Dead, Peace and War, and on Contemporary Psychohistory*, 58–79.

[220]Joseph Buckner Killebrew Autobiography, SHC.

[221]Octavia Otey Diary, Dec. 22, 1865, Wyche and Otey Family Papers, SHC.
[222]Ella Gertrude (Clanton) Thomas Journal, Nov. 30, 1870, Duke.

[223]George W. Bagby, *The Old Virginia Gentleman and Other Sketches*, edited by Thomas Nelson Page, 6.

# Bibliography

PRIMARY SOURCES

## *Manuscripts*

Alabama State Department of Archives and History, Montgomery
    Bolling Hall Papers
    Judkins-Durr Papers
    James Monroe Torbert Journal

Duke University Library, Durham, North Carolina
    Frances (Walker) Yates Aglionby Papers
    Iveson L. Brookes Letters and Papers
    Samuel Bryarly Papers
    James Chesnut, Jr., Letters and Papers
    Enoch Clark Letters
    Clement Claiborne Clay Letters and Papers
    John Clopton Papers
    Henry M. Crydenwise Letters
    George F. Davidson Papers
    Paul Hamilton Hayne Papers
    Alfred Huger Papers
    George Noble Jones Papers
    William H. E. Merritt Papers
    Munford-Ellis Family Papers
    James Burchell Richardson Letters and Papers

    Isaac Shoemaker Diary
    Ella Gertrude (Clanton) Thomas Journal
    George T. Wallace Letters
    Henry Watson, Jr., Papers
    James M. Willcox Letters and Papers

Emory University Library, Atlanta, Georgia
    Burge-Gray Papers
    John S. Dobbins Papers
    John Edmondson Family Letters
    N. W. E. Long Confederate Soldier's Letters
    Samuel David Sanders Letters

Georgia Historical Society, Savannah
    Fraser-Couper Family Papers
    Charles Colcock Jones, Jr., Papers
    George Noble Jones Papers
    Charles and Louis Manigault Records
    Telfair Family Papers
    Wayne-Stites-Anderson Family Papers

Louisiana State Department of Archives and History, Louisiana State University, Baton Rouge
    Thomas Affleck Papers
    Louis Amedee Bringier Papers
    Thomas W. Butler Papers
    Lemuel Parker Conner Family Papers
    Isaac H. Hilliard Family Papers
    Robert A. Newell Papers
    Col. W. W. Pugh Papers
    John H. Randolph Papers

North Carolina State Department of Archives and History, Raleigh
    Mrs. Catherine Ann Edmondston Diaries
    Crabtree Jones Papers

South Carolina Historical Society, Charleston
    Robert Francis Withers Allston Papers
    Thomas Chaplin Journal
    Langdon Cheves Collection
    Cheves-McCord-Miles Papers
    Dirleton Plantation Book
    Fort Motte Plantation Records
    Manigault Papers
    Mulberry Plantation Journal
    Morton Morris Pinckney Papers
    Vanderhorst Papers
    Weston Family Papers
    Miscellaneous Manuscripts

South Caroliniana Library, University of South Carolina, Columbia
    Ellis Family Papers
    S. Porcher Gaillard Plantation Book
    John Jenkins Papers
    Kincaid-Anderson Family Papers
    Middleton Family Papers
    Edward M. Stoeber Papers
    Williams-Chesnut-Manning Papers

Southern Historical Collection, University of North Carolina, Chapel Hill
    Samuel Andrew Agnew Diary
    James Lusk Alcorn Papers
    George Washington Allen Papers
    James Allen and Charles B. Allen Papers
    Peter S. Bacot Papers
    James B. Bailey Papers
    John Lancaster Bailey Papers
    Everard Green Baker Diary
    John Ball and Keating Simons Ball Books
    George Scarborough Barnsley Papers
    Oliver Beirne Papers
    John Houston Bills Papers
    Boykin Family Papers
    John Bragg Papers
    Brashear Family Papers
    John Peter Brown Papers
    Burnley Family Memoir
    William M. Byrd Papers
    Caffery Family Papers
    Henry Selby Clark Letters
    William Cooper Diaries
    John Edwin Fripp Papers
    Gale and Polk Family Papers
    David Gavin Diary
    Gibson and Humphreys Family Papers
    Graves Family Papers
    Gregorie and Elliott Family Papers
    John Berkley Grimball Diary
    Gunter and Poellnitz Papers
    Hairston and Wilson Family Papers
    Pinckney Cotesworth Harrington Papers
    Louis Hébert Autobiography
    Heyward and Ferguson Family Papers
    Hughes Family Papers
    Johnston and McFaddin Family Papers
    Cadwallader Jones, Jr., Papers
    Kean and Prescott Family Papers

Julia Louisa (Hentz) Keyes Manuscript
Joseph Buckner Killebrew Autobiography
Thomas Butler King Papers
William King Papers
William Henry King Memoirs
Edward McCrady L'Engle Papers
Mackay and Stiles Family Papers
McBee Family Papers
Andrew McCollam Papers
William H. McLaurin Papers
Lafayette McLaws Papers
William Porcher Miles Papers
John Perkins Papers
J. D. Porter Letters
William Ravenel Paper
Joseph Hubbard Saunders Papers
Slack Family Papers
Charles Smallwood Diary
Peter Evans Smith Papers
William Ruffin Smith Papers
Sparkman Family Papers
Lewis Thompson Papers
Whitaker and Snipes Family Papers
Matthew Cary Whitaker Papers
James Wilson White Papers
William Wallace White Diaries
Lewis Neale Whittle Papers
Wyche and Otey Family Papers

Tennessee State Library and Archives, Nashville
    Henry Shelton Sanford Papers (microfilm)

Tulane University Library, New Orleans, Louisiana
    Charles E. Alton Papers
    Drennan Family Papers
    Albert Sidney and William Preston Johnston Collection
    Lemann Family Papers
    Magnolia Plantation Journals
    St. Rosalie Plantation Record Book
    Weeks Family Papers

University of Georgia Library, Athens
    Colonel David Crenshaw Barrow Papers
    William J. Dickey Diaries
    Eugene Frederick Diary
    James Daniel Frederick Diary
    Archibald Carlisle McKinley Journal
    James A. Spratlin Diary

University of Virginia Library, Charlottesville
    John Hartwell Cocke Papers
    Philip St. George Cocke Papers
    Hubard Family Papers
    Robert Thruston Hubard Papers
    Watson Papers

## Official Records

*Congressional Globe*. Washington, D.C.: 1864.
*United States Census*, 1860, 1870, 1880. Washington, D.C.: Government Printing
    Office.

## Published Sources

Anderson, Charles R., ed. *Sidney Lanier: Poems and Letters*. Baltimore: The Johns
    Hopkins University Press, 1969.
Bagby, George W. *The Old Virginia Gentleman and Other Sketches*. Edited with an
    introduction by Thomas Nelson Page. New York: Charles Scribner's Sons, 1911.
Bestor, Arthur E., Jr. "Letters from a Southern Opponent of Sectionalism, September,
    1860, to June, 1861." *Journal of Southern History*, 12 (February, 1946), 106–22.
Bettersworth, John K., ed. *Mississippi in the Confederacy: As They Saw It*. Baton
    Rouge: Louisiana State University Press, 1961.
Bruce, Philip Alexander. *The Plantation Negro as a Freedman*. New York: G. P.
    Putnam's Sons, 1889.
———. "Social and Economic Revolution in the Southern States." *Contemporary
    Review*, 78 (July, 1900), 58–73.
Calhoun, John C. *A Disquisition on Government and Selections from the Discourse*.
    Edited by C. Gordon Post. Indianapolis: Bobbs-Merrill, 1953.
Calhoun, John C., II. "Life and Labor in the New South." In *The Transformation of
    American Society, 1870–1890*, edited by John A. Garraty. New York: Harper &
    Row, 1968.
Calvert, Robert A., ed. "The Freedmen and Agricultural Prosperity." *Southwestern
    Historical Quarterly*, 76 (April, 1973), 461–71.
Childs, Arney R., ed. *Planters and Business Men: The Guignard Family of South
    Carolina, 1795–1930*. Columbia: University of South Carolina Press, 1957.
Current, Richard N., ed. *Reconstruction [1865–1877]*. Englewood Cliffs, New Jersey:
    Prentice-Hall, 1965.
Dennett, John R. *The South As It Is: 1865–1866*. New York: The Viking Press, 1965.
Eggleston, George Cary. "The Old Regime in the Old Dominion." *The Atlantic
    Monthly*, 36 (November, 1875), 603–16.
Fremantle, A. J. *Three Months in the Southern States: April–June 1863*. New York:
    J. Bradburn, 1864.
Hill, Walter B. "Uncle Tom without a Cabin." *The Century Magazine*, 27 (April,
    1884), 859–64.
House, Albert V., ed. "Deterioration of a Georgia Rice Plantation during Four Years of
    Civil War." *Journal of Southern History*, 9 (February, 1943), 98–113.

256 *Bibliography*

Hundley, Daniel R. *Social Relations in Our Southern States*. New York: H. B. Price, 1860.

Kirwan, Albert, ed. *The Confederacy*. New York: Meridian Books, 1959.

Marquette, C. L., ed. "Letters of a Yankee Sugar Planter." *Journal of Southern History*, 6 (November, 1940), 521–48.

Merrick, Caroline E. *Old Times in Dixie Land: A Southern Matron's Memories*. New York: The Grafton Press, 1901.

Miers, Earl Schenck, ed. *When the World Ended: The Diary of Emma LeConte*. New York: Oxford University Press, 1957.

Morgan, John T. "The Future of the Negro." *North American Review*, 139 (July, 1884), 81–84.

Myers, Robert Manson, ed. *The Children of Pride: A True Story of Georgia and the Civil War*. New Haven: Yale University Press, 1972.

Nordhoff, Charles. *The Cotton States in the Spring and Summer of 1875*. New York: Burt Franklin, 1876.

Olmsted, Frederick Law. *The Cotton Kingdom*. New York: Alfred A. Knopf, 1953.
———. *A Journey in the Seaboard Slave States*. New York: Negro Universities Press, 1968.

Page, Thomas Nelson. "The Old Planters'." *The Century Magazine*, 78 (May, 1909), 3–21.

Percy, William Alexander, *Lanterns on the Levee: Recollections of a Planter's Son*. New York: Alfred A. Knopf, 1945.

Phillips, Ulrich Bonnell, ed. *The Correspondence of Robert Toombs, Alexander H. Stephens, and Howell Cobb*. American Historical Association. *Annual Report for the Year 1911*. 2 volumes. Washington, D.C.: Government Printing Office, 1911.

Rainwater, P. L., ed. "Letters of James Lusk Alcorn." *Journal of Southern History*, 5 (May, 1939), 196–209.

Reid, Whitelaw. *After the War: A Tour of the Southern States, 1865–1866*. Edited by C. Vann Woodward. New York: Harper & Row, 1965.

Russell, William Howard, *My Diary North and South*. 2 volumes. New York: Harper, 1954.

Sanford, Henry Shelton. "American Interests in Africa." *The Forum*, 9 (1889), 409–29.

Silver, James W., ed. *Mississippi in the Confederacy: As Seen in Retrospect*. Baton Rouge: Louisiana State University Press, 1961.

Smedes, Susan Dabney. *Memorials of a Southern Planter*. London: J. Murray, 1887.

Stone, Alfred Holt. "The Italian Cotton Grower: The Negro's Problem." *South Atlantic Quarterly*, 4 (January, 1905), 42–47.

Stroup, Rodger E. "Before and After: Three Letters from E. B. Heyward." *South Carolina Historical Magazine*, 74 (April, 1973), 98–102.

Trowbridge, J. T. *The South: A Tour of Its Battle Fields and Ruined Cities*. Hartford, Connecticut: L. Stebbins, 1866.

Williams, Ben Ames, ed. *A Diary from Dixie by Mary Boykin Chesnut*. Boston: Houghton Mifflin, 1949.

## SECONDARY SOURCES

### Books, Articles, and Papers

Alexander, Thomas B., and Beringer, Richard E. *The Anatomy of the Confederate Congress: A Study of the Influences of Member Characteristics on Legislative Voting Behavior, 1861–1865*. Nashville: Vanderbilt University Press, 1972.

Ambrose, Stephen E. "Yeoman Discontent in the Confederacy." *Civil War History*, 8 (September, 1962), 259–68.

Aufhauser, R. Keith, "Slavery and Scientific Management." *Journal of Economic History*, 33 (December, 1973), 811–24.

Barney, William L. *The Road to Secession: A New Perspective on the Old South*. New York: Praeger, 1972.

———. *The Secessionist Impulse: Alabama and Mississippi in 1860*. Princeton, New Jersey: Princeton University Press, 1974.

Belser, Thomas A., Jr. "Alabama Plantation to Georgia Farm: John Horry Dent and Reconstruction." *Alabama Historical Review*, 24 (1962), 136–48.

Belz, Herman. "The New Orthodoxy in Reconstruction Historiography." *Reviews in American History*, 1 (March, 1973), 106–13.

Berlin, Ira. *Slaves without Masters: The Free Negro in the Antebellum South*. New York: Pantheon Books, 1974.

Berthoff, Rowland T. "Southern Attitudes toward Immigration, 1865–1914." *Journal of Southern History*, 17 (August, 1951), 328–60.

———. *An Unsettled People: Social Order and Disorder in American History*. New York: Harper & Row, 1971.

Bestor, Arthur. "The American Civil War as a Constitutional Crisis." *American Historical Review*, 69 (January, 1964), 327–52.

Blassingame, John. *The Slave Community: Plantation Life in the Antebellum South*. New York: Oxford University Press, 1972.

Brandfon, Robert L. *Cotton Kingdom of the New South: A History of the Yazoo Mississippi Delta from Reconstruction to the Twentieth Century*. Cambridge, Massachusetts: Harvard University Press, 1967.

Brewer, James H. *The Confederate Negro: Virginia's Craftsmen and Military Laborers, 1861–1865*. Durham, North Carolina: Duke University Press, 1969.

Bryan, T. Conn. *Confederate Georgia*. Athens, Georgia: University of Georgia Press, 1953.

Carpenter, Jesse T. *The South as a Conscious Minority, 1789–1861: A Study in Political Thought*. New York: New York University Press, 1930.

Cash, W. J. *The Mind of the South*. New York: Vintage Books, 1941.

Clayton, Bruce. *The Savage Ideal: Intolerance and Intellectual Leadership in the South, 1890–1914*. Baltimore and London: The Johns Hopkins University Press, 1972.

Conway, Alan. *The Reconstruction of Georgia*. Minneapolis: University of Minnesota Press, 1966.

Coulter, E. Merton. "A Century of a Georgia Plantation." *Mississippi Valley Historical Review*, 16 (December, 1929), 334–46.

———. "The Movement for Agricultural Reorganization in the Cotton South during the Civil War." *Agricultural History*, 1 (January, 1927), 3–17.

Curtin, Philip D. *Two Jamaicas: The Role of Ideas in a Tropical Colony, 1830–1865*. Cambridge, Massachusetts: Harvard University Press, 1955.

David, Paul A., and Temin, Peter. "Slavery: The Progressive Institution?" *Journal of Economic History*, 34 (September, 1974), 739–83.

Davidson, Chalmers Gaston. *The Last Foray, The South Carolina Planters of 1860: A Sociological Study*. Columbia: University of South Carolina Press, 1971.

Davis, David Brion. *The Slave Power Conspiracy and the Paranoid Style*. The Walter Lynwood Fleming Lectures in Southern History. Baton Rouge: Louisiana State University Press, 1969.

DeCanio, Stephen J. *Agriculture in the Postbellum South: The Economics of Production and Supply*. Cambridge, Massachusetts, and London: The M.I.T. Press, 1974.
———. "Cotton 'Overproduction' in Late Nineteenth-Century Southern Agriculture." *Journal of Economic History*, 33 (September, 1973), 608–33.

Degler, Carl N. *Neither Black nor White: Slavery and Race Relations in Brazil and the United States*. New York: Macmillan, 1971.
———. *The Other South: Southern Dissenters in the Nineteenth Century*. New York: Harper & Row, 1974.

Destler, Chester McArthur. "David Dickson's 'System of Farming' and the Agricultural Revolution in the Deep South, 1850–1885." *Agricultural History*, 31 (July, 1957), 30–39.

Donald, David. "The Proslavery Argument Reconsidered." *Journal of Southern History*, 37 (February, 1971), 3–18.

Durden, Robert F. *The Gray and the Black: The Confederate Debate on Emancipation*. Baton Rouge: Louisiana State University Press, 1972.

Eaton, Clement. *A History of the Southern Confederacy*. New York: Macmillan, 1954.
———. *The Mind of the Old South*. Revised edition. Baton Rouge: Louisiana State University Press, 1967.
———. *The Waning of the Old South Civilization*. New York: Pegasus, 1969.

Ellem, Warren A. "Who Were the Mississippi Scalawags?" *Journal of Southern History*. 38 (May, 1972), 217–40.

Evans, W. McKee. *Ballots and Fence Rails: Reconstruction on the Lower Cape Fear*. Chapel Hill: University of North Carolina Press, 1966.

Fleming, Walter L. "Deportation and Colonization: An Attempted Solution of the Race Problem." In *Studies in Southern History and Politics Inscribed to William Archibald Dunning*. New York: Columbia University Press, 1914.
———. "Immigration to the Southern States." *Political Science Quarterly*, 20 (1905), 278–81.

Fogel, Robert William, and Engerman, Stanley L. *Time on the Cross: The Economics of American Negro Slavery*. Boston and Toronto: Little, Brown, 1974.

Foner, Eric. "The Causes of the American Civil War: Recent Interpretations and New Directions." *Civil War History*, 20 (September, 1974), 197–214.
———. *Free Soil, Free Labor, Free Men: The Ideology of the Republican Party before the Civil War*. New York: Oxford University Press, 1970.

Franklin, John Hope. "The Great Confrontation: The South and the Problem of Change." *Journal of Southern History*, 38 (February, 1972), 3–20.

Frederickson, George M. *The Black Image in the White Mind: The Debate on Afro-American Character and Destiny, 1817–1914*. New York: Harper & Row, 1971.

Freehling, William W. "The Editorial Revolution, Virginia, and the Coming of the

Civil War: A Review Essay." *Civil War History*, 16 (March, 1970), 64–72.

Freeman, Douglas Southall. *The South to Posterity: An Introduction to the Writing of Confederate History*. New York: Charles Scribner's Sons, 1939.

Friedman, Lawrence J. *The White Savage: Racial Fantasies in the Postbellum South*. Englewood Cliffs, New Jersey: Prentice-Hall, 1970.

Gaines, Francis Pendleton. *The Southern Plantation*. New York: Columbia University Press, 1924.

Gallman, Robert E. "Self-Sufficiency in the Cotton Economy of the Antebellum South." *Agricultural History*, 44 (January, 1970), 5–23.

Gaston, Paul M. *The New South Creed: A Study in Southern Mythmaking*. New York: Alfred A. Knopf, 1970.

Gates, Paul W. *Agriculture and the Civil War*. New York: Alfred A. Knopf, 1965.

Genovese, Eugene D. *The Political Economy of Slavery: Studies in the Economy and Society of the Slave South*. New York: Vintage Books, 1967.

———. *Roll, Jordan, Roll: The World the Slaves Made*. New York: Pantheon Books, 1974.

———. *The World the Slaveholders Made: Two Essays in Interpretation*. New York: Pantheon Books, 1969.

Gerteis, Louis S. *From Contraband to Freedman: Federal Policy toward Southern Blacks, 1861–1865*. Westport, Connecticut: Greenwood Press, 1973.

Grantham, Dewey W., Jr. "The Southern Bourbons Revisited." *South Atlantic Quarterly*, 60 (Summer, 1961) 286–95.

Grob, Gerald N. "Reconstruction: An American Morality Play." In *American History: Retrospect and Prospect*, edited by George Athan Billias and Gerald N. Grob. New York: The Free Press, 1971.

Gutman, Herbert G. "Work, Culture, and Society in Industrializing America, 1815–1919." *American Historical Review*, 78 (June, 1973), 531–88.

———. "The World Two Cliometricians Made: A Review-Essay of *Time on the Cross*." *Journal of Negro History*, 60 (January, 1975), 53–227.

Hackney, Sheldon. "*Origins of the New South* in Retrospect." *Journal of Southern History*, 38 (May, 1972), 191–216.

Harris, William C. "A Reconsideration of the Mississippi Scalawag." *Journal of Mississippi History*, 32 (February, 1970), 2–42.

Hartz, Louis. *The Liberal Tradition in America: An Interpretation of American Political Thought since the Revolution*. New York: Harcourt, Brace & World, 1955.

Hesseltine, William Best. *Confederate Leaders in the New South*. The Walter Lynwood Fleming Lectures in Southern History. Baton Rouge: Louisiana State University Press, 1950.

Higgs, Robert. "Race, Tenure, and Resource Allocation in Southern Agriculture, 1910." *Journal of Economic History*, 33 (March, 1973), 149–69.

Higham, John. *From Boundlessness to Consolidation: The Transformation of American Culture, 1848–1860*. Ann Arbor: William L. Clements Library, 1969.

Hill, Lawrence F. "The Confederate Exodus to Latin America." *Southwestern Historical Quarterly*, 39 (October, 1935, January, 1936, April, 1936), 100–134, 161–99, 309–26.

James, D. Clayton. "Mississippi Agriculture, 1861–1865." *Journal of Mississippi History*, 24 (July, 1962), 129–41.

Johnson, Chalmers. *Revolutionary Change*. Boston: Little, Brown, 1966.

Jordan, Winthrop D. *White Over Black: American Attitudes Toward the Negro, 1550–1812.* Chapel Hill: University of North Carolina Press, 1968.

Klingberg, Frank W. *The Southern Claims Commission.* University of California Publications in History, vol. 50. Berkeley and Los Angeles: University of California Press, 1955.

Kloosterboer, W. *Involuntary Labour since the Abolition of Slavery: A Survey of Compulsory Labour throughout the World.* Leiden, The Netherlands: E. J. Brill, 1960.

Kolchin, Peter. *First Freedom: The Responses of Alabama's Blacks to Emancipation and Reconstruction.* Westport, Connecticut: Greenwood Press, 1972.

Lang, Herbert H. "J. F. H. Claiborne at 'Laurel Wood' Plantation, 1853–1870." *Journal of Mississippi History,* 18 (January, 1956), 1–17.

Lathrop, Barnes F. "History of the Census Returns." *Southwestern Historical Quarterly,* 51 (April, 1948), 293–312.

Lerner, Eugene M. "Southern Output and Agricultural Income, 1860–1880." In *The Economic Impact of the American Civil War,* edited by Ralph Andreano. Cambridge, Massachusetts: Schenkman, 1962.

Lifton, Robert Jay. *History and Human Survival: Essays on the Young and Old, Survivors and the Dead, Peace and War, and on Contemporary Psychohistory.* New York: Random House, 1970.

Lipset, Seymour Martin. *Revolution and Counterrevolution: Change and Persistence in Social Structure.* Revised edition. Garden City, New York: Anchor Books, 1970.

Litwack, Leon F. "Free at Last." In *Anonymous Americans: Explorations in Nineteenth-Century Social History,* edited by Tamara K. Hareven. Englewood Cliffs, New Jersey: Prentice-Hall, 1971.

Loewenberg, Bert James. "Efforts of the South to Encourage Immigration, 1865–1900." *South Atlantic Quarterly,* 33 (October, 1934), 363–85.

Lowrey, Walter McGehee. "The Political Career of James Madison Wells." *Louisiana Historical Quarterly,* 31 (October, 1948), 995–1123.

Luraghi, Raimondo. "The Civil War and the Modernization of American Society: Social Structure and Industrial Revolution in the Old South before and during the War." *Civil War History,* 18 (September, 1972), 230–50.

McFeely, William S. *Yankee Stepfather: General O. O. Howard and the Freedmen.* New York: W. W. Norton, 1970.

McKitrick, Eric L. *Andrew Johnson and Reconstruction.* Chicago and London: University of Chicago Press, 1960.

McPherson, James M. *The Struggle for Equality: Abolitionists and the Negro in the Civil War and Reconstruction.* Princeton, New Jersey: Princeton University Press, 1964.

Maddex, Jack P., Jr. "Pollard's *The Lost Cause Regained:* A Mask for Southern Accommodation." *Journal of Southern History,* 40 (November, 1974), 595–612.

———. *The Virginia Conservatives, 1867–1879: A Study in Reconstruction Politics.* Chapel Hill: University of North Carolina Press, 1970.

Massey, Mary Elizabeth. "The Making of a Feminist." *Journal of Southern History,* 39 (February, 1973), 3–22.

May, J. Thomas. "Continuity and Change in the Labor Program of the Union Army and the Freedmen's Bureau." *Civil War History*, 17 (September, 1971), 245–54.

Mering, John. "Persistent Whiggery in the Confederate South: A Reconsideration." *South Atlantic Quarterly*, 69 (Winter, 1970), 124–43.

Messner, William F. "Black Violence and White Response: Louisiana, 1862." *Journal of Southern History*, 41 (February, 1975), 19–38.

Millet, Donald J. "Some Aspects of Agricultural Retardation in Southwest Louisiana, 1865–1900." *Louisiana History*, 11 (Winter, 1970), 37–61.

Montgomery, Horace. *Johnny Cobb: Confederate Aristocrat*. Athens, Georgia: University of Georgia Press, 1964.

Olsen, Otto H. "Historians and the Extent of Slave Ownership in the Southern United States." *Civil War History*, 18 (June, 1972), 101–16.

———. "Reconsidering the Scalawags." *Civil War History*, 12 (December, 1966), 304–20.

Owsley, Frank L. *Plain Folk of the Old South*. Chicago: Quadrangle Books, 1965.

Parker, William N. "Slavery and Southern Economic Development: An Hypothesis and Some Evidence." *Agricultural History*, 44 (January, 1970), 115–25.

Pereyra, Lillian A. *James Lusk Alcorn: Persistent Whig*. Southern Biography Series. Baton Rouge: Louisiana State University Press, 1966.

Perman, Michael. *Reunion without Compromise: The South and Reconstruction, 1865–1868*. London and New York: Cambridge University Press, 1973.

Phillips, Ulrich Bonnell. *American Negro Slavery: A Survey of the Supply, Employment and Control of Negro Labor As Determined by the Plantation Regime*. Baton Rouge: Louisiana State University Press, 1966.

———. "The Decadence of the Plantation System." *Annals of the American Academy of Political and Social Science*, 35 (January, 1910), 37–41.

———. "Plantations with Slave Labor and Free." *American Historical Review*, 30 (July, 1925), 738–53.

Potter, David M. "The Historian's Use of Nationalism and Vice Versa." *American Historical Review*, 67 (December, 1962), 924–50.

Quarles, Benjamin. "Lord Dunmore as Liberator." *William and Mary Quarterly*, 15 (October, 1958), 494–507.

Ransom, Roger L., and Sutch, Richard. "Debt Peonage in the Cotton South after the Civil War." *Journal of Economic History*, 32 (September, 1972), 641–69.

———. "The Ex-Slave in the Post-Bellum South: A Study of the Economic Impact of Racism in a Market Environment." *Journal of Economic History*, 33 (March, 1973), 131–48.

———. "The 'Lock-In' Mechanism and Overproduction of Cotton in the Postbellum South." *Agricultural History*, 49 (April, 1975), 405–25.

Rawick, George P. *From Sundown to Sunup: The Making of the Black Community*. Westport, Connecticut: Greenwood Press, 1972.

Reid, Joseph. "Sharecropping as an Understandable Market Response: The Post-Bellum South." *Journal of Economic History*, 33 (March, 1973), 106–30.

———. "Sharecropping in History and Theory." *Agricultural History*, 49 (April, 1975), 426–40.

Reynolds, Donald E. *Editors Make War: Southern Newspapers in the Secession Crisis*.

Nashville: Vanderbilt University Press, 1970.

Rister, Carl Coke. "Carlotta, A Confederate Colony in Mexico." *Journal of Southern History*, 11 (February, 1945), 33–50.

Rogers, George C., Jr. *The History of Georgetown County, South Carolina*. Columbia, South Carolina: University of South Carolina Press, 1970.

Roland, Charles P. *Louisiana Sugar Plantations during the American Civil War*. Leiden, The Netherlands: E. J. Brill, 1957.

Rolle, Andrew F. *The Lost Cause: The Confederate Exodus to Mexico*. Norman: University of Oklahoma Press, 1965.

Rose, Willie Lee. "Masters without Slaves." Paper presented at the annual meeting of the American Historical Association, New York, December, 1966.

———. *Rehearsal for Reconstruction: The Port Royal Experiment*. New York: Vintage Books, 1964.

Rothstein, Morton. "The Cotton Frontier of the Antebellum United States: A Methodological Battleground." *Agricultural History*, 44 (January, 1970), 149–65.

Saloutos, Theodore. "Southern Agriculture and the Problems of Readjustment, 1865–1877." *Agricultural History*, 30 (April, 1956), 58–76.

Scarborough, William K. *The Overseer: Plantation Management in the Old South*. Baton Rouge: Louisiana State University Press, 1966.

Scott, Anne Firor. *The Southern Lady: From Pedestal to Politics, 1830–1930*. Chicago: University of Chicago Press, 1970.

Sellers, Charles Grier, Jr. "The Travail of Slavery." In *The Southerner as American*, edited by Charles Grier Sellers, Jr. New York: E. P. Dutton, 1966.

Shalhope, Robert E. "Race, Class, Slavery, and the Antebellum Southern Mind." *Journal of Southern History*, 37 (November, 1971), 557–74.

Shugg, Roger W. *Origins of Class Struggle in Louisiana: A Social History of White Farmers and Laborers during Slavery and After, 1840–1875*. Baton Rouge: Louisiana State University Press, 1939.

———. "Survival of the Plantation System in Louisiana." *Journal of Southern History*, 3 (August, 1937), 311–25.

Silver, James W. *Confederate Morale and Church Propaganda*. New York: W. W. Norton, 1967.

Simkins, Francis Butler, and Patton, James Welch. *The Women of the Confederacy*. New York and Richmond: Garrett and Massie, 1936.

Sitterson, J. Carlyle. "The McCollams: A Planter Family of the Old and New South." *Journal of Southern History*, 6 (August, 1940), 347–67.

———. "Magnolia Plantation, 1852–1862: A Decade of a Louisiana Sugar Estate." *Mississippi Valley Historical Review*, 25 (September, 1938), 197–210.

———. *Sugar Country: The Cane Sugar Industry in the South, 1753–1950*. Lexington, Kentucky: University of Kentucky Press, 1953.

———. "The Transition from Slave to Free Economy on the William J. Minor Plantations." *Agricultural History*, 17 (October, 1943), 216–24.

———. "The William J. Minor Plantations: A Study in Ante-Bellum Absentee Ownership." *Journal of Southern History*, 9 (February, 1943), 59–74.

Stampp, Kenneth M. *The Peculiar Institution: Slavery in the Ante-Bellum South*. New York: Vintage Books, 1956.

———. *The Southern Road to Appomattox*. Cotton Memorial Papers. El Paso: Texas Western Press, 1959.

Staudenraus, P. J. *The African Colonization Movement, 1816–1865*. New York, Columbia University Press, 1961.

Stephenson, Nathaniel W. "The Question of Arming the Slaves." *American Historical Review*, 18 (January, 1913), 295–308.

Stephenson, Wendell Holmes. "A Quarter-Century of a Mississippi Plantation: Eli J. Capell of 'Pleasant Hill.' " *Mississippi Valley Historical Review*, 23 (December, 1936), 355–74.

Sterkx, H. E. *Partners in Rebellion: Alabama Women in the Civil War*. Rutherford, New Jersey: Fairleigh Dickinson University Press, 1970.

Tatum, Georgia Lee. *Disloyalty in the Confederacy*. Chapel Hill: University of North Carolina Press, 1934.

Taylor, Joe Gray. *Louisiana Reconstructed: 1863–1877*. Baton Rouge: Louisiana State University Press, 1974.

———. "Slavery in Louisiana during the Civil War." *Louisiana History*, 8 (Winter, 1967), 27–33.

Taylor, Paul S. "Plantation Agriculture in the United States: Seventeenth to Twentieth Centuries." *Land Economics*, 30 (May, 1954), 141–52.

Taylor, William R. *Cavalier and Yankee: The Old South and American National Character*. Garden City, New York: Doubleday, 1963.

Thomas, Emory M. *The Confederacy as a Revolutionary Experience*. Englewood Cliffs, New Jersey: Prentice-Hall, 1971.

Thompson, Edgar T. "The Planter in the Pattern of Race Relations in the South." *Social Forces*, 19 (December, 1940), 244–52.

Tindall, George Brown. *The Persistent Tradition in New South Politics*. The Walter Lynwood Fleming Lectures in Southern History. Baton Rouge: Louisiana State University Press, 1975.

Toplin, Robert Brent. *The Abolition of Slavery in Brazil*. New York: Atheneum, 1971.

———. "The Specter of Crisis: Slaveholder Reactions to Abolitionism in the United States and Brazil." *Civil War History*, 18 (June, 1972), 129–38.

Trelease, Allen W. *White Terror: The Ku Klux Klan Conspiracy and Southern Reconstruction*. New York: Harper & Row, 1967.

———. "Who Were the Scalawags?" *Journal of Southern History*, 29 (November, 1963), 445–68.

Trexler, Harrison A. "The Opposition of Planters to the Employment of Slaves as Laborers by the Confederacy." *Mississippi Valley Historical Review*, 27 (1940), 211–24.

VanAucken, Sheldon. "A Century of the Southern Plantation." *Virginia Magazine of History and Biography*, 58 (July, 1958), 356–87.

van den Berghe, Pierre L. *Race and Racism: A Comparative Perspective*. New York, London, Sydney: John Wiley & Sons, 1967.

Vandiver, Frank E. *Their Tattered Flags*. New York: Harper & Row, 1970.

Wagstaff, Thomas. "Call Your Old Master—'Master': Southern Political Leaders and Negro Labor during Presidential Reconstruction." *Labor History*, 10 (Summer, 1969), 33–53.

Wallace, Anthony F. *Culture and Personality.* New York: Random House, 1961.

Weaver, Blanche Henry Clark. "Confederate Emigration to Brazil." *Journal of Southern History,* 27 (February, 1961), 33–53.

Weaver, Herbert. *Mississippi Farmers, 1850–1860.* Nashville: Vanderbilt University Press, 1945.

Wesley, Charles H. "The Employment of Negroes as Soldiers in the Confederate Army." *Journal of Negro History,* 4 (July, 1919), 239–53.

White, William W. *The Confederate Veteran.* Tuscaloosa, Alabama: Confederate Publishing Company, 1962.

Wiener, Jonathan M. "Planter-Merchant Conflict in Reconstruction Alabama." *Past and Present,* 68 (August, 1975), 73–84.

———. "Planter Persistence and Social Change: Alabama, 1850–1870." Paper presented at the annual meeting of the Organization of American Historians, Boston, April, 1975.

Wiley, Bell Irvin. *Confederate Women.* Westport, Connecticut: Greenwood Press, 1974.

———. *The Plain People of the Confederacy.* The Walter Lynwood Fleming Lectures in Southern History. Baton Rouge: Louisiana State University Press, 1944.

———. "Salient Changes in Southern Agriculture since the Civil War." *Agricultural History,* 13 (April, 1939), 65–76.

———. *Southern Negroes, 1861–1865.* New Haven: Yale University Press, 1938.

———. "Vicissitudes of Early Reconstruction Farming in the Lower Mississippi Valley." *Journal of Southern History,* 3 (November, 1937), 441–52.

Williams, T. Harry. "An Analysis of Some Reconstruction Attitudes." *Journal of Southern History,* 3 (November, 1937), 441–52.

———. *Romance and Realism in Southern Politics.* Eugenia Dorothy Blount Lamar Memorial Lectures. Athens, Georgia: University of Georgia Press, 1961.

Williamson, Joel. *After Slavery: The Negro in South Carolina during Reconstruction, 1861–1877.* Chapel Hill: University of North Carolina, 1965.

Wilson, Theodore Brantner. *The Black Codes of the South.* University, Alabama: University of Alabama Press, 1965.

Wolfenstein, Martha. *Disaster: A Psychological Essay.* Glencoe, Illinois: The Free Press, 1957.

Wood, Forrest G. *Black Scare: The Racist Response to Emancipation and Reconstruction.* Berkeley and Los Angeles: University of California Press, 1970.

Woodman, Harold D. *King Cotton and His Retainers: Financing and Marketing the Cotton Crop of the South, 1800–1925.* Lexington: University of Kentucky Press, 1968.

Woodward, C. Vann. "Emancipations and Reconstructions: A Comparative Study." Paper presented at the Thirteenth International Congress of Historical Sciences, Moscow, August, 1970.

———. *Origins of the New South, 1877–1913.* Vol. 9 of *A History of the South,* edited by Wendell Holmes Stephenson and E. Merton Coulter. Baton Rouge: Louisiana State University Press, 1951.

———. "The Strange Career of a Historical Controversy." In C. Vann Woodward, *American Counterpoint: Slavery and Racism in the North-South Dialogue.* Boston, Toronto: Little, Brown, 1971.

Wooster, Ralph A. *The People in Power: Courthouse and Statehouse in the Lower South, 1850–1860.* Knoxville: University of Tennessee Press, 1969.

———. *The Secession Conventions of the South.* Princeton, New Jersey: Princeton University Press, 1962.

Wright, Gavin. " 'Economic Democracy' and the Concentration of Agricultural Wealth in the Cotton South, 1850–1860." *Agricultural History*, 44 (January, 1970), 63–93.

———. "New and Old Views on the Economics of Slavery," *Journal of Economic History*, 33 (June, 1973), 452–66.

Zeichner, Oscar. "The Transition from Slave to Free Agricultural Labor in the Southern States." *Agricultural History*, 13 (January, 1939), 22–32.

## Unpublished Theses and Dissertations

Baltimore, Lester B. "Southern Nationalists and Southern Nationalism, 1850–1870." Ph.D. dissertation, University of Missouri, 1968.

Corbett, Melville Fort. "A Preliminary Study of the Planter Aristocracy as a Folk Level of Life in the Old South." M.A. thesis, University of North Carolina, 1941.

Coyner, Martin Boyd, Jr. "John Hartwell Cocke of Bremo: Agriculture and Slavery in the Ante-Bellum South." Ph.D. dissertation, University of Virginia, 1961.

Durant, Susan Speare. "The Gently Furled Banner: The Development of the Myth of the Lost Cause, 1865–1900." Ph.D. dissertation, University of North Carolina, 1972.

Fisher, John E. "Statesman of the Lost Cause: R. M. T. Hunter and the Sectional Controversy, 1847–1887." Ph.D. dissertation, University of Virginia, 1968.

Flusche, Michael A. "The Private Plantation: Versions of the Old South Myth, 1880–1914." Ph.D. dissertation, The Johns Hopkins University, 1973.

Gilmour, Robert Arthur. "The Other Emancipation: Studies in the Society and Economy of Alabama Whites during Reconstruction." Ph.D. dissertation, The Johns Hopkins University, 1972.

Grier, Douglas Audenried. "Confederate Emigration to Brazil, 1865–1870." Ph.D. dissertation, University of Michigan, 1968.

Hilliard, Sam Bowers. "Birdsong: Sequent Occupation on a Southwestern Georgia Plantation." M.A. thesis, University of Georgia, 1960.

Johnson, Michael P. "Secession and Conservatism in the Lower South: The Social and Ideological Bases of Secession in Georgia, 1860–1861." Ph.D. dissertation, Stanford University, 1973.

Lathrop, Barnes Fletcher. "The Pugh Plantations, 1860–1865: A Study of Life in Lower Louisiana." Ph.D. dissertation, University of Texas, 1945.

McCrary, James Peyton. "Moderation in a Revolutionary World: Lincoln and the Failure of Reconstruction in Louisiana." Ph.D. dissertation, Princeton University, 1972.

Menn, Joseph Karl. "The Large Slaveholders of the Deep South, 1860." Ph.D. dissertation, University of Texas, 1964.

Myers, John B. "Black Human Capital: The Freedmen and the Reconstruction of Labor in Alabama, 1860–1880." Ph.D. dissertation, Florida State University, 1974.

Noble, William Allister. "Sequent Occupance of Hopeton-Altama, 1816–1956." M.A. thesis, University of Georgia, 1956.

Olsberg, Robert Nicholas. "A Government of Class and Race: William Henry Trescot and the South Carolina Chivalry, 1860–1865." Ph.D. dissertation, University of South Carolina, 1972.

Robbins, John Brawner. "Confederate Nationalism: Politics and Government in the Confederate South, 1861–1865." Ph.D. dissertation, Rice University, 1964.

Sides, Sudie Duncan. "Women and Slaves: An Interpretation Based on the Writings of Southern Women." Ph.D. dissertation, University of North Carolina, 1969.

Smith, Samuel Boyd. "Joseph Buckner Killibrew and the New South Movement in Tennessee." Ph.D. dissertation, Vanderbilt University, 1962.

Tebeau, Charlton Watson. "The Planter in the Lower South, 1865–1880." Ph.D. dissertation, University of Iowa, 1933.

Wallenstein, Peter. "From Slave South to New South: Taxes and Spending in Georgia from 1850 through Reconstruction." Ph.D. dissertation. The Johns Hopkins University, 1973.

# Index